How to Succeed at University

SAGE Study Skills

How to Succeed at University

An Essential Guide to Academic Skills,
Personal Development and Employability

Bob Smale & Julie Fowlie

2nd Edition

Los Angeles | London | New Delhi
Singapore | Washington DC | Boston

Los Angeles | London | New Delhi
Singapore | Washington DC

SAGE Publications Ltd
1 Oliver's Yard
55 City Road
London EC1Y 1SP

SAGE Publications Inc.
2455 Teller Road
Thousand Oaks, California 91320

SAGE Publications India Pvt Ltd
B 1/I 1 Mohan Cooperative Industrial Area
Mathura Road
New Delhi 110 044

SAGE Publications Asia-Pacific Pte Ltd
3 Church Street
#10-04 Samsung Hub
Singapore 049483

Editor: Jai Seaman
Assistant editor: Lily Mehrbod
Production editor: Victoria Nicholas
Proofreader: Kate Campbell
Indexer: Judith Lavender
Marketing manager: Catherine Slinn
Cover design: Stephanie Guyaz
Typeset by: C&M Digitals (P) Ltd, Chennai, India
Printed and bound by CPI Group (UK) Ltd,
    Croydon, CR0 4YY

Library of Congress Control Number: 2014950830

British Library Cataloguing in Publication data

A catalogue record for this book is available from
the British Library

ISBN 978-1-4462-9546-5
ISBN 978-1-4462-9547-2 (pbk)

MIX
Paper from
responsible sources
FSC® C013604

Contents

List of Figures and Tables

Figures

Tables

Biographical Details

Bob Smale is a Senior Lecturer at University of Brighton Business School where he has been closely involved in developing the undergraduate business skills programme with Julie Fowlie. His teaching includes employee relations, together with aspects of organisational behaviour and human resource management, and his research interests include employee relations and pedagogy. Bob has a background in the banking industry and employee relations. He was formerly a part-time professional musician and is also a qualified aromatherapist. He has worked in further, adult and higher education for almost three decades, as well as delivering personal skills training, mostly in the public and voluntary sectors.

Julie Fowlie is a Principal Lecturer at University of Brighton Business School, where she has been closely involved in developing the undergraduate business skills programme with Bob Smale. Her teaching includes aspects of management, organisational behaviour and human resource management. She has research interests in emotional intelligence and pedagogy. Julie previously worked in the finance industry in a senior management position, also having had experience as a bond dealer. She is also a qualified swimming coach and lifeguard. Julie has taught in further, adult and higher education and runs her own training business, most recently designing and delivering a management development programme for a private sector organisation.

Preface to the Second Edition

This second edition builds upon the first edition, published in 2009, and has been written to reflect the changing demands on students in terms of academic achievement and future employability. In particular this edition includes: 'thumbnail' definitions of commonly used terms; and increased emphasis on the application of technology to academic work and the implications for avoiding plagiarism, together with the importance of developing and maintaining a digital presence in order to enhance employability.

Acknowledgements

We recognise that first developing a taught skills programme and then writing a skills book is not so much a work of invention, but rather involves bringing disparate ideas into an integrated, understandable and cohesive format. We have tried to acknowledge in the text the source of particular ideas, but we also recognise that some are in the public domain and are ultimately unattributable. However, we would like to take this opportunity to thank all those who have contributed to this area and from whom we have learnt so much.

In terms of the development of this book we would like first to thank Jai Seaman, our Commissioning Editor at Sage Publications, for her advice and encouragement. We must pay tribute to all our colleagues, past and present, who have supported and defended an undergraduate skills programme at Brighton Business School and contributed so many ideas to it. We also need to thank our students, from whom we have not only learnt so much, but also upon whom we have tested and developed many of our ideas. Finally, we must thank Ralph Timberlake for reading and commenting on the first draft of both editions. However, all errors and omissions remain our own responsibility.

Introduction

Overview

- Why do you need to upgrade your skills to succeed at university?
- Why do you need to read this book?

Why do you need to upgrade your skills to succeed at university?

This book has been written to help you to develop the personal, academic and employability skills you will need to succeed in higher education, in employment or whatever else lies ahead. Complete the short self-scoring test below to assess your own level of confidence in relation to developing the skills you will need both to complete your course successfully and for your life beyond university.

✍ Activity: Why do you need to read this chapter?

You need to self score each question on a scale from 0 to 10, where 0 is low and 10 is high.

1. How confident do you feel about starting your course and meeting new people?	
2. How much attention have you given to planning your future development?	
3. How organised do you feel you are in terms of your studies?	
4. How good are you at living independently?	
5. How good are you at completing assignments?	
6. How much do you know about conducting research?	
7. How good are you at taking examinations?	
8. How confident do you feel that you can complete your course?	
9. How confident are you about getting a job after your course?	
10. How confident are you about developing yourself after university?	
Total score	

Interpretation

What did you score?

- Less than 50%   You will definitely find a lot of help in this book.
- 50%–75%   There is still plenty to learn in this book.
- 75%–100%   You are very confident – read on to confirm your understanding!

Why do you need to read this book?

This book is primarily intended for new undergraduate students in higher education but will also be useful to established undergraduates and post-graduates. We know from experience that not all students achieve their full potential, either in their academic work or long-term employability, because they lack some of the basic personal, academic and employability skills. There are clearly winners in higher education and employability, so our question to you is: **'Why shouldn't you be one of them?'**

Much of our work in recent years has been to help students develop their skills, not only in skills modules but also throughout their studies. This book reflects our commitment to you the student, our desire to share our ideas and to help you develop your skills while in higher education and beyond. We do not seek to be dogmatic but rather aim to provide you with ideas and inspiration, and to encourage you to think for yourself about what you need to develop. We provide a framework for you to reflect upon and set your own goals, and to develop your own path in order to achieve those goals.

Producing good academic work is largely about understanding certain conventions that operate. Imagine trying to play football or tennis if no one ever told you the rules. We do not believe that the processes of learning and assessment should be a guessing game and part of our aim is to demystify the process for you.

However, success in higher education is not all about academic skills; in order to achieve good results you need good personal skills too. It is no good writing a brilliant essay if you miss the hand-in date and score zero per cent, or if you work hard at your revision and then dry up in the exam hall. So issues such as time management and handling stress are important, together with a wide range of other personal skills.

For most of you, the long-term goal of higher education will be to improve your employability. Many academic and personal skills are what we call **transferable skills**, which means these will stand you in good stead both when looking for employment and in your future careers. There are some particularly valuable employability skills that we really want to share with you, skills that can give you an edge in the competitive labour markets and help you to get the right job. We also include some content on developing yourself both within your future professional career and/or in higher education as well some ideas on entrepreneurship and self-employment as an alternative to formal employment.

The book follows the logic of our teaching and is highly interactive. Short sections of narrative are interspersed with activities providing many opportunities for reflection and action. To facilitate this, each chapter contains the following pedagogic features:

- **Overview** – bullet points outline the content of each chapter.
- **Diagnostic test** – a short self-scoring skill set questionnaire is provided for you to assess your own needs in relation to the content of each chapter.
- **Introduction** – a short narrative explaining the content and why it might be important to your becoming a successful student.
- **Activities and narrative** – activities are interspersed with sections of narrative. The activities are designed to help link the ideas introduced in the narrative sections to your particular needs.

- **Experience boxes** – these relate real students', lecturers' and in some cases other people's experiences to illustrate points.
- **Thumbnails** – provide short definitions of commonly-used terms.
- **Follow-up activities** – these include checklists of skill development activities to follow up on.
- **Further reading and websites to look up** – these are provided for further exploration of the subject area.
- **Review and reflection** – these provide spaces for you to log reflections on each chapter in response to some trigger questions.

We are committed to helping students succeed in higher education and beyond, but it's up to you how you use the book. You can work through the book systematically, chapter by chapter, or dip in here and there to support your development – perhaps using the diagnostic tests at the start of each chapter to help identify your needs. However you use the book, we wish you every success with your studies and your life beyond, and it is our sincere hope that this book helps you achieve success in your journey through life.

PART I

How to Develop Your Personal Skills

1

How to Prepare Yourself for Higher Education

Overview – what's in this chapter?

- Why do you need to upgrade your personal skills?
- Handling the transition into higher education
- Orientating yourself to your studies
- Recognising your own motivation to learn, grow and develop
- Understanding your emotions in the developmental process
- Developing your self-efficacy and self-confidence
- Follow-up activities, further reading and websites to look up
- Time for review and reflection

Why do you need to upgrade your personal skills?

Try completing the short self-scoring test overleaf, to assess your own level of confidence in relation to developing your own personal skills in order to complete your course successfully.

✎ **Activity: Why do you need to read this chapter?**	
You need to self score each question on a scale from 0 to 10, where 0 is low and 10 is high.	
1. How confident do you feel about starting your course?	
2. How confident do you feel about meeting new people?	
3. How organised do you feel you are in terms of your studies?	
4. How confident do you feel about your study skills?	
5. How motivated do you feel about completing your course?	
6. How confident do you feel about overcoming any barriers?	
7. How able are you to handle the emotional side of your course?	
8. How clearly can you visualise your next role after your course?	
9. How well do you think you present yourself to other people?	
10. How confident do you feel that you can complete your course successfully?	
Total score	
Interpretation What did you score? • Less than 50% You definitely will find a lot of help in this chapter. • 50%–75% There is still plenty to learn in this chapter. • 75%–100% You are very confident – read on to confirm your understanding.	

What do you want to achieve by studying in higher education?

This is a question that you may already be asking yourself. Understanding your answer will have a lot to do with you successfully completing your course.

This chapter starts by helping you to make a successful transition into higher education. How was your induction? You may have felt confused or overloaded by the end of day one. Then there are the problems of meeting new people, settling into accommodation, maybe living away from home for the first time and getting your studies organised.

The chapter next considers your motivation – what you hope to achieve and why. What barriers there are to be overcome and how will you do this? How anxious are you about the process? Keeping motivated and handing any anxieties will be vital to you in achieving success at university. The chapter then goes on to look at how you can handle your emotions in what will be a developmental process.

The chapter also looks at **self-efficacy** and how you can build self-confidence in order to succeed in your studies, in employment and in all that lies ahead. You might think that this is rather too soon and that perhaps it should be later in the book, and may be something to look at the end of your course – but read on, it's what it's all about!

> **Self-efficacy** – concerns our confidence in our ability to succeed.

Finally there are some follow-up activities, suggested further reading, websites to look up, and some space for review and reflection. Reflection will be a recurring theme of this book. It is simply about thinking – but in a structured way – in order to help us learn, grow and develop.

Handling the transition into higher education

Things to do before you arrive

There are quite a few things you can do before you arrive to smooth your transition into university life. Being prepared will help you feel more relaxed and confident when you arrive. Try to work through our suggestions in the following activity.

 Activity: Getting prepared

- Check through all the information you have been sent and look at the university website. You may find a 'new student area' on the website which will be dedicated to helping you make this transition.

- Look for student groups on social networking sites. Increasingly students find there is a group dedicated to their course or location and if not, you can start one. This can be really useful in developing a 'starter pack' of friends before you arrive.

- Talk to anybody you know who has been to university and find out what their experience was and what you can learn from this.

- Make a list of everything you want to take with you, including some home comforts to make your university accommodation more like home.

How did you feel on the first day?

The first day in higher education can be quite traumatic for many new students. There will almost certainly be an induction programme organised for you and it could last for a whole week or even for two. Many people feel that they are subject to **information overload** as a series of well meaning 'talking heads' supply endless information – all of which, they tell you, is absolutely essential.

 Activity: How did you feel at the start?

1. Write a paragraph expressing how you felt on the first day in higher education.

2. Write another paragraph about how you felt at the end of the first week. Was it better or worse?

3. Write a paragraph about how you felt at the end of the first month. You might need to make a diary date to do this.

What is culture shock?

Culture shock is experienced when people are first exposed to a new and alien culture. They may feel confused and disorientated. When people enter higher education there is always an element of culture shock, because virtually everyone was somewhere else with a different culture before they arrived. **International students** are often more prone to suffering from culture shock, not only because of differences in the education system, but also because of language and cultural differences. Similarly, if you are a **mature student** or studying **part-time**, then you may also feel it more. Indeed it is generally true to say that the greater the difference between where

> **Culture shock –** feelings individuals experience when entering a new and alien culture; these will tend to be greater the more different the new culture is.

you came from and where you are now, the more likely you are to feel the effects of culture shock.

There are good and bad ways to help overcome culture shock. Consider the following two lists.

Good ways …	Bad ways …
Get connected socially (see next section).	Avoid everybody, especially anybody from your course.
Eat in the refectory.	Eat in your room.
Visit the Students Union and see what is on offer.	Do not attend classes.
	Don't do any work.
Go to the 'freshers' fayre', join student societies, attend meetings and activities etc.	Deny what is really happening.
	Resort to drink or drugs.
Read and file away all that 'stuff' from induction.	Think about leaving.
Get your studies organised, check out your timetable, etc.	Go home for good!
Log onto the computer system and check student websites, blogs, etc.	
Visit the library and check out the facilities and the nearest book shop.	

 Activity: Overcoming culture shock

1. Have a look through the 'good ways' outlined above and make a list of things that you need to do over the first few days and weeks.
2. Keep the list in a place where you can see it and tick off things as you achieve them. It's important to record your successes!

Do you feel homesick or like leaving your course?

Culture shock can lead to homesickness, and you may feel like packing up and going home. It's very common to feel like this, particularly if you feel overwhelmed by the workload, the place or the people – perhaps all three!

Leaving your course is a really big life-changing decision and so deserves really thorough consideration. Knowing *why* you want to leave or why you want to stay will be really important if you are going to make the right decision for you.

✎ Activity: Thinking of leaving your course?

1. Try making two lists to consider your reasons for going or staying.

Reasons for going…		Reasons for staying…	
•		•	
•		•	
•		•	
•		•	
•		•	
•		•	
•		•	
•		•	

2. Now consider:

• Are your reasons more emotional or rational?

• Are any of your reasons short term and likely to change?

• Where do you see yourself in the future?

• What help and support could you access? (See next section.)

Here are some more things you really should do before leaving:

- Talk it over with your friends/other people on the course. You may be surprised at how much they want you to stay.
- Talk it over with your course leader, personal tutor or any other member of the academic staff you feel comfortable talking to.
- You may have accommodation problems or just be unhappy where you are. There should be an accommodation officer or department you can talk to about this.
- You may be an international student, in which case you may have an International Tutor and/ or International Office to support you and you should be able to access language support.

- You may have special needs that can be accommodated by the institution and there should be someone to talk to about this, probably a whole department called 'student services' to check out.
- You may actually feel depressed or be suffering from anxiety problems. This is not necessarily a reason for leaving, but may rather be a reason for staying and working through your problems. You should be able to get support through a student counsellor who will probably be accessed through your student services department or student medical centre.
- Your students' union can also help with welfare and academic problems and will be experienced in giving advice and support.

Finally, if you have worked through the two lists in the previous activity and accessed the support you need, you will know if you are making a rational or emotional decision to leave. It's very easy to make a snap decision and then regret it. While it may be harder to stay and work through your reasons in the short term, it will be more rewarding in the long term.

A student told us ...

One student told us that, having arrived from one of the remotest corners of the world, she found she had no friends and felt nothing in common with anyone in her halls or on her course. She was so homesick that she just wanted to get on a plane and go back home. We encouraged her to hang in and join some student societies in order to meet more people. By the end of the first year she felt sufficiently confident that she didn't even go home for the summer vacation.

How are you with meeting new people?

Meeting new people tends to happen quite naturally for most people in the first few days at university, but maybe you found it difficult or met the wrong people, or maybe it has all gone a bit quiet now. This could be an area that you need to work on in order to integrate and settle in happily at your university or college.

The first time you meet someone is very important. First impressions really do count. People can sense intuitively in the first 30 seconds of an encounter what basic impression they will have of the other person after 15 minutes – or half a year. For instance, when people watch just 30-second snatches of staff giving a lecture, they can assess each teacher's proficiency with about 80 per cent accuracy (Ambady, 1993). Almost the same level of accuracy has been found from brief observations in 44 other studies, including one of people's interactions with bosses, peers and subordinates (Ambady and Rosenthal, 1992).

Activity: Meeting new people

Take a few minutes to reflect upon the following questions:

- Who was the first person you met on your first day?
- What were your first impressions?

Social phobia – irrational or exaggerated fear of involvement in social situations and possible implications or outcomes of doing so.

Some people find it particularly difficult to talk to strangers and will tend to avoid making new connections. This is known as a **social phobia**, but it can be overcome with perseverance. See also Chapter 4 on handling stress and developing relaxation techniques.

Here are some 'golden rules' for overcoming a fear of talking to new people – remember:

- You have a perfect right to speak to strangers.
- It doesn't matter what they think of you, because you are still you.
- It doesn't matter how many rejections you get because eventually you will get into meaningful conversation with someone.
- The more you do it, the better it will go and the more your fears will reduce.
- You are OK!

 Activity: Overcoming social phobias

1. Put yourself in a social situation such as a common room at lunch time or student union bar in the evening. Avoid anywhere that is so loud you can't talk or so quiet that you are feeling self-conscious.

2. Think about what you will say to open a conversation. Open questions such as 'how is it going?' are a good start (see also Chapter 3 on developing your questioning and listening skills).

3. Look out for someone who looks friendly and is also on their own.

4. Try out your opening question and try to back this up with friendly questions, exploring what they told you and then perhaps sharing something of your experience.

5. Make sure you keep doing this until you get into a meaningful conversation.

6. Review how it went and try again another time – soon. Avoidance breeds more anxiety, so it's better to keep at it (see also Chapter 4 on handling stress and developing relaxation techniques).

Not believing in the last of these 'golden rules' – you are OK – underpins our fears and phobias. If you can't truly believe it, try pretending that you are OK, acting a role, when you speak to someone. You may be surprised how quickly you begin to believe it! See also Chapter 3 on understanding the role of emotions – transactional analysis.

How well focused are you on other people?

You can improve the quality of the conversations you have with other people. Three critical factors are: energy, openness and mind focus. These largely determine the presence we can muster and maintain in any given interaction.

 Activity: Presence assessment

1. Ask yourself the following questions to measure your current ability to offer others your full presence:

   - On a scale of 1 to 10 (with 10 indicating a mind homing in like a laser beam of pure attention and 1 being a state of total mind-meandering), what is **your focus level** right now?

   - On a scale of 1 to 10, what is your level of **open-mindedness** and **open-heartedness** at this very moment towards other people?

   - On a scale of 1 to 10, what is your energy level right now, in terms of the reserves of **mental and physical vitality** and **vigour** you can bring to the moment?

2. Now consider how you can use these techniques:

   - You can perform the above simple self-awareness exercise at any time, mentally calculating your score in order to gauge your current level of presence.

   - Consider using it just prior to an interaction with others, initially to prepare yourself emotionally, then midway through an interaction to increase your emotional intelligence competencies and alertness, and finally as you leave an interaction to assess your overall presence throughout.

   - Used with regularity, the assessment becomes a self-correcting mechanism. Conscious attention to self-awareness can increase your ability to get on with other people.

Orientating yourself to your studies

What is your attitude to work and study? How do you approach study? Although you may be new to higher education, you will know how you were at school or college.

Activity: How were you at school or college?	
Did you:	**Tick**
attend classes regularly?	
participate enthusiastically when you were there?	
do all the work that was set?	
read to support the work in class?	
file your notes away neatly?	
start your assessments early so as to complete them on time?	
revise thoroughly for exams?	

Whatever you did before, it's now time to get organised for higher education. The emphasis will be much more on **independent study**, so being organised will be much more important – and if you don't get organised it is going to get very tough.

Contact time with staff may be much more limited in higher education than you were used to in school or college. The emphasis will probably be much more on you becoming an **independent learner**. Therefore knowing what you are supposed to be doing, when and where, and how to access the support facilities that you need, will become much more important.

Here are some ideas to consider:

- **Get connected** – get logged onto the university computer system as soon as you can in order to access online information. There will probably be a new student area which you can access even before you arrive.
- **Check your timetable** – sounds obvious, but you need to be in the right place at the right time. You should be able to check it out online and there is most likely to be an app you can access. Not everything runs to timetable, so make sure you have a system for remembering what you should be doing such as using a diary, personal organiser or mobile phone.
- **Full participation** – again it sounds obvious, but it's essential. It's usually true that failure rates correlate very closely to poor attendance patterns. You don't have to be especially gifted to pass, but you do need to turn up and to participate when you get there. Be there in mind and body!
- **Pre- and post-session work** – try to look upon pre- and post-session work as essential parts of the course and not as a nuisance or a 'bolt on'. Actual taught sessions in higher education tend to be relatively short, typically one hour, so post-session work will help to reinforce and extend what you have started to learn in a session and pre-session work or 'prep' will help you understand the next one.

- **Library and bookshops** – finding your way around the library and checking out bookshops are all useful things to do in your first few days and will really help you when the pressure builds up later.
- **Notes/folders** – how are you with paperwork? If it's all in a messy heap in the corner, it will be a serious setback to your studies. So the first few days is a good time to buy some files and start to learn to love filing! Taught programmes go by very quickly, with new material to take on board every week. Filing things away is good for revision as it helps to refresh your memory about what you studied. In addition it's all there waiting for you when you need material in order to complete assessments or to revise for exams.

 Activity: Getting organised for study

1. Make a list of things you think you need to do over the next few days and weeks.
2. Keep the list in a place where you can see it and tick off things as you achieve or complete them. It's important to record your success!
3. When you are a couple of weeks into your course, try playing **Freshers' bingo**, which is the next activity, to see how you are doing.

 Activity: Freshers' bingo

1. Take a few minutes to tick the boxes as honestly as you can. There is no prize – it's just for you!
2. Consider what you have learnt from doing this and what else you could do to establish yourself at university.

So have you…

Made friends and developed a social life?	Read for all your modules?	Attended taught sessions regularly?	Contributed your fair share to group work?
Done the required preparation for taught sessions?	Got your notes and folders organised for your studies?	Joined any student societies or sports clubs?	Checked your university emails regularly?
Wanted help but didn't like to ask anyone?	Been to the library and/or used library resources?	Been punctual for taught sessions?	Been homesick or thought about leaving the course?
Settled into your accommodation?	Felt overwhelmed?	Learnt new skills?	Engaged with online course materials?

Recognising your own motivation to learn, grow and develop

Motivation – has to do with the motives or drives we have for taking or avoiding actions.

Motivation is simply about having a motive to take some action. For example, consider these three questions. Why do people study? Why do people go to work? Why do they get up at all? It is clear that people do not all have the same motivations, but each of us has to find what motivates us in order to complete a course, get a job or whatever. The questions are: what is going to motivate you to succeed in your course, then in finding a job and in life as a whole?

Try completing the activity box below in order to find out what is going to motivate you and why, what the barriers to your achievement are and what new skills you might need to learn.

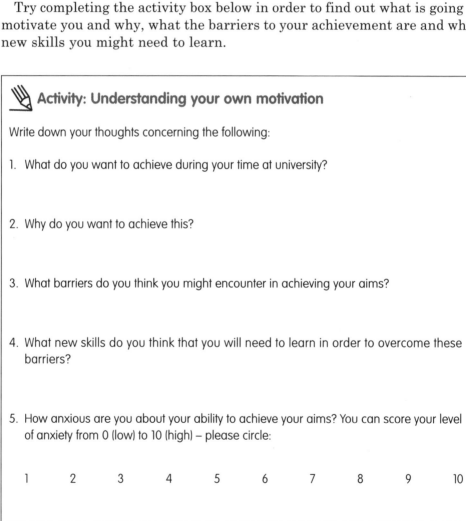

Activity: Understanding your own motivation

Write down your thoughts concerning the following:

1. What do you want to achieve during your time at university?

2. Why do you want to achieve this?

3. What barriers do you think you might encounter in achieving your aims?

4. What new skills do you think that you will need to learn in order to overcome these barriers?

5. How anxious are you about your ability to achieve your aims? You can score your level of anxiety from 0 (low) to 10 (high) – please circle:

   1   2   3   4   5   6   7   8   9   10

Identifying what you want to achieve and why at the start of your course is important, because there will always be days when you wonder what you are doing it all for. Many people also feel seriously anxious about their ability to complete their studies. If you are considering leaving your course, and many students do, remembering why you are studying and your motivation to achieve can pull you through on dark days (see earlier section in this chapter, on handling the transition into higher education).

 Activity: Comparing your motivation to succeed

1. Get someone else to complete the questions in the previous activity and then compare your answers. You might want to consider:

   - Are your answers the same or similar?
   - Do you think that they should be so?

2. Note down any differences which you feel are important.

Succeeding in higher education will require you holding onto your dream. Here are a few things you might want to try out:

- Try **visualising** yourself in a future time, perhaps at graduation or starting a new job. Paint the picture in your mind and put yourself clearly in it (there is more on visualisation in Chapter 2, Visualising your success).

  > **Visualisation** – picturing and recording in our mind a future event to help us achieve a better outcome

- Try using **affirmations**. An affirmation is something we say to ourselves because we need to say it. It is always a positive statement of your intention and starts with 'I', so your affirmation could be as simple as 'I know that I can succeed in my course'. It is a lie until we don't need to say it anymore. Try repeating affirmations every day until they become redundant. You'll know when that is!

  > **Affirmations** – statements we choose to make in order to reconceptualise.

- Try putting your affirmations on notes and put them up in your room to remind yourself what you are doing and why. This can seem quite daft when you are starting your course in the heady days of September or October, but by the dark days of November or February, they could be your salvation.
- Similarly, try putting up pictures or carrying them with you. Many people find friends, family or partners are an inspiration, or maybe it could be a car or a house you aspire to own. If you want to live in another part of the world, try carrying a picture of that place around with you to remind you of your dream.

A student told us ...

One student told us that his ambition was to be an accountant, but clearly this relied upon him completing his course successfully. He imagined himself in his new life, driving a black BMW. To remind himself, he put a picture of one from a magazine over the desk in his room.

Understanding your emotions in the developmental process

The science of moods

One of the biggest and perhaps least talked about factors in your development will be your ability to understand and work with your own emotions and those of others. At the core of this is the idea that, as human beings, we are 'hard wired' to respond to the behaviour and subsequent emotional reactions of other people. One person transmits signals that can alter hormone levels, cardiovascular functions, sleep rhythms and even immune functions inside the body of another. In all aspects of social life, our physiologies intermingle.

Emotional intelligence (EI) – is concerned with the science of emotion and emotional reactions.

In recent years a science of emotion has developed which is known as **emotional intelligence**. This has been defined as:

> The ability to express emotion, assimilate emotion in thought, understand and reason with emotion and regulate emotion in self and others. (Mayer and Salovey, 1990)

and as:

> The capacity for understanding our own feelings and those of others, for motivating others and ourselves whilst using leadership, empathy and integrity. (Goleman, 1998: 82)

Why are our emotions a potential threat to our success?

Amygdala takeover – when we are taken over by negative emotions

Negative emotions can get in the way of our succeeding, not only in our studies but also in employment and life generally. When we are taken over by negative emotions, this is referred to as an **amygdala takeover**. This can be

20

defined as an inappropriate and uncontrolled emotional response. It has four components:

- A trigger, which is a catalyst that stimulates because it generates an impulse.
- A strong emotion that is felt, such as anger, desire or frustration.
- An instant, impulsive, irrational or uncontrolled reaction that is usually inappropriate.
- A subsequent feeling of regret, after the feelings have passed.

When are we at risk of amygdala takeovers?

Predisposing factors	Trigger	Responses
• Tiredness	• Frustration	• Shouting
• Build-up of stress – 'the last straw'	• Value conflicts	• Crying
	• Personal criticism	• Shutting down
• Lots of effort into something	• Unfairness	• Swearing
	• Aggressive behaviour from others	• Physical violence
• Alcohol		

 Activity: Amygdala takeover

Think about an amygdala takeover you have experienced.

1. What triggered it?
2. What was your response (that you regretted)?
3. Can you identify anything that made you predisposed to a takeover?

Emotions involve an orchestration of activity in circuits throughout the brain, particularly the frontal lobe, which houses the brain's executive facilities (such as planning); the amygdala, which is particularly active during the experience of negative emotions such as fear; and the hippocampus, which adjusts actions to context (Davidson quoted in Goleman, 2003: 186–7).

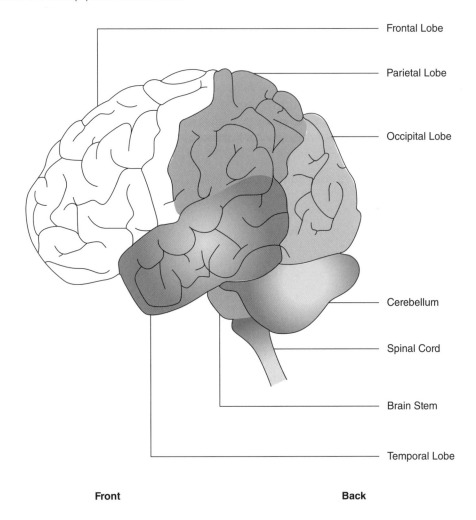

FIGURE 1.1   Regions of the human brain

Source: http://www.science.ca/images/Brain_Witelson.jpg

Emotional intelligence competencies – refers to discrete aspects of emotional intelligence which we may have to a greater or lesser extent, e.g. self-awareness.

What are emotional intelligence competencies?

Goleman (2001) has conducted research into **emotional intelligence competencies** which can be observed when an individual is considered to be emotionally intelligent. He went on to develop the competencies framework in the next activity.

Activity: Understanding your emotional intelligence competencies

1. Review the four lists of emotional intelligence competencies, ticking those you feel competent in. You are competent in a cluster when you can tick the majority in the box.

Self (personal competence)	Other (social competence)
Self-awareness	**Self-management**
Understand own strengths, areas for development, needs and drives	Manage feelings and impulses
	Choose words carefully
Recognise how feelings affect self	Avoid hasty judgements
Openness to feedback for development	Behave in accordance with values
	Follow through on promises
Self-confidence based on real strengths	Open to new ideas and adaptable in the face of new situations
	Motivate self to achieve
	Take action to make the most of opportunities in the future
Social awareness	**Relationship management**
Listen to others	Are skilled at winning people over
Understand others' perspectives	Listen well, seek mutual understanding and welcome sharing of information fully
Sense how others are feeling	Foster open communication and stay receptive to bad news as well as good
Understand how the organisation works	Handle difficult people and tense situations with diplomacy and tact
Committed to helping others (e.g. patients/clients)	Lead by example
	Model the change expected of others
	Balance a focus on task with attention to relationships
	Collaborate, sharing plans, information and resources

2. Review the four lists of emotional intelligence competencies again, this time identifying your strengths and areas for development, opportunities and threats, and record your findings in the 'SWOT Analysis' below.

(Continued)

(Continued)

What do you see as your **strengths** in terms of the emotional intelligence competencies?	What do you see as your **weaknesses**/areas for development in terms of the emotional intelligence competencies?
What **opportunities** do you see to develop your emotional intelligence competencies?	What **threats** do you see to you developing your emotional intelligence competencies, or barriers that may need to be overcome?

Can emotions be learned?

An American study into the source of happiness that has followed the lives of 268 men from youth to old age has shown that happiness is not down to the attributes that you are born with. George Vaillant, the current director of the study from Harvard Medical School, told the *Today* programme's Evan Davis: 'happiness is the wrong word... happiness is too close to hedonism and getting lucky'. He explained that happiness is more about 'emotional intelligence' and 'skill at long-term relationships'. 'If you want to be happy and you don't have a six-month-old baby to trade smiles with, get yourself a puppy' (*Today Programme*, 2012).

 Activity: Recognising your success competencies

Spencer and Spencer (1993: 336) have also identified the following competencies that predict success at work and in life:

- **Achievement orientation** – the desire to attain standards of excellence and do better, improve performance.
- **Initiative** – acting to attain goals and solve problems before being forced to by events.
- **Information seeking** – digging deeper for information.
- **Conceptual thinking** – making sense of data and using algorithms to solve problems.
- **Interpersonal understanding** – hearing the motives and feelings of diverse others.
- **Self-confidence** – a person's belief in their own efficacy, or ability to achieve goals.
- **Impact and influence** – a person's ability to persuade others to his or her viewpoint.
- **Collaborativeness** – working effectively with others to achieve common goals.

1. Review the above list of success competencies, ticking those you feel competent in.
2. Add your findings to the SWOT analysis you made in the previous section.

Developing your self-efficacy and self-confidence

Self-efficacy is about our confidence in our ability to succeed, whether it is in higher education, employment or life generally. Spencer and Spencer (1993: 80) offer a more detailed definition of self-confidence:

> **Self-efficacy** – concerns our confidence in our ability to succeed.

> Self-confidence is a person's belief in his or her own ability to accomplish a task. This includes the person expressing confidence in dealing with increasingly challenging circumstances, in reaching decisions or forming opinions, and in handling failure constructively.

Spencer and Spencer (1993) state that self-confidence is a component of most models of superior performers, although they also state that self-confidence may or may not be an independent variable: 'Is someone successful because they have self- confidence, or do they have self-confidence because they are successful?' Both may be the case in a positive self-perpetuating cycle, as illustrated in Figure 1.2

Building your self-confidence will mean doing new things and developing new skills. Whenever we step into new territory we are likely to feel anxious, but we develop confidence by keeping at it and pushing through. Your decision to enter higher education will inevitably mean doing new, different and sometimes difficult things, but the rewards will come from achieving them and from the increased self-confidence that you can take into employment and life.

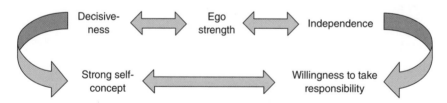

FIGURE 1.2   Self-confidence – self-perpetuating cycle

Source: Adapted from Spencer and Spencer, 1993: p 81

Follow-up activities

It is quite common in the first couple of weeks of a course not to have much academic work to do, so this may be a good time to invest some effort in what will be important for you over your time in higher education.

Activity: Developing your self-confidence

1. Reviewing your SWOT analysis, think of something you could do to build your self-confidence. It may be something you would normally avoid doing or something you have been putting off.
2. Make a definite plan to do something different in your life and then activate it.
3. How did it go? Make a note of what happened.

Time for action – Checklist

Have you:

- got connected to the university's internet/intranet and explored the new student area if there is one?
- made good efforts to get socially integrated?
- checked out your academic timetable and located rooms?
- started dealing with the information overload by setting up files etc.?
- checked out the library and bookshop?
- explored any online reading lists if these are available?
- accessed any other support services that you will need?
- considered your motivation and how it compares to that of a friend?
- recognised the role of your own emotions and self-efficacy in your development and success?

Further reading

Burns, T. and Sinfield, S. (2012) *Essential Study Skills: The Complete Guide to Success at University,* 3rd edn. London: Sage.

Cameron, S. (2009) *The Business Student's Handbook*, 5th edn. Harlow: Pearson.

Cottrell, S. (2013) *The Study Skills Handbook*, 4th edn. Basingtoke: Palgrave Macmillan.

Feldman, R. (2000) *Power Learning, Strategies for Success in College and Life.* Maidenhead: McGraw-Hill Higher Education.

Fowlie, J. A. and Wood, M. (2009) 'The emotional impact of leaders behaviours', *Journal of European Industrial Training*, 33 (6): 559–72.

Goleman, D. (2003) *Destructive Emotions and How We Can Overcome Them.* London: Bloomsbury.

Jeffers, S. (2012) *Feel the Fear and Do it Anyway*, Revised edn. London: Random House.

Lee-Davies, L. (2007) *Developing Work and Study Skills*. London: Thomson.

Pedler, M. and Boydell, J. (1999) *Managing Yourself*. London: Lemos and Crane.

Race, P. (1995) *Who Learns Wins*. London: Penguin.

Race, P. (2007) *How to Get a Good Degree: Making the Most of your Time at University*. Buckingham: Open University Press.

Thompson, M. (2013) *Winning Strategies for Sport and Life*. London: Gabrielle Lea Publishing.

Websites to look up

- Most universities and colleges of higher education will have areas on their website with titles such as 'arriving at university', 'accommodation', 'international student support', 'dealing with homesickness', 'culture shock', etc.
- The National Union of Students also provides information at:
  www.nus.org.uk
- Information for international students is available from UKCISA at:
  www.ukcisa.org.uk

Time for review and reflection

This is your space to log your reflections on this chapter, to think about what you have learnt, how you will use it and what else you need to find out.

There will be more on reflection and why and how we can use it to learn, grow and develop in Chapter 2, in the sections on recognising your own strengths, and planning your continuing personal development.

What were the key learning points of this chapter?
What are your strengths in the areas covered by this chapter?
What areas did you identify for development?

What have you learnt about yourself?
How will you use this knowledge?
What else do you need to learn or find out about in relation to this chapter?

2

How to Plan Your Personal Development

Overview – what's in this chapter?

- Why do you need to plan your personal development?
- Recognising your own strengths and areas for development
- Planning your continuing personal development
- Visualising your success and putting the past behind you
- Overcoming resistance to change
- Reviewing your progress and updating your plans
- Follow-up activities, further reading and websites to look up
- Time for review and reflection

Why do you need to plan your personal development?

Try completing the short self-scoring test overleaf, to assess your own level of confidence in relation to planning your own personal development.

✎ **Activity: Why do you need to read this chapter?**

You need to self score each question on a scale from 0 to 10, where 0 is low and 10 is high.

1. How much thought have you given to planning your future development?	
2. To what extent have you decided upon clear targets you want to achieve?	
3. How clearly can you specify your plans or state your targets?	
4. How committed are you to turning your plan into reality and to achieving your targets?	
5. How convinced are you that your plans can become a reality?	
6. How much effort have you put into achieving your targets so far?	
7. How likely are you to resist the process of change?	
8. How likely are you to let obstacles deter you from achieving your targets?	
9. How clearly can you visualise yourself achieving your targets successfully?	
10. Have you set a clear timescale to achieve your goal or dates to review your plans?	
Total score	

Interpretation

What did you score?

- Less than 50%   You will definitely find a lot of help in this chapter.
- 50%–75%   There is still plenty to learn in this chapter.
- 75%–100%   You are very confident – read on to confirm your understanding.

We all need to change in order to grow and develop. Some of this process happens spontaneously; for example, you might make a friend who can teach you a new skill such as using a computer package, or who helps you to get a vacation job. It's usually good to take up the opportunities which life hands to you, but there is a lot of chance involved in this and it's important to recognise that the process can also be planned. You have a much better chance of achieving what you want if you approach the process systematically.

As a student you might have some fairly obvious targets. Typically our students tell us that they want to make new friends, graduate with a good degree and be offered a great job! However, what you want out of university doesn't just happen by accident – it's far more likely to happen if you consciously think about exactly what *you* need to do to meet your targets.

Personal development planning is the process of actively planning and reviewing your personal development, and mirrors the processes of **professional development planning** and **continuing professional development** (CPD) programmes in the workplace. The whole concept of continuing professional development reflects the idea that an initial qualification such as a first degree or professional qualification is not enough and that, in a changing world, updating our knowledge and skill competencies is essential in order to remain a competent professional.

In answer to the question, 'why would people want to change?' Boyatzis (2001; in Cherniss and Goleman, 2001) suggests:

- to increase personal effectiveness or promotion potential;
- to become a better person;
- to help others develop.

Boyatzis goes on to identify four **discontinuities** in the change process, which are those periods when our consistent behaviour suddenly changes, perhaps surprising others and ourselves. The four discontinuities, which can be seen as steps, are:

> **Personal development planning** – process of actively planning and reviewing your personal development.

> **Professional development planning** – process of actively planning and reviewing your professional development.

> **Continuing professional development** – structured and ongoing process of learning, which aims to maintain professional competence after initial qualification or appointment.

> **Discontinuity** – a break in the normal flow of activity.

1. Deciding who am I and what I want to be – i.e. real self and ideal self.
2. **The balance between preservation and adaptation**. It may be better to focus upon our strengths rather than our deficiencies, and to decide what we want to keep and build upon.
3. **The decision to change** – the move from contemplation to preparation, making choices and creating your own learning agenda.
4. **The decision to act** – may include a period of experimentation and receiving feedback from other people including friends, family, tutors, etc.

Change may have repercussions when 'they' don't understand (Jeffers, 1991). They may be your friends, peers, families and tutors; in a work context they might be bosses, colleagues, subordinates. However, resistance to change may also be internal, as we may fear the process and resist doing what we need to do to grow and develop (see also the section in this chapter on overcoming resistance to change).

Ultimately, if we are not changing, growing and developing we are likely to start contracting. The status quo is not an option; standing still in a changing world tends to lead to us being left behind. This chapter is therefore designed to help you facilitate the process of change and is based upon what we have learned from others and through our own experience of our personal journeys. We invite you to join us!

 Activity: What were your targets and what was your motivation?

1. Can you remember your targets for university which you established in the 'Understanding your own motivation' activity in Chapter 1? If so, write them here:

2. If you can't remember what your targets were or didn't complete the activity, have a look back at Chapter 1 and complete the motivation activity.

3. Are these targets still important to you?

4. How are you doing at achieving your targets?

In this chapter we aim to help you identify your own strengths and areas for development, to plan your continuing personal development, visualise your success, overcome resistance to change, review your progress and update your plans. Finally there are some follow-up activities, suggested further reading, websites to look up, and space for review and reflection.

Recognising your own strengths and areas for development

Developing a realistic picture of who you are is the first step in planning your personal development. In particular, it is important to identify your strengths, your areas for development, and your opportunities for development together with any threats or barriers to achievement. You can also include strengths and areas for development, opportunities and threats from outside life. Making a personal SWOT analysis, as in the next activity, involves looking at the following areas:

- **Strengths** – knowledge, skills and abilities that you already have and may be able to build on. Remembering your strengths is a good starting point and can make you feel more positive about the process.
- **Weaknesses** – potentially these are areas for development if you can work on them in order to turn them from negatives to positives.
- **Opportunities** – these are your life chances and they are all there to be exploited. Even an area for development can become an opportunity to develop.
- **Threats** – these are likely to stop you achieving your targets. What are they? Are there barriers which will need to be overcome?

> **SWOT Analysis** – technique for analysing **s**trengths, areas for development, (**w**eaknesses), **o**pportunities and **t**hreats.

✎ **Activity: Who do you think you are?**

1. Try to complete the following SWOT analysis:

What are your *strengths* that you may build upon?	What are your *weaknesses* or areas to develop and work on?
What *opportunities* do you see to develop yourself?	What *threats* do you see to your personal development or barriers that may need to be overcome?

2. What did you learn about yourself in the process?

You will find more activities in Chapter 9 (e.g. What skills do I have to offer?) and in Chapter 10 (e.g. What are my personal qualities?) which will help you to identify your skill set and personal qualities. Doing this sort of preparation can really help to inform your personal development planning and also has the potential to expose new areas for your continuing personal development.

Planning your continuing personal development

In thinking about our personal development we can draw an analogy with a railway journey from one town to another, passing through various stations. Personal development planning is about planning our personal journey through life, and just like a rail journey it can sometimes seem as if we are on a particular track; however, our journey can include a number of stops along the way. These 'stops' are our **review dates**. Reviews allow you to re-confirm or change your objective. In terms of the analogy, we can stop for a while and reconsider – maybe even change trains if we think we are on the wrong track or simply a bit off course.

We can also recognise the idea of the **off course model** (Jeffers, 1991: 126–8) as in the case of a plane or boat which can be off course for as much as 90 per cent of the journey but keeps returning to its heading or course. So personal development is not always a straightforward journey from point A to point B. Our lives often contain many twists and turns. Reviews just help us to take stock, see where we are, re-plan and move on again, so that ultimately you can achieve what *you* want. So it's vitally important to have clear targets, to record them and review your progress towards them regularly. We need aims if we are to achieve anything, because without them we are literally 'aimless'. So targets give us aims in life and can help to keep us on track.

> **Off course model –** developed by Susan Jeffers, recognises that we spend much of our life being off course but that the key to successful development is to keep getting back on course.

What do you want to develop?

There is no limit to what you can plan, nor do you need to stick to immediate or academic targets, although they should not be excluded. Typical areas for personal development planning include:

- Study skills and study outcomes such as progression, grades and final awards.
- Job and career aspirations including career path and salary.
- Health and fitness concerns including improving exercise, diet and reducing stress levels.
- Personal goals such as climbing a mountain, playing a sport or musical instrument, seeing the pyramids, forming a relationship or whatever else you want to do.

Many students formulate general targets about their degree or job but just what you consider a 'good degree' or a 'good job' is relative – it depends upon what your aspirations are. Think of the image of the medal podium at the Olympic Games. You might typically see one athlete ecstatic because he/she is the best in the world, while another is in despair at 'only' getting silver, and sometimes a third is overjoyed because he/she was a complete outsider who unexpectedly got a bronze when nothing at all was expected. Here we see laid bare people's aspirations when compared with the outcomes they actually achieve.

Activity: What do you want to achieve?

1. Brainstorm ideas for things you might potentially want to achieve in life.
2. Next revisit your list and decide what is really important to you.
3. Put what is left into a priority order which you can use in your personal development plan (PDP).

Making your targets SMART

To make your personal development planning really effective you need to set **SMART targets**, i.e. targets which are:

> **SMART targets** – targets which are **s**pecific, **m**easurable, **a**chievable, **r**ealistic and **t**imed.

S = Specific

M = Measurable

A = Achievable

R = Realistic

T = Timed

Example of a SMART goal

- *Objectives: What do I want to learn*? To improve my time management skills.
- *What will I do to achieve this*? Break larger tasks down into smaller tasks, make a 'to do list', set deadlines, give myself rewards when I have completed a task.
- *What resources or support will I need*? Work lists, a diary, an available app or books (e.g. Fiore, N. (2007) *Now Habit: A Strategic Program for Overcoming Procrastination and Enjoying Guilt-free Play*. London: Penguin Books, also available as a Kindle book).
- *What will my success criteria be*? All tasks on my to do list either completed or rescheduled each day, no work taken home and two hours per week devoted to my continuing professional development (CPD).
- *Target date for review and completion*? Review date: 7 February.

If your targets are not SMART you will be less likely to achieve them, and a common reason for failing to achieve is related to making loose targets such as:

- 'I will get better results next semester'
- 'I will be less nervous about exams'
- 'I will get a good job'.

The problem here is deciding what words such as 'better', 'less' and 'good' actually mean. A SMART target for results, if this was realistic and achievable, could be:

'I will get an overall 2.1 next semester'

Making a goal which involves measuring your own performance, such as examination nerves, can be more problematic. You could start by making an assessment of yourself on a scale of 1 to 10 and then setting a realistic point to aim for. If 0 was no anxiety and 10 was high anxiety you might make a goal as follows, if you felt this was realistic and achievable:

'I will reduce my level of examination anxiety from seven to three'

 Activity: Making a SMART target

1. Try making a SMART target that you might include in your personal development plan (PDP).
2. Now check your target. Is it: specific, measurable, achievable, realistic and timed? If not, try re-working it until you are happy that it is.

Making your personal development plan (PDP)

In making a successful personal development plan, we recommend that you adopt a systematic approach which includes the following stages:

- Do your preparation first. Complete your 'Who do you think you are?' SWOT analysis activity (see above) so that you have a clearer view of who you are before you start.
- Think before you write. What are your priorities, what is achievable and what is realistic? You can't do everything, and if you try to, you are likely to become demotivated very quickly.
- Set a realistic number of targets and specify each one clearly. What do you want to achieve? Focusing your energy on a smaller number of targets may well bring you more success.
- Think what you will need to do to achieve each aim. There could potentially be several actions for each objective.
- Identify all the resources you will need to achieve each objective. Again there could be several for each of your objectives.

- Consider carefully how you will measure your success. For some targets the outcome can be clearly measured, as for example 'Achieve 2.1 degree' or 'save £200 from my part-time job for Christmas presents'. For others such as increased confidence or reduced anxiety you will have to create your own scale, as suggested earlier in this section.
- Make sure you fix both specific review dates and clear mechanisms for doing it. It is sometimes quite useful to have a 'meeting with yourself' – and you can make a note in your diary, mobile phone or personal organiser to remind you to do it.

 Activity: Making a PDP

1. Try completing a personal development plan, using the following format:

Aims:	Actions:	Resources:	Measurement:	Review and timescale:
What do I want to achieve/ learn?	What will I do to achieve this?	What resources/ support will I need?	What will my success criteria be?	Date and method of review?

2. Critically review your completed PDP or get a friend to look it over. The key questions are:

- Are your targets really SMART?
- Have you fixed a time and method for review?
- Is it just a plan or are you really going to do it?

Research has shown that individuals who set goals are more likely to see behavioural changes if the goals set are highly specific, appropriately difficult, targeted, and remembered – and where the individual remains highly committed (McShane, 2011). The more detailed and appropriate the level of difficulty, then the greater the self-directed change and the more this increases the possibility of achieving the goal. Therefore, people who specify their targets are more likely to achieve them and the more clearly they specify them, then the more likely they are to achieve.

Visualising your success and putting the past behind you

Visualisation – picturing and recording in our mind a future event to help us achieve a better outcome.

Guided **visualisation** is a key technique in **Neuro-Linguistic Programming** (or NLP) and involves us changing our **subjective experience** or thoughts. Since our brains record all memories, visualisation enables new memories to be recorded, helping us to overcome past disasters and to look positively at the future. It doesn't change what happened, but rather how we feel about it.

Neuro-Linguistic Programming – collection of techniques developed by Bandler and Grinder, drawing on neurology and linguistics.

NLP was developed by Bandler and Grinder (1976; 1979, cited in O'Connor and Seymour, 2002: 2) and has become the basis of much work in the area of human communications. There are many branches to NLP, but central concerns include:

- emotional states and how we might change them;
- studying patterns or language and behaviours as evidenced in situations;
- building rapport and trust in interpersonal relations, perhaps by mirroring or matching words or behaviours;
- setting motivational targets and overcoming barriers to achievement;
- modelling behaviour – discerning the sequence of ideas or behaviours required to successfully achieve a task;

Subjective experience – has to do with the individual's internal perception of reality.

- reprogramming subjective experience in order to overcome negative thought patterns, such as phobias, or to allow for successful achievement of targets.

In the following two activities, we first try to put something from our past behind us, before turning our attention to what we want to achieve for the future. In both cases you will need to work with a partner.

✍ Activity: Putting the past behind us

1. Working individually, recall something you didn't manage to succeed at or where you felt you under-achieved – perhaps something that plays on your mind.

2. Note down how you are feeling emotionally at this very minute, while you are recalling the experience.

3. Now working with a partner, close your eyes and ask your partner to slowly talk you through the following steps. You can either nod or say yes when you want them to move on to the next stage, but do not share your thoughts with your partner during the process.

- Visualise your memory.
- Put a frame around the picture.
- Turn off any sounds associated with it.
- Push it away from you so it's about ten feet away.
- Paint it onto glass so that it's fragile and brittle.
- Turn it to black and white.
- Push it far, far away, until it's in the distance.
- In your mind, pick up a stone and throw it with perfect accuracy at your picture.
- Watch the glass shatter and the picture break into a million black and white pieces that then dissolve into dust in space.

4. At the end of your visualisation, write down how you felt emotionally at that moment.

 Activity: Visualising your successes

1. Working individually, identify something that you want to achieve.
2. Note down how you are feeling emotionally at this very minute.
3. Now working with a partner, close your eyes and ask your partner to talk you slowly through the following steps. You can either nod or say yes when you want them to move on to the next stage, but do not share your thoughts with your partner during the process.

   - Visualise what you want to achieve.
   - Put yourself in the picture.
   - Add any sound or music you would like.
   - Check that you are happy with the picture and make any changes you want.
   - Indicate that you are happy with it.
   - Now increase the brilliance of the picture.
   - Check out how you look, breathe and speak, together with any other impressions.
   - What emotions do you feel?
   - What physical sensations do you feel?
   - What are you saying?
   - What kind of person are you?

4. At the end of your visualisation, write down how you felt emotionally at that moment.

Visualisation also links well with other techniques such as meditation and autogenic training (see also Chapter 4 on handling stress and developing relaxation techniques), and normally involves picturing and recording how we think things realistically might be. If we build a picture in our mind of how we might handle a difficult situation better, we are more prepared when we meet it, because we have already built some of the psychological structures of the experience. For example, if you fear examinations you can try to visualise yourself being relaxed and confident while taking them.

Overcoming resistance to change

Resistance may be internal or external, in other words it could be other people that stop us moving on, but also it could be ourselves. The root of almost all resistance to change is fear and included in this is the fear of failure – getting it wrong, doing badly and maybe being worse off than you are now. Personal development is partly about getting unstuck from wherever we are stuck and moving on. However, getting stuck would seem to be part of the human condition and most of us seem to suffer from some level of **inertia** at points in our lives. When you catch yourself saying 'but I always ...' you could be well and truly stuck!

Inertia – being stuck and unwilling or resistant to movement or progress.

Inertia gives us some hope of security, but it may be a false hope. It is very easy to get trapped in a **comfort zone** and this, of course, avoids the discomfort of having to take steps outside of it. Your comfort zone may in fact be quite uncomfortable, but staying stuck can seem preferable to taking the steps you need to take in order to move on, grow and develop. Here are some examples of false comfort zones:

Comfort zone – an area of life in which an individual avoids risk and anxiety.

- Sticking with a group of 'friends' you don't particularly like or respect because it feels safer than making new ones.
- Avoiding your studies because it seems easier in the short term not to go to class or pick up a book.
- Staying in substandard accommodation where you find it hard to study because it is too much hassle to move.

Getting unstuck takes one thing only: commitment to achieving what you want. Making a personal development plan is a sign of your commitment to your own development and so is reviewing it. Getting into the habit of **planning, acting**

and reviewing as an ongoing cycle will allow you to see how you are doing. If you are still stuck when you review, then getting unstuck will have to become a target in itself.

One technique for overcoming your own resistance is to try to think in a way which at first **disassociates** you from the problem. In the next activity you will see a classic disassociative question, which asks you why you think other people in your situation might resist change. From there it's a short step to ask yourself: What about me then? Why might I be resisting?

> **Disassociation** – psychological concept describing some level of detachment from a situation.

 Activity: Overcoming resistance to change

1. Try to think why some other people might resist change, if they were in your situation.

2. Might you be doing the same thing? If so, how might this resistance be overcome?

3. Think where you expect external resistance might come from. Who or what might want to keep you stuck – and why?

4. How might this resistance be overcome?

As you start to change, you might face resistance from family, friends and significant others in your life who don't understand what is happening to you. Jeffers (1991: 89–108) devotes a whole chapter to this problem entitled 'When "they" don't want you to grow'. This is a problem that many students report when they return home. While they have changed, back home everybody is going round in the usual circles and it can be surprising and distressing to find that you don't fit in anymore. Worse still to find that they think there is now something wrong with you, as often expressed in terms such as 'huh, is that what they teach you then?'

It is usually good to explain your plans to those around you and to try to get positive support. We are generally more effective when we have positive people around us who appreciate what we are trying to do. However, if you get only negative feedback from any or all of the people in your immediate circle, then it is time to look for a new **cheering squad**. As Jeffers puts it (1991: 90):

> It is amazingly empowering to have the support of a strong, motivated and inspirational group of people.

41

Reviewing your progress and updating your plans

According to the old adage, 'the road to hell is paved with good intentions'. Making a plan is all well and good, but it could just be fine words if a plan is all that it is. Your plan needs to be activated and you need to review your progress regularly. As we suggested earlier in this chapter, your personal development can be seen as being like a journey, with stops along the way which provide opportunities for you to review your progress, to confirm or change your plans and to make a new review date.

Review dates are not the same as end dates. We sometimes see students setting a target such as 'Get overall 2.1 this year' with a review date to coincide with the release of results. However, that is at a point where they can no longer influence the result. Let's face it, everyone reviews their progress on results day. What they needed was a *series* of review dates over the course of their studies to make sure they were on track and a *final* review date when results come out.

There are many ways of reviewing your progress. You could have a **meeting with yourself** as suggested earlier, or you might have a friend or colleague to buddy up with for some form of peer review of each other's progress. Your institution should have some form of **personal tutor** scheme, so another option would be to ask your tutor to review your plan with you.

Follow-up activities

Time for action – Checklist

Have you:

- reflected upon your progress to date?
- completed the SWOT analysis in order to see what you have already and what you want to develop?
- identified your targets for development?
- made your targets SMART?
- made a personal development plan?
- visualised what you want to achieve?
- identified what resistance you might face and considered how to overcome it?
- fixed review date(s) and method(s) for review and updating of your plans?

One outcome of every review should be to make a new plan or at least to update the existing one, so that you always have a plan in operation. You must also, of course, fix a new review date. So the process is ongoing – a cycle of reviewing, planning, acting and then reviewing, planning and acting again – so that it becomes a form of **habitualised behaviour**.

> **Habitualised behaviour** – behaviour pattern that become routine as a result of repetition.

Further reading

Buckingham, M. and Clifton, D. O. (2005) *Now, Discover Your Strengths*. London: Simon & Schuster.

Burns, T. and Sinfield, S. (2012) *Essential Study Skills: The Complete Guide to Success at University*, 3rd edn. London: Sage.

Cameron, S. (2009) *The Business Student's Handbook*, 5th edn. Harlow: Pearson.

Cherniss, C. and Goleman, D. (ed.) (2001) *The Emotionally Intelligent Workplace*. San Francisco: Jossey-Bass.

Cottrell, S. (2013) *The Study Skills Handbook*, 4th edn. Basingstoke: Palgrave Macmillan.

Cottrell, S. (2010) *Skills for Success: The Personal Development Planning Handbook*, 2nd edn. Basingstoke: Palgrave Macmillan.

Fiore, N. (2007) *Now Habit: A Strategic Program for Overcoming Procrastination and Enjoying Guilt-free Play*. New York:, Penguin Group (USA) Inc. (also available as a Kindle book).

Goleman, D. (2013) *Focus: The Hidden Driver of Excellence*. New York: Harper Collins.

Goleman, D. (1998) *Working with Emotional Intelligence*. London: Bloomsbury Paperbacks.

Jeffers, S. (2012) *Feel the Fear and Do it Anyway*, Revised edn. London: Random House.

McShane, B. (2011) *The Few That Do: How Winners Set and Reach Their Goals*. Rossa Publishing.

O'Connor, J. (2002) *The NLP Workbook: A Practical Guide to Achieving the Results you Want*. London: Element.

O'Connor, J. and Seymour, F. (2002) *Introducing NLP: Psychological Skills for Understanding and Influencing People*, 3rd edn. London: Element.

Thompson, M. (2013) *Winning Strategies for Sport and Life*. London: Gabrielle Lea Publishing.

Websites to look up

- For help and support with personal/professional development planning:
  www.uncommon-knowledge.co.uk/personal_development/plan.html
  www.palgrave.com/skills4study/pdp/about/index.asp
- For help and information with visualisation:
  www.stress.org.uk

Time for review and reflection

This is your space to log your reflections on this chapter, to think about what you have learnt, how you will use it and what else you need to find out.

What were the key learning points of this chapter?
What are your strengths in the areas covered by this chapter?
What areas did you identify for development?
What have you learnt about yourself?
How will you use this knowledge?
What else do you need to learn or find out about in relation to this chapter?

3

How to Improve Your People Skills

Overview – what's in this chapter?

- Why do you need to upgrade your people skills?
- Developing your questioning and listening skills
- Preparing for formal interviews
- Understanding the role of emotions
- Recognising non-verbal communications
- Resolving conflict with other people
- Asserting yourself when it is appropriate
- Developing your influencing skills
- Giving and receiving feedback
- Follow-up activities, further reading and websites to look up
- Time for review and reflection

Why do you need to upgrade your people skills?

Try completing the short self-scoring test overleaf, to assess your own level of confidence in relation to improving your people skills.

✎ Activity: Why do you need to read this chapter?

You need to self score each question on a scale from 0 to 10, where 0 is low and 10 is high.

1. How good are you at talking to new people?	
2. How good are you at framing questions in order to get people talking?	
3. How good are you at listening to other people, for example in lectures and seminars?	
4. How good are you at saying clearly what you want to say?	
5. How good are you at handling your emotions?	
6. How aware are you of other people's body language?	
7. How good are you at resolving conflict with other people?	
8. How frequently do you assert yourself in situations with people?	
9. How good are you at influencing people?	
10. How open are you to receiving feedback from others?	
Total score	

Interpretation

What did you score?

- Less than 50%   You will definitely find a lot of help in this chapter.
- 50%–75%   There is still plenty to learn in this chapter.
- 75%–100%   You are very confident – read on to confirm your understanding.

Whatever you want to do or achieve in life will definitely involve working and interacting with other people. Clearly we all have a level of skill in this area, but some of us are better than others. The good news is we can all develop our people skills.

However, it's not just a case of developing our own communication skills, because when dealing with other people we are also *interacting* with them and their reactions may be quite unpredictable. We all have bad days and catching someone you know at the wrong moment may require you to change your approach or even to back off altogether.

We all have to handle a myriad of **interpersonal situations** in life and they include:

- **Formal situations** – such as attending a tutorial or supervision with one of your lecturers, conducting your own research interviews for completion of an academic assignment or a recruitment interview for a job, placement or internship.
- **Informal situations** – such as meeting new friends, catching up with old ones or 'chatting up' in a night club.

Whatever the situation, there are key skills that we can all learn and develop to help us be effective in our interpersonal communications, including:

- question formulation;
- listening and hearing;
- reading body language;
- understanding the emotional content of interpersonal communications;
- conflict resolution;
- asserting ourselves;
- influencing others;
- giving and receiving feedback.

No one handles every interpersonal situation perfectly, but the skills listed above are ones that we can all keep developing through life. These are **transferable skills,** that is, skills learnt in one context which can be used in another. Skills learned here can be developed in social situations and then used to further our studies and careers.

> **Transferable skills –** skills learnt in one situation which can be readily transferred to another, e.g. communication skills developed in social situations and then used in the workplace.

In this chapter we aim to help you to develop your interpersonal skills and abilities in handling relationships. We will focus in particular upon questioning and listening skills, preparing for formal interviews, the role of emotions, non-verbal communications, resolving conflict, asserting yourself and influencing others, together with giving and receiving feedback. Finally there are some follow-up activities, some suggested further reading, websites to look up, and some space for review and reflection.

Developing your questioning and listening skills

Asking better questions

We all use questions for a variety of purposes including to get people talking, to find out information, and to give direction and reinforcement to our conversations. However, some questions can be more productive than others. We can distinguish three types of question:

- **Open-ended questions** – these generally produce longer answers and get people talking. They usually start with words such as who, what, when, where, which, why, how or tell me. They demand longer answers, so you get more information by asking fewer questions and your conversation becomes more productive. The most open question is probably, 'tell me about your life'.
- **Closed or directional questions** – these tend to produce short answers because they can be answered with a simple yes or no. They start with words such as do, did, are, might, if, can, does, have, is, etc. Closed questions do help with direction. For example, in a job interview you might ask, 'will there be any opportunities for further training and development?' If the answer is 'yes', you can follow this up with an open question. Most often this is the real value of a closed question, in establishing whether an area is worthy of further exploration.
- **Reflective questions** – these ask the other person to expand upon their answer. For example, you might be chatting with a friend who mentions planning a holiday in Greece. There are two possibilities here. You could simply repeat the word 'Greece' with an upturn in your voice to indicate a question, which is an example of so-called 'up-speak'. Almost certainly your friend will then go on to tell you more about the trip. Alternatively you can ask a question such as 'can you tell me more about that?'

 Activity: Developing your questioning skills

- Try writing some sample questions of each of the three types listed above.
- Next try dropping them into everyday conversations.
- Reflect upon your results. Which questions were most effective and why?

Selecting the right questions comes with experience. People who are nervous frequently ask too many questions in general and too many closed questions in particular. It is just a case of practising your questioning skills, reflecting on how it went and gradually improving your technique.

Listening and hearing

Perhaps one of the most frustrating things that can happen in an interpersonal situation, be it socially, in a formal interview or seminar, is when you feel that you are not being listened to. It typically happens something like this: You are asked, 'what are you doing at the moment?' You answer, 'I am studying engineering at university.' Then they ask you, 'And what are you studying at university?' Why does this sort of thing happen? Well clearly the interviewer wasn't listening to your answer, and you might ask why. The most likely reason is that he or she was distracted and probably more concerned with thinking about the next question, rather than listening to the answer to the one in hand.

Listening is the second great interpersonal skill after question formulation, but listening isn't enough. It may sound completely obvious to say, but we also have to **hear** what is said and that is not the same thing at all.

Imagine you are listening to a band or orchestra at a gig or in a concert hall. You listen to the music, but do you hear it all? You might be interested in what one musician is playing, so you focus in on that performance. You hear it, while listening to the whole. It takes attention and concentration and this is what we need for interpersonal communication. This is what we call **active listening.**

Active listening involves:

- being fully engaged or 'switched on' to the situation;
- not speaking unless you are absolutely sure that the other person has finished what they are saying;
- maintaining eye contact;
- displaying open body language;
- triggering the other person to say more with nods or smiles.

> **Active listening –** requires the listener to be fully engaged and focused on the other person and what they are saying.

Active listening is also highly relevant to your participation in lectures, seminars and workshops. Being fully engaged and focused will help you to get more out of the learning experience by enabling you to absorb more of what is said, take more accurate notes, make more relevant contributions and formulate better questions to ask.

Silence is golden! This old expression is very true, because you usually find that people will say much more when you give them space and time. A good rule here is, ask less and listen more!

 Activities: Listening and hearing

Here are two activities that will help you to improve your listening and hearing skills:

1. Working with a friend, take turns to interview each other. The interviewer only asks one open question, and then relies upon nods, smiles and other facial expressions in order to get responses.

2. When you are in a social situation try asking someone an open question and then try to refrain from saying anything else for as long as possible, once again triggering the other person with nods, smiles and so on.

Note down how long you managed to make these activities last. With practice you will be able to ask less, but elicit more from people.

Preparing for formal interviews

Structured interview – questions are pre-scripted around a pre-set agenda.

In preparing for a formal interview, it is important to recognise what type of interview you are planning to conduct. There are three options and each of the following has advantages and disadvantages:

- **Structured interviews** tend to revolve around a pre-set agenda and scripted questions. They can in one sense be very thorough, because some thought has been put into deciding what needs to be covered and also into formulating the questions. However, these can be very stilted in practice and the formality can intimidate the interviewee. Also the interviewer may miss something really important altogether, because no pre-prepared question covered it.

Informal interview – questions are not pre-scripted and the interview is allowed to flow.

- **Informal interviews** are often the best because you can be very relaxed and this will encourage the other person to open up and talk. However, they may be quite unsystematic, rambling around from point to point and again may miss some points in the process.

Semi-structured interview – has some structure but allows for flexibility and supplementary questions.

- **Semi-structured interviews** are a compromise and have the advantage of having some structure whilst allowing some flexibility. They allow points to be introduced and then to be explored more fully with supplementary questions.

✎ Activity: Developing interview questions

- Before you conduct an interview, do some preparation by making a *mind map* (see Chapter 5 on using mapping) in which you identify all the areas you want to explore.
- Rather than scripting questions in advance, try using your mind map as a crib sheet during the interview. Use closed questions to open up new areas when necessary and then open questions to explore them.
- Afterwards reflect upon how it went, making a note of what went well, what did not go so well and what you would do differently next time.

When conducting an interview it may be useful to consider adopting the following systematic approach:

- Think in advance what you want to achieve from the interview and what you want to know. Making a mind map – as in the last activity – can often help focus your thoughts.
- Seek a *comfortable* environment in which to conduct the interview – somewhere that both your interviewee and yourself will feel comfortable. It should ideally be clean, tidy,

well-ventilated and neither too hot nor too cold. Not being comfortable can be a major distraction from the interview process.

- Try to avoid any interruptions by putting a notice on the door, putting any extension phone on divert and switching your mobile to silent or, better still, off completely. There is nothing worse than somebody crashing in or a phone ringing just as you have asked the most difficult question. The moment can be lost forever.
- Organise the furniture, avoid putting a desk or table between yourself and your interviewee and, if possible, sit side by side as face to face can be confrontational.
- Think about personal space – too far away is too distant and too close is threatening (see also the following section, on recognising non-verbal communication).
- Start your interview by making introductions; be welcoming, friendly and use first names to relax your interviewee.
- Always explain the purpose of the interview, stating how long it is likely to take and what is going to happen. Doing this will help to relax and reassure your interviewee.
- Consider making your opening questions easy and non-threatening, in order to help relax your interviewee and get them talking. For example, you could ask them about their journey and if they found their way to you with no trouble, or simply how they are doing.
- Ask your questions giving your interviewee plenty of time to reply, and also give your interviewee opportunities to ask questions.
- Summarise the interview and explain what will happen next.

Four **golden rules** of interviewing are:

1. Always listen closely to answers.
2. Give time and space.
3. Don't interrogate.
4. Don't be judgemental/prejudiced.

 Activity: Developing your interview skills

Working in a group of three, take turns to play the role of:

1. An interviewer working for an employment agency, who is trying to find out as much as possible about the interviewee.

2. A student interviewee seeking work who is unsure as to what work he or she might best be able to do.

3. An observer who will time the activity, take notes and give constructive feedback after the interview, using the following questions:

   - What questions were used (i.e. open, closed, reflective)?

   - How well did the interviewer listen to the answer and was sufficient time given for the interviewee to reply?

   - What body language was displayed?

Understanding the role of emotions

What is Transactional Analysis?

Transactional Analysis – system of analysis developed by Eric Berne for understanding emotions in interpersonal communication.

Transactional Analysis was developed by Berne (1968; 1975) and provides us with an invaluable tool for understanding the emotions which underpin interpersonal communications. However, he also gives us:

- a theory of personality;
- a model of interpersonal communication;
- a method of analysing patterns of behaviour.

Stewart and Joines (2012) have provided a workable textbook on Transactional Analysis and for the most part, this section follows the key concepts they have identified. Try working through them one concept at a time, recording your thoughts in the activity box that follows each one.

The ego state or PAC model

Berne (1968; 1975) argues that emotional responses are encoded in childhood, before the age of five, and stored in three sets: parent, adult and child. As we learn child responses through our experience of childhood, concurrently we learn parental responses from those who brought us up. We all have these emotional responses at our disposal, but some will be more developed in some people than in others.

- Our **parent** is our protector, guardian and critic and is divided into controlling or **critical parent** and **nurturing parent**. Today, each is frequently subdivided into positive and negative aspects.
- Our **adult** is our rational self, but it is not an ideal state, as we need our parent to warn us and our child for play.
- Our **child** is also divided. The **free, natural, rebellious** or **glee child** is happy and playful, while the **adapted child** or **depressed child** conforms to rules and societal norms but may be difficult, petulant or irritable. They are also often now subdivided into positive and negative parts.

According to Berne (1968; 1975) all our emotional responses can be categorised under one of these headings. We have all learnt and encoded a range of emotional responses and are constantly **switching** between them. You may easily observe this in yourself and others, when something triggers a **switch**. For example, an otherwise calm and rational individual, who normally drives very well, may suddenly react with road rage when triggered by some relatively minor incident.

It may be that one ego state is dominant, and that you may be predominantly drawing upon your critical or nurturing parent, rational self, free or adapted child.

 Activity: Ego states

1. Try to come up with an example of ego state behaviour, drawn from your own experience of life, for your:

   - critical or controlling parent
   - nurturing parent
   - adult
   - glee child
   - depressed child.

2. Which do you think is your dominant ego state or states?

Transactions

The **transaction** is seen as the basic unit of interpersonal communication and all transactions are seen to involve an exchange of communications between two or more individuals. Transactions may be:

- **Complementary** (lines parallel)
- **Crossed** (lines not parallel)
- **Ulterior** (contains covert message).

Two examples of complementary transactions:

Parent to child: You should be careful with saving that work, you know what happened last time.

The implication is I'm OK and you are not OK.

Child to parent: 'I really don't need you to keep reminding me about saving the work.'

The implication here is you're not OK, I'm OK, but *you* don't realise.

Adult to adult: 'So, how is the work going?'

Adult to adult: 'It's going fine thanks.'

The implication here is I'm OK, you're OK, and we can discuss the work without it being an issue.

An example of a crossed transaction:

Boss asks calmly: 'Have you finished the report yet?'
  The transaction is ostensibly adult/adult and the implication is, I'm OK/ you're OK.

Subordinate replies hysterically: 'Report, report, what do you want, blood or something!'
  Here the depressed child is responding to a perceived critical parent. The implication is, you're not OK and neither am I.

Two examples of an ulterior transaction:

Boss asks tersely: 'Have you finished that report yet?'
  The overt message here is adult to adult, but the covert message is critical parent to child, 'You should have finished it by now' – i.e. you're not OK.

Subordinate asks boss: 'Will everybody be kept on after the merger?'
  The overt message is adult to adult but the covert message is depressed child to parent, 'Will I be kept on?' i.e. I'm not OK.

Strokes, over stroking and stroke deprivation

Strokes in Transactional Analysis are emotional acknowledgments we give to and get from other people rather than physical strokes. These can be either positive or negative, including encouragement and chastisement. Strokes give us feedback and therefore are part of how we know how we are doing.

Activity: Emotional stroking

Here are some examples of positive and negative strokes:

Positive strokes	Negative strokes
You look good today!	You look awful!
You made a really good job of this!	I see you managed that eventually!
That really suits you!	Did you have to wear that?
You always cheer me up!	You always get on my nerves!

Consider the following questions and jot down what you think.

- Do you give out more positive or more negative strokes?

- Do you give out too many or too few strokes?

- How might giving more positive strokes change a relationship you have?

Stroke deprivation is when no one gives you strokes or tells you how you are doing. Managers who forget to thank and praise their staff should expect a demotivated workforce!

Over stroking is experienced when people give you so many positive and negative strokes that it leads to confusion.

Your stroking skills will tend to condition the relationships that you have with those around you. If you love someone, don't forget to tell them!

Life script

Life script is the life story which we wrote in childhood and stored away in our subconscious mind, but of which we may now be quite unaware. There are three possibilities:

- If you had a good life you might have developed a **winning script**, in which case you would expect to be a success.
- If you had a nasty life you might have developed a **losing script** and you might expect to be a failure.
- You might have developed something in between called a **non-winning script** in which you might expect life to be just OK.

The question is, are life scripts deterministic? The really important point here is that our scripts do not determine whether or not we are winners or losers, but rather how we feel about what happens to us in life. When interviewed, celebrities will often say words to the effect of either, 'I always knew I would get to the top' or 'I still can't believe it's all happened'. In these kinds of statements, they reveal their life scripts.

Activity: Examining your life script

Consider the following questions and jot down what you think:

- What do you say about your anticipated future life to yourself?
- What do you say about your anticipated future life to others?
- Do you need to say anything different to yourself or others and, if so, what?

Remember, what you say about your life chances to yourself and others will tend to expose your life script.

A student told us...

One student said in a moment of despair, 'Why should I achieve anything, when no one in my family ever has before?'

Discounting, redefining and rackets

Discounting is when we blank out our perception of reality to fit the script. For example someone might tell you, 'I never had a lucky break', but you know he actually passed up every one that came along.

Redefining is when we distort our perception of reality to fit the script. For example, someone might say, 'Everything I do always goes wrong', but she can't explain the excellent degree that she got and the top job she now holds.

Rackets are emotional responses that you were permitted to have during childhood in order to get strokes and which get replayed in adult life. For example, if you fell over in the park when you were four years old, you screamed and screamed and then they bought you an ice cream to keep you quiet, think about what you learnt about the world. People who use emotions in adult life to get a payoff may well be drawing on what they learnt in childhood.

 Activity: What rackets did you learn?

Consider the following questions and jot down what you think.

- Which emotional responses do you employ in adult life in order to get what you want?
- What happened in childhood which might have led you to learn this response?

Stamps

Stamps are when we experience a racket feeling and store it up rather than expressing it. We bottle up emotions like people sticking stamps on a card to save up for something. One day we may choose to redeem that card, and when we do the 'flood gates' will open and everything will pour out in a tirade. Typically we are likely to say, 'and another thing ...'

Games and payoffs

A **game** in Transactional Analysis is a series of pre-rehearsed transactions being replayed. We all know some games that are neither sports nor fun games, but instead are life games, played to achieve an outcome or **payoff**. A payoff leads to one party gaining at another's expense. In your working life you will certainly meet some people who will play power games with their colleagues. Some examples of games discussed by Berne (1968) include:

- **NIGYSOB** – 'Now I've got you, you son of a bitch' is the classic 'wind-up' game.
- **SWYMD** – 'See what you made me do' is a blaming game that allows one actor to gain protection from further interruption.
- **WHAM** – 'Why does it always happen to me' allows one actor to play the victim role.
- **ITHY** – 'I'm only trying to help you' is where one player seeks psychological advantage over another by providing unwanted support.

When you get drawn into a game, you may feel that you have played it before. The truth is that you probably have, as most games are well known, especially in close relationships found in families and workgroups. However, there are ways to break a game. The first step is to recognise when a game is being played and that you may have unconsciously consented to be an actor in it. There are then a number of options including:

- Refusing to play by saying, 'I don't want to play this game anymore'. You may be surprised by the fact that even those completely unaware of this game concept will understand that you are terminating the game.
- Take on another role within the game by 'switching' ego states.
- Start playing another game. That really confuses them!

 Activity: Recognising game playing!

Consider the following questions and jot down what you think.

- Are you aware of ever playing or being drawn into life games?
- If you answered yes, what could you do to break the game?

In general we can perhaps see game playing as a negative activity and ultimately destructive because it undermines our relationships with other human beings. Learning that we don't need to play games is part of recognising our next point, **autonomy**.

Autonomy

Autonomy involves realising our full potential by updating the strategies we adopted as children. We can do what we want, once we realise that we can. This is the really good news that comes out of TA.

 Activity: Claiming your birthright – autonomy!

Consider the following questions and jot down what you think.

- How autonomous are you?
- When you don't do what you want, what stops you? It's a tough one to answer, but look out for words like 'should' and 'ought' which are very 'scripty'.
- What do you need to do in order to become more autonomous?

Potential criticisms of TA

Nature and nurture – nature suggests we are the product of our genetic inheritance whereas nurture sees human development as resulting from life experiences.

Berne (1968, 1975) is sometimes criticised for being 'Post-Freudian' because he considers that personality is formed in childhood, i.e. by **nurture** rather than by **nature**. The latter view is to some extent supported by the more recent recognition of the impact of DNA. There are also the still controversial arguments about the effects of both our life in the womb and of our often traumatic experience of birth. Therefore TA is perhaps at its weakest as a theory of personality development. So what is the point of using Transactional Analysis?

We suggest that TA is invaluable for:

- **Self analysis** – to understand ourselves better, to become less the product of deeply internalised past experiences and more autonomous human beings.
- **Interpersonal skills** – to understand and improve our communications with those around us; to break unfortunate communication patterns; and to create more harmonious relationships.

Activity: Updating your emotional strategies

Consider the following questions and jot down what you think.

- If you have a negative relationship with somebody in your life, try introducing more positive strokes. Note how the relationship changes over time.

- Listen to your friends; what do they say about their likely successes in relation to examinations, course outcome, careers and life generally? They will almost certainly expose their life script to you very quickly.

- Ask yourself to what extent you are autonomous and to what extent your life script rules you.

Recognising non-verbal communications

A big part of dealing with other people better lies in how we read and react to **non-verbal communication**. Mehrabian (1971) has claimed that in terms of our understanding of interpersonal communications:

- 7 per cent of meaning is in the words spoken;
- 38 per cent of meaning is paralinguistic, i.e. in the way that the words are said;
- 55 per cent is in facial expression.

> **Non-verbal communication or body language** –
> refers to visual communications that we signal to other people.

What we display to others and how we read other people's non-verbal communications is a language in itself, often referred to simply as **body language**. We all make extensive use of non-verbal signals or body language in everyday communications and commonly observed signals include the following:

- Maintaining **eye contact** and **nodding** from time to time shows interest, whereas positively averting the gaze can clearly signal disinterest.
- General **physical proximity**. Closeness or distance may indicate emotional closeness or distance. We tend to get closer to the people we feel closest to. Similarly, we can feel very uncomfortable when people we don't like get too close to us.
- **Leaning forward** in meetings, interviews or in any discussion tends to show interest, while leaning back tends to show disinterest.
- **Pointing** with elbows or knees may indicate interest in the person pointed at and, perhaps, a sexual interest in a social situation.
- **Matching** or **mirroring** each other's body language tends to show agreement, perhaps even with nodding in unison. These are known by salespeople as *buying signals*.
- Signs of **defence** include crossed arms and/or legs; hiding behind desks, books or folders, big glasses, beards, moustaches; or long hair over the face, etc.

Non-verbal communications are often seen in clusters which makes them more convincing. For example, if you are interviewing someone who sits behind a desk with arms crossed and looks out of the window rather than at you, then you are probably fairly safe in assuming a high level of disinterest. However, it is easy to misread a signal. For example, someone with crossed arms may simply be cold rather than defensive. There may also be cultural variations, as for example in parts of the Far East, where it is considered rude to look people in the eye. Contrast this with the Western view which sees avoiding eye contact as a sign of dishonesty.

 Activity: A fly on the wall!

Try doing this activity when you are alone but in a crowded place. Travel termini are especially useful places to do this and it helps to fill the time when you get delayed.

- Observe the non-verbal communications of the people you can see who are involved in interactions with others.
- Think how much of their communication you can interpret, without necessarily hearing what is said.
- How many ego states (see previous section) can you read, from people's body language?
- Consider how what you observed in this activity might be useful in helping you to deal more effectively with other people in your everyday life.

Understanding something about non-verbal communications also allows us to take some control of situations by signalling more clearly to others what we want to communicate. Non-verbal communication is not just about body language; we can also think about how to signal things to people in other ways, and for example when we set up the chairs for an interview or presentation. In the case of interviews, putting chairs in a circle will, potentially, create a friendlier meeting whereas arranging them face to face will be a more confrontational set-up.

Resolving conflict with other people

Conflict resolution – the active process of trying to resolve conflict between parties.

There are many causes of conflict in the world from full-scale wars over borders, ethnic or religious differences, to the more mundane washing-up crisis experienced in many student households. Completing group assignments is also frequently a cause of conflict and you will find that much of the content of this chapter will be helpful in smoothing that particular path (see also Chapter 5 on completing group assignments successfully). Fortunately, there are many techniques which can be used to resolve conflicts.

 Activity: Evaluating methods of conflict resolution

Consider what advantages and disadvantages there might be to the following methods of conflict resolution:

- **Coercion** or **force** – one party forces the other to submit, e.g. terrorism.
- **Manipulation** – facts are intentionally distorted or a situation is dramatised, e.g. political spin.
- **Acquiescence** – one party gives in to the other.
- **Convergence** – ideas are synthesised when the parties 'come together'.
- **Democracy** – people vote and the majority view prevails.
- **Compromise/negotiation** – both parties agree to give something to get something.
- **Conciliation** – a third party acts as go-between and gets the parties talking.
- **Mediation** – a third party suggests what might happen.
- **Arbitration** – a third party decides what will happen.
- **Avoidance** – parties avoid a resolution and conflict remains.
- **Denial** – the parties pretend there is no problem.

This activity raises the question: is there a best way to resolve conflict? We suggest that there is not, and that different situations require different methods. Clearly avoidance and denial are not, in reality, methods of conflict resolution.

When there are arguments, knowledge of Transactional Analysis and non-verbal communications (as discussed earlier in this chapter) can be useful, in order to understand first what is going on and second how to change it. Some top tips for reducing tension are:

- Lower your voice and speak as quietly as possible. This lowers the overall volume and the other person will normally lower their voice eventually.
- Be on the same level as the other person. Ask the other person to sit if possible or you could stand up if they won't.

Cooling off period – parties take time out to allow the emotions to diminish in the hope of returning for a more informed and rational discussion.

- Ask, 'Can we make another time to discuss this?' in order to allow for a **cooling off period** and perhaps to gather more information, if this is appropriate.
- Ask the other person, 'Can we discuss this rationally?' This is an attempt to force them into the adult rational ego state (see the above section on Transactional Analysis and the role of emotions). They may, however, say no and walk off.
- Ask the other person to put the problem in writing to you. This forces the other party to think more about the issue and often marks an end to the affair.
- Use 'we' instead of 'you' and 'I'. Changing the personal pronouns changes the context. For example phases such as 'we seem to have a problem' and 'could we think about a solution?' move the situation from conflict to a joint problem-solving situation.

Conflict is common and sometimes inevitable when dealing with other people, but developing some skills and techniques can help to minimise and hopefully resolve it. In general, it's better to focus upon common ground, possible solutions and positive outcomes.

Asserting yourself when it is appropriate

What is assertiveness and why is it important?

Assertiveness – involves asserting your rights in contrast to either aggression or acquiescence.

Are you saying what you really want to say? Do you sometimes fear saying what you mean to say or fear the reaction of others?

From our prehistoric ancestors we have retained two basic responses to trouble, namely **fight** and **flight** (see also Chapter 4 on handling stress and developing relaxation techniques). This is evidenced in non-assertive behaviour patterns in which we may either fight or take flight as follows:

Fight or flight – tendency to either 'stand and fight' or 'take flight' in response to perceived danger.

- **Fight = aggression**, which is evidenced by violent language or behaviours.
- **Flight = avoidance**, in which we avoid and 'bottle up' problems and are diminished in the process.

However, neither fight nor flight is a satisfactory response to most everyday situations and both lead to unwanted physiological changes in our body chemistry through increased adrenaline, causing short-term and long-term symptoms. The alternative approach is for us to learn to be assertive.

Every incidence of non-assertive behaviour requires two players, a 'manipulator' and a 'nice guy'. For example, consider the following scenario:

> You kindly give me a lift to the supermarket every Friday after work, then one week I say, 'Look I am feeling really tired tonight, and also there is something on the television I want to see. If I give you some money and a list, can you get my shopping for me and drop it round later? After all, I am on your way home.'

If you are such a nice guy that you get my shopping for me, have you allowed me to manipulate you? What would be the implication of you refusing to get the shopping?

 Activity: How assertive am I?

Assess how assertive you are by taking the following test. Circle the letter for the response that, in your opinion, best answers each of the following questions.

1. You are in a long line to pay for your lunch. Someone walks up and moves into the line in front of you. The assertive thing to do is:

   a. to complain to others around you in a loud voice.
   b. to ask the person to go to the end of the line.

2. Which of the following is a reason to be assertive?

   a. to achieve your goals.
   b. to show who is right.

3. The definition of assertiveness usually includes the following:

   a. 'deny the rights of others'.
   b. 'ask for what you want'.

4. A non-assertive person may respond to a situation with non-verbal cues such as:

   a. a whiny voice.
   b. direct eye contact.

5. Aggressive words from others violate your right to courtesy and respect. Which of the following is an aggressive comment?

   a. 'Don't be such a fool.'
   b. 'Would you mind very much if we skip the formalities?'

6. Which of the following is an appropriate assertive response?

   a. keeping your opinions to yourself when you are angry with someone such as a tutor or a boss.
   b. asking that person for a meeting in which you can express your point of view.

The correct answers are: 1: b   2: a   3: b   4: a   5: a   6: b

---

Learning some assertiveness techniques

Assertiveness techniques help us to express our needs in a way that is polite and generally acceptable to others. Most of the time people are cooperative and thoughtful, but when conflict arises people respond in different ways. Some act aggressively, some passively, and some assertively. Here are some techniques that can help you become more assertive:

- Remember that no one can manipulate you, unless you allow him or her to do so.
- Avoid *knee jerk* reactions. In a busy life it is easy to feel that we have to respond to every situation immediately.
- Give yourself thinking time. Take stock and think what you should say or do. It could be nothing!
- Learn to say no, when it is appropriate to do so.
- Learn how to say no, avoiding 'I can't' which is negative and diminishing in favour of 'I won't', which is your positive choice.
- Learn to say yes when you *want* to and not because you think you *ought* to.
- Be persistent when necessary. Smith (1975: 73–87) talks about the **broken record**: 'I won't, no I won't', etc. Eventually they will get the message.

> **Broken record –** technique for enforcing an assertive message by repetition.

If faced with a threat of violence it may be better not to act assertively, but rather **non-assertively**. If you are being held at knifepoint or a car is speeding towards you, an assertion will be of little use. Flight and/or fight are still appropriate responses in dangerous situations, which is what 'Mother Nature' designed them for.

 Activity: How do I know when to be assertive?

1. Smith (1975: 28–71) has given us ten assertiveness rights. Try working through them and tick any that you have difficulty with:

   - You have the right to judge your own behaviour, thoughts and emotions, and to take responsibility for their initiation and consequences yourself.
   - You have the right to offer no excuses to justify your behaviour.
   - You have the right to judge whether you have the responsibility for finding the solutions to other people's problems.
   - You have the right to change your mind.
   - You have the right to make mistakes and to be responsible for them.
   - You have the right to say 'I don't know'.

- You have the right to be independent of the goodwill of others before coping with them.
- You have the right to be illogical in making decisions.
- You have the right to say 'I don't understand'.
- You have the right to say 'I don't care'.

2. Review the items you ticked in the list.

3. To gain ongoing benefit from the work you have done on assertiveness, complete the following tasks:
   - Identify situations where either you did not feel that you asserted yourself or perhaps that you did it in an inappropriate way.
   - Think what you need to do differently in the future.
   - Make a diary date to review your progress after, say, one month.

Developing your influencing skills

Achieving your goals (see Chapter 2 on planning your continuing personal development) often involves influencing those around you, in order for you to develop and progress. However, people don't like to feel they are being used or manipulated and it is easy to make enemies in the process. The good news is that most people seem to like being helpful, if they are approached in the right way, and so it is important to win people over to your cause. Cooperation will be a key word.

There is no one way to influence people around you, but here are some ideas to work through.

- **Goals** – being clear on your goals and what you want to achieve is a good starting point. Your goals can become a focus for everything else you do. Try practising what you learnt in Chapter 2, reminding yourself regularly of your goals and visualising your success.
- **Interpersonal skills** – improving these involves developing the skills covered in this chapter. This will help you to achieve your goals by improving the interactions you have with others. This development will include your interview skills, understanding emotions, non-verbal communication, and being able to assert yourself when required.
- **Networking** – this is an active process in which you commit yourself to building your network of contacts with others. You never know when a contact will become useful, so it is always worth asking for their contact details and giving them yours.
- **Relationship building** – this is also an active process, not this time involving casual contacts but rather those who will help and encourage you. In higher education this will include both your friends and friendly tutors. It is good to work out who is going to be important to you and to give them your attention.

- **Leadership** – some situations require you to put yourself out front, for example when completing a group assignment. Someone will have to take the lead and they will most probably have the biggest influence on the final result, so, why not make sure it's you? See also Chapter 5, Completing group assignments successfully.
- **Confidence** – people will be much more likely to react positively to someone who displays confidence in what they are doing. Try to act as if you count, even if you are not sure whether you do. It's amazing how confidence grows when you start to do this and people start to take you seriously. However, avoid arrogance as that will tend to alienate those you need to help you. There is a fine line between confidence and arrogance – and it's very important to recognise it.

Activity: How can I develop the art of persuasion?

Cialdini (2001) suggests that we can harness the 'science of persuasion'. Read through the table below, noting down what you need to do differently in order to become more persuasive.

Liking: People like those who like them.	Uncover real similarities and offer genuine praise.
Reciprocity: People repay in kind.	Give what you want to receive.
Social proof: People follow the lead of similar others.	Use peer power whenever it's available.
Consistency: People align with their clear commitments.	Make your commitments active, public, and voluntary.
Authority: People defer to experts.	Expose your expertise; do not assume it is self-evident.
Scarcity: People want more of what they can have less of.	Highlight the benefits of exclusive information.

In terms of influencing and persuading, it is essential to consider how you approach people. It's not just a question of what you say and how you say it, but also to whom, when and where.

Letters tend to get filed, or worse still binned, and emails overlooked or deleted, so face-to-face or telephone communications are always preferable. If you do have to write, make sure you call first to get a name, address and position. If you don't get a reply you can always back this up with a phone call, politely asking if the named recipient received your letter or email.

A student told us...

A student told us that he had telephoned a major corporation (which will remain name-less) for help with a research project and that they had been very unhelpful. When asked how many people he had spoken to he replied, 'One'. He was then informed that the corporation currently had in the region of 160,000 employees and that he might just have been unlucky. He tried again, and got the help he needed.

When calling an organisation, it is often best to explain who you are and what you want, and then to ask who could help you. It doesn't matter how many times you get transferred if you get to the right person in the end.

When you are referred from one person to another, try to get the name of the person referring you as well as the person you are passed on to. You can then introduce yourself by saying, 'Mr/Ms X suggested I talk to you'. It helps to break the ice.

If someone works in a busy office, can you set up a time to take him or her for a coffee, in order to sit down quietly and have chat? Alternatively, can you make an appointment to see him/her?

 Activity: Developing your influencing skills

- Consider who you need to influence in order to achieve your goals.
- Consider how you might best approach them, what to say, when and how – i.e. the best way, best time, best place.
- Activate your plans, review how they are going and be prepared to change your approach if it is not working.

Giving and receiving feedback

We all learn about the world through **feedback** (see Chapter 5, Recognising why reflection is important to learning) but the quality of feedback we receive, how we receive it and how we use it is highly variable. We all give and receive feedback quite naturally, even without speaking we use body language, including eye contact – or the lack of it! See also the discussion above on recognising non-verbal communications.

Feedback – information reported back as in a 'feedback loop' which potentially allows learning to occur and decisions to be made based upon updated information.

Imagine taking a draft of your report or essay – over which you have worked long and hard – to your tutor for some feedback. Which of the following responses would be the most useful:

- Its rubbish!
- It's brilliant!
- You make some very good points here. There are a couple of other things that you should say which I have noted in the margin. You use a good variety of sources. I notice that one, which I have underlined, does not trace to your bibliography. The presentation is generally good. You should start a new page for your bibliography.

Emotive language – language carrying emotional rather than rational messages.

Sandwich technique – involves reporting negative feedback between positive feedback.

Linking words – are used to join two messages, but may diminish the former in relation to the latter.

The first two examples are highly **subjective** and use what we can call **emotive language**. They actually tell us nothing about what is right or wrong, or indeed good or bad, about the work because they reflect only the emotions of the reader. In contrast the third example appears to give a more **objective** commentary on the work. It employs the **sandwich technique**, which is often used to deliver the bad news more kindly and within a more objective context. It avoids the use of **linking words** such as, 'but', 'although' and 'however', which tend to diminish the earlier statement, as for example, when your tutor says, 'This is generally a good piece of work, but...'.

As a student, you will need to get regular feedback in order to progress. This may come in many forms, but if you find yourself in a feedback vacuum, don't be afraid to ask, 'How am I doing?'

Much of your feedback may be in written form, in particular when you get assignment work returned to you by your tutors. Increasingly, feedback is being given online and this may include some combination of written comments, a marking grid and audio comments. When assignments are returned or online feedback released, notice how many students are only concerned about the grade and ignore the other feedback. To get the most out of your feedback we suggest that you try the following steps:

- Read and or listen to everything carefully, including all the feedback you have received, whether it be written on the work or accessed online.

- Ask questions of your tutor if there is anything you don't understand or simply can't read. If he or she is too busy at the time, ask for an appointment or send him/her an email.
- Think about what has been written, what you can learn from it and what you might need to do differently in the future.

A student told us...

A final year student told us that he was very disappointed with the first semester grade we had given him and was concerned about the impact on his final degree. We went through his work with him and pointed out the feedback which highlighted the obvious errors he was making in terms of intellectual argument, source referencing and presentation. He told us the same sort of issues had come up in other modules and so we suggested it was time to start taking his tutors feedback on board.

The feedback we give impacts upon others just as much as the feedback we receive does. You may well also be in the position of giving feedback to others and this might include:

- when working in teams or on group assignments;
- as a mentor to other students as part of a mentoring programme;
- when reviewing another student's work informally or as part of a formal peer assessment programme;
- when completing feedback documentation on your course and/or modules.

There are some clear guidelines for giving feedback effectively (adapted from video material, Davis, 1999) and these include the following:

- Feedback should be objective rather than subjective or emotive.
- Base feedback upon identified criteria. With assignment work, the objectives should be clearly stated in the brief. If they are not, ask your tutor for them, preferably before you start on the work.
- Make your feedback specific rather than generalised, in order to tell the person what is actually right and wrong.
- Try to be descriptive, so as to provide a useful level of detail. 'Could do better' is not acceptable in this day and age!
- Structure your feedback so as to cover everything point by point.
- Your feedback should stick to what the person **needs to know** rather than what is merely **nice to know** – in other words, stick to essentials and avoids waffle.
- Be constructive rather than destructive, because the aim should always be to help the person to develop.
- Be non-evaluative, because giving feedback on a person's work is not the same as judging them.

With regard to the process:

- Fixing a convenient time and finding a suitable place is important. Being rushed or uncomfortable will naturally detract from the process and for feedback the *corridor meeting* – although much loved in universities – is not acceptable.
- Feedback can often usefully start by asking the other person how they felt the activity went. Often we are our own sternest critics, and the role of the person giving feedback can then become to put our own thoughts into perspective.
- There should always be time for a two-way discussion and for the person receiving the feedback to ask questions.
- The process should end by making a plan for future action and perhaps making a date to meet again, if this is appropriate.

When we receive feedback we have to be prepared to listen and take it on board. Goleman (1998: 263) suggests that

> Feedback can be a priceless tool for self-examination and for cultivating change and growth.

Baddeley (1990) suggests that when we look at a particular situation, we see it through the lens provided by the mental models we have built up through past experience, education or training. We approach situations we encounter with a mindset, a recipe we have acquired from the past, and we use that to understand what is happening and to decide what response/action to take. The mental models we create may or may not be the most appropriate given the situation, or we have not had enough experiences, education or training to develop the most appropriate response to a given situation.

 Activity: How good am I at receiving feedback?

This self-assessment will help you measure your current skills in receiving feedback. For each of the statements, tick the 'rarely', 'sometimes', or 'often' box to indicate how consistently you use the described behaviour.

		Rarely	Sometimes	Often
1.	I truly listen to what feedback givers are saying.			
2.	I keep feedback in perspective and do not over-react.			
3.	I try to learn from all feedback, even if it is poorly given.			

		Rarely	Sometimes	Often
4.	I am willing to admit to and learn from questions about my performance or behaviour.			
5.	Rather than avoiding feedback, I attempt to turn every feedback session into a useful encounter.			
6.	I accept redirections, reinforcing rather than denying them.			
7.	I accept responsibility for my role in achieving individual, team and organisational goals.			
8.	I accept responsibility for searching for solutions to performance and behavioural problems that threaten goals.			
9.	I accept responsibility for keeping my emotions in check during feedback discussions.			
10.	I am committed to listening and learning from all feedback sessions.			

In general when receiving feedback we suggest that you:

- Listen! It is so easy to go into **private circuits**, especially if you are still thinking about the last point when the next one comes up.
- Try to confirm what has been said by using reflective questions (see the section in this chapter on questioning and listening skills), e.g. 'Could you explain that?' or 'I'm not sure but did you say…?'
- Take notes, because you won't remember everything that is said.
- Conclude positively, thanking the person for their comments – whether negative or positive, and whether you agree with them or not.
- Consider what has been said and be open-minded. It's all too easy to be defensive about criticism or even praise if you under-estimate yourself.

 Activity: How am I doing?

- Consider the question: How do I know how well I am doing?
- Review the feedback you have received to date.
- Ask for additional feedback if necessary.
- Consider what all this tells you about how you are doing and what you need to do as a result.

Finally, we ask you to not be afraid to ask for feedback from your tutors, your peers and anyone else who can help. Ensure that you are clear about assessment requirements and don't wait until you get a disappointing mark before asking for help. Try to be open to the feedback process and learn as you go. Too many students fear the process, especially when they are struggling, and so avoid it and then fail.

Follow-up activities

Time for action – Checklist

Have you:

- practised your interpersonal skills by asking closed, open and reflective questions?
- learnt to recognise both your own emotional responses and those of others?
- considered how you can use your knowledge of non-verbal communications?
- thought about how you might use alternative strategies to resolve conflict?
- asserted yourself when you had the need to do it?
- considered when and where you need to use persuasion techniques?
- asked for feedback on how you are doing?

Further reading

Berne, E. (1968) *The Games People Play*. London: Penguin.

Berne, E. (1975) *What Do You Say After You Say Hello?* London: Corgi.

Cameron, S. (2009) *The Business Student's Handbook*, 5th edn. Harlow: Pearson.

Goleman, D. (2003) *Destructive Emotions and How We Can Overcome Them*. London: Bloomsbury.

Guirdham, M. (2002) *Interpersonal Skills at Work,* 3rd edn. Harlow: Pearson.

Hunsaker, P. L. (2005) *Management – A Skills Approach,* 2nd edn. Upper Saddle River, NJ: Pearson.

Lee-Davies, L. (2007) *Developing Work and Study Skills*. London: Thomson.

Mehrabian, A. (1971) *Silent Messages*. Belmont, CA: Wadsworth.

Moon, J. (1999) *Reflection in Learning and Professional Development*. London: Kogan Page.

Moon, J. (2006) *Learning Journals: A Handbook of Reflective Practice and Professional Development*, 2nd edn. Abingdon: Routledge.

O'Connor, J. (2002) *The NLP Workbook: A Practical Guide to Achieving the Results You Want*. London: Element.

Pease, A. (2006) *The Definitive Book of Body Language*. New York: Bantam.

Russell, T. (1998) *Effective Feedback Skills*, 2nd edn. London: Kogan Page.

Smith, M. J. (1975) *When I Say No I feel Guilty*. New York: Bantam.

Stewart, I. and Joines, V. (2012) *TA Today*, 2nd edn. Nottingham: Lifespace.

Thompson, M. (2013) *Winning Strategies for Sport and Life*. London: Gabrielle Lea Publishing.

Websites to look up

- For general help with people skills/interpersonal communications:
  www.ezinearticles.com/?People-Skills:-Eight-Essential-People-Skills&id=12294
- For further information on transactional analysis:
  www.ericberne.com/transactional-analysis
- For more information on body language/non-verbal communication:
  www.peaseinternational.com
- For information on assertiveness:
  www.assertiveness.org.uk
  www.h2g2.com/edited_entry/A2998551
- For information on conflict resolution:
  www.mindtools.com/pages/article/newLDR_81.htm
- For information on influencing styles:
  www.ezinearticles.com/?Understanding-The-Different-Influencing-Styles&id=340096

Time for review and reflection

This is your space to log your reflections on this chapter, to think about what you have learnt, how you will use it and what else you need to find out.

What were the key learning points of this chapter?
What are your strengths in the areas covered by this chapter?

What areas did you identify for development?
What have you learnt about yourself?
How will you use this knowledge?
What else do you need to learn or find out about in relation to this chapter?

4

How to Look After Yourself and Upgrade Your Self-Nurturing Skills During the Developmental Process

Overview – what's in this chapter?

- Why do you need to look after yourself and upgrade your self-nurturing skills?
- Living independently
- Managing your money
- Managing your time
- Handling stress and developing relaxation techniques
- Getting to sleep
- Looking after your health, including diet, exercise and health problems
- Accessing help and support
- Follow-up activities, further reading and websites to look up
- Time for review and reflection

Why do you need to look after yourself and upgrade your self-nurturing skills?

Try completing the short self-scoring test overleaf, to assess your own level of confidence in relation to your nurturing skills, to help you complete your course successfully.

✎ **Activity: Why do you need to read this chapter?**

You need to self score each question on a scale from 0 to 10, where 0 is low and 10 is high.

1. How confident are you about living independently?	
2. How are you with managing your money?	
3. How good are you at getting to places on time?	
4. How likely are you to meet deadlines that are set for you?	
5. How good are you at managing stress?	
6. How easy do you find it to relax?	
7. How good are you at eating a balanced diet?	
8. How regularly do you exercise?	
9. How likely are you to ask for help if you have a health problem?	
10. How aware are you of the support systems available to you?	
Total score	

Interpretation

What did you score?

- Less than 50%   You definitely will find a lot of help in this chapter.
- 50%–75%   There is still plenty to learn in this chapter.
- 75%–100%   You are very confident – read on to confirm your understanding.

Studying in higher education can be tough! There are many pressures to achieve academically and many of you will be living in a new situation with new people, perhaps living independently for the first time. Skills such as washing, cooking and cleaning may seem somewhat mundane when starting a university course in your chosen discipline, but they are essential for completing it. You may, depending upon your course, have far less contact time with academic staff than you were used to in school or college. Therefore developing the ability to live and work independently will become very important. For others these will be skills that you already have.

What we are looking at in this chapter are **survival skills**. Too many students leave because they are not equipped to deal with the experience of higher education. Some get into debt, others get sick through poor diet and lack of exercise, while others develop destructive behaviour patterns.

In this chapter we will look at a range of issues, including the problems of living independently, managing your money, managing your time, handling stress, developing relaxation techniques and getting to sleep, together with the need to look after your health, including diet, exercise and dealing with health problems. Finally there are some follow-up activities, some suggested further reading, websites to look up, and some space for review and reflection.

Living independently

 Activity: What is good and bad about independent living?

There are many pros and cons related to living away from home. If you are doing this for the first time, try working through the following questions:

- What are you looking forward to?
- What are you not looking forward to or are most anxious about?

Adjusting to living independently

For many students, the biggest adjustment they have to make when moving into higher education is learning to live independently from family and friends for the first time. The good news is that you can make a lot of new friends and that these new friendships are made with others who are in a similar situation to yourself.

If you make good friends they will become your support network, so this is a priority and will probably happen quite naturally (see also Chapter 1 which looks at the transition into higher education and gives you ideas on meeting new people).

Other considerations include managing your money, accommodation, getting to sleep, and dealing with domestic chores such as shopping, cooking, washing and cleaning – all issues which are discussed in this chapter.

Living in a student room

A university or college room can look very bare when you move in, and a good start is to make it your own space. Some ideas include:

- Bring some things from home such as your favourite posters, books or mugs.
- Invest in an electric kettle and some supplies of tea and coffee – it will save you money in the long run and may encourage visitors to your room.

- Make friends with your neighbours. They need not become your closest friends, but it is good to be on friendly terms with them, to be mutually supportive and to avoid any unnecessary conflict.
- Leave your door open when you want company and close it when you want to work. Others will soon get the message and, if not, a 'do not disturb' sign works wonders.

It is a question of defining your space and making your room a 'home from home'. It will be your lounge, bedroom and study for the next year and you are going to spend quite a bit of time there, working and entertaining, so it's a good idea to make it as comfortable as possible.

 Activity: What do I want to take?

If you are going to be living in a student room in 'halls' or a college, try making a list of things you will want to take with you.

Living in a shared house

Living in a shared house can bring special challenges in terms of sharing common spaces such as the lounge (if there is one), bathroom and kitchen. Common areas of conflict are the recurring 'washing-up crisis', or people not cleaning the bath. While these are irritating, more serious problems can occur over shared payment of bills, etc. Some tips for house sharing include the following:

- Hold a house meeting to agree rules at the outset – in terms of how it is going to be, who does what and how bills are to be divided (your bank may have a facility which allows you to split the bills).
- Set a really good example yourself by being respectful of others and practising what you have agreed. If the person in the next room played loud music till five in the morning and kept you awake, doing the same to him the next night is not an amicable – or effective – solution!
- Try to be on good terms with everybody, being helpful and flexible. If you are making a cup of tea, why not offer to make the others one?
- Don't leave nasty little notes around the place, saying 'Who didn't do ...' or such like. It's guaranteed to antagonise your housemates and poison the atmosphere. It is better to try and approach things directly and in an adult rational manner. See Chapter 3, How to improve your people skills.
- Assert yourself appropriately, when it is right to do so. See also Chapter 3, How to improve your people skills – particularly the sections on resolving conflict and on asserting yourself.

Private landlords can be highly variable in terms of the treatment you get, and some are notorious, so it's usually better to rent properties on the approved list from your university or college. However, even this may not be a guarantee of fair treatment. If you do get into problems you should seek advice from your university or college accommodation office and/or students' union welfare office.

House sharing can be a very positive experience but horror stories abound, so it is advisable to try and manage the situation from the start and to deal with problems as and when they arise. Be prepared for some rewards and some problems.

Managing your money

A student told us ...

A student told us that he had a really good time in the first term, going out every evening and getting taxis back to his halls. Unfortunately he very quickly ran out of money, had to get two jobs to pay off his debts and very nearly had to leave university!

Making a budget and sticking to it

How much do you imagine you will spend – or do spend – a week? Completing the following activity has proved truly shocking for some students, but it's an essential starting point in achieving a realistic grasp of your finances.

✍ Activity: Making your own budget

Try estimating how much you either will spend or expect to spend, expressing each figure in terms of a weekly amount.

Weekly expenditure	£
• Books, stationery and any other study materials you need for your course	
• Rents for lodgings, shared house, or college room or halls. Housekeeping if living at home	
• Mobile phone and internet connection etc.	
• Other bills for services including gas, electricity, etc.	
• Food prepared for you, including meals taken in the refectory, fast foods, etc.	

(Continued)

(Continued)

• Food you prepare, plus other household shopping such as cleaning materials, washing powder, toiletries, etc.	
• Clothing, repairs and renewals	
• Entertainment and socialising, cinema, gigs, etc.	
• Sports and any other hobbies	
• Travel, including to and from where you stay to where you study	
• Weekends away, visiting home or friends and holidays, if you plan to get away in the vacations	
• A reasonable contingency for any unanticipated expenditure	
Total	
Weekly income	**£**
• Student loans	
• Grants or bursaries	
• Allowances from parents/family, etc.	
• Paid work	
• Other	
Total	
How is it looking? If your expenditure is more than your income, it is time to think about how to change it. Try reading the next two subsections on minimising expenditure and maximising your earning potential, and then make a new budget.	

Minimising your expenditure

There are some really simple tips for minimising expenditure, including:

- **Think before you spend!** If you are an impulse buyer, try to develop a habit of stopping yourself and taking time to think before you spend. Do you really need it and is it a good deal? Being a financially solvent student might mean not wearing the latest fashions!
- **Where to eat?** Eating in halls or in the refectory may be cheaper than eating out. Making your own food will probably be even cheaper and may potentially be more nutritious than ready-made food or takeaways. See also the section below on looking after your health.
- **Investigate student deals**. Student deals will often be cheaper and are worth looking at. Companies like to attract people while they are students in order to develop loyalty to their brand later on, but you need to shop around.
- **Do student things**. Student gigs will normally be much cheaper than commercial ones, as will student bars. Student travel is usually designed for the 'hard of pocket'. Your students' union will also know where you can get student discounts locally.

- **Manage your time.** Managing the balance between academic work, paid work and social life can really help with controlling your expenditure. See also the section below on managing your time.

Maximising your earning potential

Many students rely on part-time and vacation work in order to help support their studies. While too much paid work can seriously undermine your academic performance, a reasonable level of work can provide you with extra money and also a number of other benefits including:

- new friends – as you come into contact with another group of people, many of whom may also be students;
- valuable work experience – this is especially true if you can find something relevant to your line of study (even at a lowly level you are likely to learn something useful and maybe some transferable skills);
- savings in expenditure, particularly on entertainment – most obviously if you are serving behind a bar rather than drinking at it!
- Discounts – working in clothing, food, book or other types of stores often means that you get really useful discounts on purchases;
- Free food – working in catering often means you get fed at the start or end of your shift.

However, some students get better paid jobs than others. See Chapters 9 to 11 for material on getting jobs, internships and placements.

A student told us ...

A student who worked in a well-known clothing store at weekends told us that when the weekend supervisor's job came up, he applied and then got the job, using the employability skills that we had taught him (see Chapters 9 to 11). This increased his earnings considerably as well as providing useful managerial experience.

Managing financial problems

It's easy to say that the best way to avoid problems is to avoid debt. However, in the current climate of student loans and tuition fees, debt may be hard to avoid. The first step is to have a clear budget for your expenditure (as outlined in an earlier activity) and the second is to try to stick to it as far as possible. Remember your 'contingencies' allocation is there for **unforeseen emergencies**.

If you have real financial problems, the best advice everyone will give you is: don't avoid them. Interest and bank charges will literally compound and increase your debt. It is a good idea to talk to everyone who can help and get the best advice, including:

- **your bank**, which may be far more sympathetic than you might imagine – ask to see a customer advisor, who will be able to talk you through the options;
- **the student services department**, which will probably have either a specialised debt counsellor or at least somebody with significant experience in this area;
- **the students' union**, which will have a welfare adviser who is experienced in advising upon student debt problems;
- **the local Citizens Advice Bureau**, which will have specialised debt counsellors.

Managing your time

Why manage your time?

Time is unique! It is the only resource which we all have equally and it is the most valuable resource we have. Once used, it has gone forever; unlike many resources, time cannot be stored or hoarded, it cannot be borrowed and it cannot be given away.

As a student you need to plan your academic workload, employment, social life and domestic commitments so that you allocate the required amount of time to all your modules. More time may be needed for some subjects, so be sure that you are aware of your strengths and areas you need to give more time to.

Improving your time management can give you a better perspective on forthcoming activities and priorities, more opportunities to be creative, less stress, more leisure time and greater achievement of goals and objectives.

 Activity: How do I use my time?

Try completing this activity as honestly as possible, in order to review how you use your time and how you could improve your time management.

Question:	Analysis: How well do I spend my time?	Strategy: What will I do to improve this?
Do I use time efficiently? How do I waste time?		
What or who distracts me from study?		
Do I need to plan out my time: • **for the year?** • **for the term?** • **for the week?** • **for the day?** • **for each piece of work?**		

Do I waste time getting started?		
Do I make the most of spare moments?		
Do I find time passes and I do not know what has happened?		

- Reflecting on the analysis column, what are your major concerns?
- What strategies did you come up with to overcome these issues?
- Make a plan to overcome these problems and a date to review your progress. See also Chapter 2, especially the section on planning your personal development.

Understanding some terminology

Understanding the following terminology can help us to develop better time management skills and gives us a vocabulary with which to discuss it:

- **Type A and Type B personality.** Are you 'high drive' (Type A) or 'low drive' (Type B)? Both obsessive 'workaholics' and committed 'lazybones' are guilty of the abuse and misuse of time. Some students do too little work and fail to achieve their goals, while some others completely overdo it and burnout.

  > **Type A & Type B Personality** – refers to people who tend to be driven (Type A) or who tend to lack drive (Type B).

- **Presenteeism.** This is where people stay at work for an excessive number of hours and can be the result of many factors including heavy workload, inefficiency, trying to impress the boss or colleagues and an unhappy home life. Similarly, some students feel that they have to know everything or do everything to get good marks, but they tend to become confused in the process.

  > **Presenteeism** – people who stay at work or study for an excessive number of hours.

- **Absenteeism.** This may also be related to work or home factors such as poor motivation or commitment to a job, or domestic or family problems. Some students frequently cut classes, but how often does this benefit them in achieving their goals? Who is winning here?

  > **Absenteeism** – people who are absent from work or study for no legitimate reason.

- **Task mesmerisation.** This is when we allow ourselves to be side-tracked, concentrating on some task or tasks to the exclusion of others. We usually do it because we feel secure in the area of mesmerisation, and because we fear the other tasks we have to do. Some students absorb themselves in a particular module or topic to the exclusion of others, while others avoid their bogey subject altogether – perhaps hoping it will go away.

  > **Task mesmerisation** – concept derived from the work of Franz Mesmer, of individuals becoming fixated on a particular task to the exclusion of all others.

Time bandits –
people who steal your
valuable time.

Time structuring –
excessive attention to
the structuring of time.

Me time – time for
you to think, relax,
exercise and recharge
your batteries.

Mindfulness – idea
drawn from Buddhism
which involves
focusing completely
on what you sense.

- **Time bandits**. These are people who rob you of your pre-cious time, making unreasonable demands upon it. If they stole money from your wallet or purse, how would you react? Is your time any less valuable? Controlling time bandits is essentially about asserting ourselves and our own self worth (see Chapter 3, on asserting yourself when it is appropriate). As a student there are always possibilities for happy interruptions to your studies, but make sure that you are really doing what you want to do.
- **Time structuring** is an excessive attention to the structuring of time, so that it becomes a barrier to any flexibility. Can you tell the time at any time during the day without looking at your watch? Do you say, 'But I always do this at that time'? If so, maybe it's time for a bit more flexibility.
- **Me time**. This is the time – which we all need – to think, relax, exercise and recharge our batteries. It is yours, you deserve it, and you worked for it, so take it and don't feel guilty! There is an awful tendency in modern life to feel that you should always be doing something, be it work or play, but stopping and resting are important too. It is now almost a lost art that we have to re-learn. See also the discussion of stress control and relaxation later in this chapter and the idea of '**mindfulness**'.

Self-management skills

Time management is the management of the activities we engage in during our life. Time management is a key element in self-management because if you can't manage your time, then clearly it is hard to achieve anything else. Therefore, managing your time is essential to achieving your goals (see also Chapter 2 on planning your continuing personal development).

As with managing anything else, self-management involves certain skills, including:

- setting goals/objectives;
- prioritising;
- planning;
- implementing;
- controlling;
- evaluating.

If you are both concerned about how you are spending your time and serious about improving, consider the following:

- **Commitment** – there are no gimmicks or short cuts. Sloppy time management is just a bad habit. You must be committed to doing something about it.
- **Analysis** – you must have data on where you spend your time, what your problems are, and the causes. Time logs and other forms of analysis are essential.
- **Planning** – you may be saying 'I don't have time to plan', but effective management always requires planning, whether you are managing a family budget, a business, or your studies. An hour of planning will save you many hours doing the wrong things, fighting crises and avoiding the unimportant.
- **Follow-up and re-analysis** – a plan will not work very well, no matter how good it is, if you don't monitor results, detect problems, and modify the plan accordingly.

What kind of time manager are you?

As a student it might be useful to consider yourself as a manager of your own time. Do you manage your time or does it manage you?

 Activity: Fire fighter or town planner?

Contrast these two polar opposites and consider which model you feel you most closely resemble, placing yourself on the continuum below.

FIRE FIGHTER		TOWN PLANNER
The fire fighter is totally reactive and spends all day dealing with crises, and crisis has become a habit – a way of life. Fire fighters find it hard to delegate or to trust subordinates, in case they fail. Thus they do fail, and crisis is assured. The fire fighters have no wider vision, or big picture.	5–4–3–2–1–0–1–2–3–4–5	The town planner is totally proactive; everything is planned, every moment of every day, and everything has a purpose. It sounds ideal but town planners cannot recognise the need to react to a crisis, unless it has been included in their planning. Thus the town planner is totally inflexible and lacks any sensitivity to immediate issues.

Procrastination

Procrastination – putting off starting things that need to be done.

Do you have difficulty getting started on projects, leave things till the last minute, or put off until another day what you could have done today? If the answer to any of these questions is yes, then you have a tendency to **procrastinate**.

 ### Activity: Find your procrastination score

Take the following test to find out just how much you procrastinate. Circle the number that best applies for each question.

I invent reasons and look for excuses for not acting on a problem.

| Strongly agree | 4 | 3 | 2 | 1 | Strongly disagree |

It takes pressure to get me to work on difficult assignments.

| Strongly agree | 4 | 3 | 2 | 1 | Strongly disagree |

I take half measures that will avoid or delay unpleasant or difficult tasks.

| Strongly agree | 4 | 3 | 2 | 1 | Strongly disagree |

I face too many interruptions and crises that interfere with accomplishing my major goals.

| Strongly agree | 4 | 3 | 2 | 1 | Strongly disagree |

I sometimes neglect to carry out important tasks.

| Strongly agree | 4 | 3 | 2 | 1 | Strongly disagree |

I schedule assignments too late to get them done as well as I know I could.

| Strongly agree | 4 | 3 | 2 | 1 | Strongly disagree |

I am sometimes too tired to do the work I need to do.

| Strongly agree | 4 | 3 | 2 | 1 | Strongly disagree |

I start new tasks before I finish old ones.

| Strongly agree | 4 | 3 | 2 | 1 | Strongly disagree |

When I work in groups, I try to get other people to finish what I do not.

| Strongly agree | 4 | 3 | 2 | 1 | Strongly disagree |

I put off tasks that I really do not want to do but I know that I must do.

| Strongly agree | 4 | 3 | 2 | 1 | Strongly disagree |

Scoring: Total the numbers you have circled. Your score: ....

Interpretation:

- If your score is below 20, you are not a chronic procrastinator and you probably have only an occasional problem.
- If your score is 21–30, you have a minor problem with procrastination.
- If your score is above 30, you procrastinate quite often and should work on breaking the habit.

The problem is that procrastination can become a habit. Some people say they just can't get started, while others leave everything to the last minute. It may well affect what kind of degree or job you get – or even if you get one at all. So if you have a problem, it's time for action!

 Activity: Overcoming procrastination

- Think about the last time you procrastinated. Describe it as completely as you can. What was the task?
- What did you do rather than doing what needed to be done?

Planning your time

So far in this section we have looked at how you use and perhaps abuse your time. Students often complain early in their courses about having too much time between lectures, seminars and workshops. Yet later on there are often desperate attempts to complete assignments on time, with students sometimes completing the work overnight.

Part of what we have to learn, both as students and through life, is how to use our time more effectively in order to achieve our objectives. So how will you use your time in the future?

 Activity: Planning your time

In order to achieve your objectives it would be useful for you to complete the following two time plans:

1. **Weekly schedule**: try taking your academic timetable and fitting in other things you have to do around it, so you can get into a workable routine. For example you might plan times to go to the library between lectures on a Monday and to do your washing after seminars on a Tuesday and so on.

(Continued)

(Continued)

2. **Work schedule**: try taking your academic year diary and fill in assignment deadlines. Then add earlier deadlines to start researching, reading and writing up each piece of work, so that your final deadlines are just for submission.

Fix review dates in your diary in order to monitor your progress. Be prepared to change and update your plans, so that you achieve your goals.

Handling stress and developing relaxation techniques

What is stress and what causes it?

> **Stress** – physical or psychological pressure or tension.

Many people complain of **stress** or being 'stressed out', but what is stress? Many stress symptoms can be identified, but what underlies these is more complex. Mental stress will cause physical symptoms, as for example when we complain of 'butterflies in our stomach' before making a speech or an oral presentation. Stress is therefore a cause, while physical symptoms are effects.

Long-term stress that comes from working in a stressful environment or living in a stressful situation is frequently less perceptible or immediately apparent. We may complain of a sickly feeling, sleeping badly, or experience physical symptoms which may or may not be stress related (as in conditions such as asthma for example). We may have a stress-related illness but not necessarily relate it to our occupational or domestic stress. However, just as there is no smoke without fire, there is no effect without a cause.

> **Eustress** – positive stress associated with achievement and exhilaration.

Is stress necessarily bad for you? There are different kinds of stress, for example:

> **Distress** – negative stress associated with feelings of helplessness and hopelessness.

- **Eustress** – this is the positive stress associated with achievement and exhilaration which gives us energy and motivation.
- **Distress** – this is associated with negative feelings of helplessness, hopelessness, etc.

It is true to say but perhaps harder to accept that stress is caused not so much by what happens to us, but by the way we as individuals react to external events. For example, pressure of work is frequently blamed for stress, but so is unemployment. While some people become stressed in these situations others do not. This is not to say that excessive pressure of work or long-term unemployment are desirable, but rather that we need to understand the way in which we react to life events and, in particular, the role of anxiety, fear and phobias.

Anxiety results from personal fears which may, to a greater or lesser extent, be rational. The **flight or fight syndrome** refers to the situation in which the body produces extra adrenaline in response to perceived danger. It may lead to a persistent low level 'sickly' feeling or a classic **panic attack**, where the individual feels overwhelmed by psychological fears and as a result produces physiological symptoms, typically including hyperventilation, due to excessive adrenaline production.

Fear is at the root of all anxiety feelings – it is our normal and natural emotional protection from a dangerous world but it becomes a problem when our fears are either groundless or exaggerated, as in a phobia. **Phobias** are persistent and exaggerated fears based either on irrational fears, such as fearing that the sky might fall down on you, or more commonly based upon exaggerations of rational fears, such as fearing that your plane might crash.

Overcoming our fears

In order to overcome fears, we need to confront unrealistic fears and get realistic fears into perspective – for example, accepting that flying is safer than crossing the road! To do this we may need to embark upon a systematic programme of desensitisation. There are essentially two ways of doing this:

- **Flooding –** as exemplified by jumping in at the deep end of a swimming pool if you are scared of water, going to the top of

---

Anxiety – condition resulting from fears which may be to a greater or lesser extent rational or irrational.

Flight or fight syndrome – condition in which the body produces additional adrenaline in response to perceived danger in order to fight or take flight.

Panic attack – episode in which an individual feels overwhelmed by fear and produces physical symptoms in response to excessive adrenaline production, including hyperventilation.

Phobia – persistent and exaggerated fear based upon either irrational or exaggerated fears.

Flooding – confronting fears immediately and completely.

**Progressive
desensitisation –**
confronting fears
gradually and in
stages.

a tall building if you fear heights, or getting straight back on a horse if you have fallen off. This may work dramatically to resolve the problem or further reinforce fears.

- **Progressive desensitisation** is achieved in combination with relaxation techniques (see next section on controlling our own stress), by confronting fears in easy stages: doing small things first and gradually building up confidence. For example the fear of flying might be confronted first by looking at pictures of planes and then visiting airports before finally boarding a plane.

If you have a serious phobic problem or long-term unresolved anxieties, you should seek professional help. Your first port of call might well be your university or college medical centre or student services department.

Controlling our own stress

It is really important not to let stress take over your life, as not only can it seriously affect your health but also your performance in every aspect of your life. For help in controlling the day-to-day stresses of student life, some practical ideas for stress control include the following:

- **Learning to breathe!** Breathing is as important to stress control as it is to life itself. It was the first thing you did when you were born and the last thing you will do on this Earth. A little time spent every day retraining yourself to breathe slowly and deeply from the abdomen will provide a technique which you can draw upon in any sedentary situation. Try it in lectures, seminars, in traffic jams and any time you get delayed and eventually it will become automatic. It also helps with vocal projection and public speaking. See also Chapter 7, on giving effective presentations.
- **Taking more exercise!** Sport and exercise help to burn off surplus adrenaline and release endorphins to create a feeling of well being by changing our body chemistry. Gentle walking, cycling and swimming all provide valuable opportunities for thought and reflection, and regulate breathing – generally they are rhythmic and centring activities for the mind and body (see also the section below on building in the right kind of exercise).
- **Talking to someone!** It's not good to 'bottle things up'. It is much better to share problems regularly, making time for good quality communications with friends, housemates, family, tutors, your doctor, a counsellor or whoever else you feel is most appropriate.
- **Writing it down!** Writing up notes, reports, or keeping a diary or journal can all be cathartic and in a sense the paper can be the best counsellor, because it is absolutely neutral. Many courses now encourage various forms of reflective practice and this too provides a space for you to write down things you think and feel. See also Chapter 5 on why reflection is important to learning.

- **Stopping blaming and starting accepting!** Blaming is a common activity and builds negative connections in the brain which may lead us into depression. It's well worth asking yourself who you blame, for what, and why. Try to break the blaming habit, recognising that it is preferable to achieve a positive outcome by trying to do something positive about a negative situation, rather than going on about it. A good rule is to change what you can change and accept what you can't. See also Chapter 3 on asserting yourself when it is appropriate.
- **Making time for yourself!** Good time management helps you to use your time effectively. Prioritise work, and use diaries and charts to plan your time. This should also involve creating time for you – or **me time** – which means making a date with yourself in order to unwind, relax, and get in touch with your emotions. See also the previous section, on managing your time.
- **Meditating.** This is an excellent way of creating 'me time', and involves learning techniques for relaxation and exploring the inner space of our own psyche. You may be able to learn meditation techniques through a local Buddhist group or centre. **Mindfulness** is the idea drawn from Buddhism which is practised in meditation and involves focusing completely on what you see and sense, without preconception, and is often taught as part of a meditative technique.

> **Mindfulness** – idea drawn from Buddhism which involves focusing completely on what you sense.

- **Learn a relaxation technique.** Relaxation CDs, apps and books frequently teach relaxation response techniques, in which you will learn to relax when you 'pull' a psychological trigger – usually a key word which you have learnt to associate with relaxation. **Autogenic training** teaches a particular set of mental techniques used to help with relaxation, stress control, off-loading and positive thinking (Bird and Pinch, 2002; Kermani, 1996).

> **Autogenic** – meaning 'coming from within'.

- **Visualise yourself not being stressed. Visualisation** links well with meditation and relaxation techniques, and involves picturing and recording how, realistically, we think things might be. If we build a picture in our mind of how we might handle a difficult situation better, we are more prepared when we meet it because we have already built some of the psychological structures of the experience. For example, if you fear examinations, visualise yourself being relaxed and confident while taking an examination. See also Chapter 2 on visualising your success and Chapter 8, How to develop successful examination techniques.

> **Visualisation** – picturing and recording in our mind a future event to help us achieve a better outcome.

- **Get professional help if you need it.** If you have serious and unresolved issues, it's good to get help with them. See the section below, on accessing help and support, for ideas on where to go and who to ask.

Activity: Overcoming stress

- Take a few minutes to review the list above.

- Consider the question: What do I need to do differently in order to avoid stress? Jot down your ideas here and make a diary date to review your progress every week.

- Keep a 'stress diary' for one month. Spend a few minutes every day first reflecting and then recording both good and bad events that have happened through the day, putting a stress level against each on a scale of 1–10. Also note what you did to control your stress and which relaxation techniques you used each day.

- Review your stress diary. After one month, and perhaps before, you should be able to identify causes of stress and successful stress control strategies.

Getting to sleep

It is not unusual for new students to have sleep problems and also for these to occur before key points in academic life, such as before assignment deadlines and examinations. For most people these are short-term disruptions, but if you have long-term unresolved sleep problems you should seek advice from your doctor or university medical centre. They may be able to help you directly or in extreme cases they could refer you to a specialist hospital sleep clinic.

A student told us ...

A student told us that this was her first time living away from home and that she had serious sleep problems. She was having difficulty both getting to sleep and then waking up. She had missed a lot of morning lectures and seminars and was feeling permanently tired.

The paradox with sleep is that we routinely do it quite naturally, but when we try to do it we often seem to fail. To sleep successfully, we normally need three things:

- You need to be tired. This might sound obvious, but it's amazing how many people go to bed early the night before an exam and then can't sleep. So don't go to bed until you are tired.
- You need to be relaxed. This is why worrying about not sleeping keeps you awake. Fortunately there are many things you can do to help achieve a deep state of relaxation, without the use of drugs or alcohol.
- You normally need to be comfortable, although if you are very tired you may fall asleep without being so, for example when travelling.

If you can create a situation where all three states – tired, relaxed and comfortable – occur at the same time, you will almost certainly sleep. The next activity gives you some ideas which might help.

 Activity: Improving your chances of getting to sleep quickly

Consider putting the following twenty points into action:

- Don't go to bed until you are tired. Early nights might be ok if you are really tired, but going to bed too early is fighting what your body is telling you.
- Avoid too much late night entertainment just before attempting to sleep such as television, social media or playing computer games.
- Avoid eating too much, too late.
- Avoid caffeine altogether in the evening.
- Do eat a little to stop your blood sugar level dropping overnight and your body waking you up.
- Create a quiet time before bedtime to reflect upon the day and put it in perspective.
- Make a note of anything you have to do the next day. Use notes, lists or a diary so you don't have to remember those things all night.
- Write down any things that are on your mind before you try to sleep, as this will help to prevent you thinking about them during the night.
- Make sure that you have enough bedclothes so you won't be cold and not so many that you will overheat, because either being too hot or too cold may wake you up.
- Do set alarm clocks or the alarm on your mobile phone if you need to be up at a certain time, otherwise you may spend all night worrying about whether you will oversleep or not.
- Put a few drops of a soothing aromatherapy oil such as chamomile or lavender underneath your pillow. Avoid using an oil burner overnight as the flame will give a flickering light and it is also a fire risk.
- Make yourself comfortable, perhaps starting on your back, even if this is not your normal sleeping position.
- Try to avoid thinking about sleep altogether, because it generally happens when you're not thinking about it.
- See your mission not as sleep but rather as achieving a deep state of relaxation, telling yourself that if you are relaxed, tired and comfortable then you will sleep.
- Start breathing slowly and regularly, evenly and deeply.

(Continued)

(Continued)

- Breathe down into your body rather than up into your head. This takes your attention into your body, which you want to refresh in sleep, rather than into your brain, which you want to relax.

- Focus your thoughts on your breathing, allowing any intrusive thoughts to pass through your mind, and remember always to return to thinking about your breathing.

- With every breath, feel yourself going further down, more and more into a deep state of relaxation.

- Take at least twenty such conscious breaths every night.

- When you feel ready, move into your normal sleeping position.

- If all this fails, try staying awake all night. This usually fails and results in a good night's sleep!

1. What do you think you might do differently in order to put these ideas into action?

2. Try making a sleep strategy incorporating the ideas you have identified as being most useful to you.

3. Try your new sleep strategy for a week and then review your progress.

Looking after your health, including diet, exercise and health problems

If you can stay healthy, it really helps you to improve your chances of achieving your goals, both in terms of your studies and your wider goals in life. Conversely, falling ill can seriously undermine performance. Many students are quite healthy when they start their courses but fall sick during their first year due to poor nurturing skills and/or lifestyle decisions. Some students under-achieve, some have to intermit (take a year or so out), while a few leave altogether.

In this section we look at some of the things you can do to help your body stay fit and prevent health problems adversely affecting your studies. In particular we will look at diet, exercise, smoking, drinking, drugs, and dealing with health problems including sexual health. However, many health problems are stress related, so keep the section above in mind. You should also see the section above, on handling stress and developing relaxation techniques.

Improving your diet

Eating a balanced diet is standard health education advice and you will probably already know that you should get your daily share of vitamins, proteins and carbohydrates, but many students do get run down because of poor diet, particularly during their first winter away from home.

Following advice and eating five to seven portions of fruit and vegetables is a good start. If your shopping does not include much that is fresh and green, you might need to spend more time in the supermarket's greengrocery section. Local food markets, greengrocers, farm shops and farmers markets are also worth looking out for and can prove cheaper than the supermarket. While fruit juices can be used to supplement your fruit and vegetable intake, eating fresh rather than processed greengrocery also helps us get the trace elements we need, which are often missing from the processed alternatives.

We definitely need proteins too, but eating meat every day is both expensive and unnecessary provided you get protein from other sources such as fish, dairy products, rice, pulses and nuts. There are plenty of very healthy vegetarians! As for carbohydrates, though they are often seen simply as a filler, the body needs these for energy and you will get some vitamins as well. Potatoes, pasta and rice are good standbys for any kitchen and can be rotated for variety.

Breakfast can be the most important meal of the day. Taking a few minutes to make porridge can make for a good warming start, especially in the winter. Oats are also good for absorbing fats. Breakfast is also a good time to start adding extra fibre to the diet through cereals, but eating plenty of fruit, vegetables and whole grains through the day will also support this. Try to avoid snacking and fast foods. These tend to be relatively expensive, full of additives and often of limited nutritional value.

Plan your shopping. It is much better to have a list rather than just grabbing things that take your eye in the supermarket. Taking five minutes to make a list before you go can save a lot of time, waste and unnecessary expense. However, it is also good to look for bargains and be prepared to change your plans if something is really worth buying instead of what you had planned. In particular, fruit and vegetables get marked down if there is a glut or a sudden change in the weather. Avoiding waste is important, because it is just costing you money for nothing. So do watch those 'consume by' dates and if you buy too much of something, try to think what else you can make out of it.

Many students learn to cook at university partly through necessity, because it saves money, but also because it can be fun. You can make cooking an adventure, trying a new recipe every week. You can now find lots of recipes on the internet, some with instructional video clips. In shared accommodation it can be good idea to have a rota for cooking. Not only can this be more time efficient, as you may well only have to cook a couple of times a week, but also it can mean you have a more sociable house as people are committed to eating together. Cooking with or for friends and having the occasional dinner party can be fun – and a lot cheaper than eating out.

Activity: Are you what you eat?

1. Take a minute to think about your diet. Here are a few questions to consider:
   - Do you eat too much or too little food, or just enough to sustain you?
   - Do you get a good balance of vitamins, proteins and carbohydrates?
   - Do you snack rather than eating more balanced meals?
   - Do you shop well for food, getting good nutritional value for your money?

2. Try making a food plan or shopping list for the next week. How does it differ from what you ate last week?

Cardiovascular system – the body system which has to do with the circulation of the blood.

Lymphatic system – the body system which has to do with the circulation of lymph.

Adrenaline – hormone produced in the body at times of stress and excitement that acts as a neurotransmitter.

Endorphins – neurotransmitters associated with pleasure or euphoria.

Neurotransmitters – chemicals which carry messages in the brain and body.

Building in the right kind of exercise

If you want to be in really good shape for your studies, the best advice is to take regular **cardiovascular exercise**. This means using big muscles – as in walking, running, cycling and swimming – to work the heart and to get the blood and **lymphatic systems**, which have a number of functions in maintaining a healthy body and keeping it working really well. While weights may help you build the body beautiful, they do not provide the heart with the right type of workout it needs to see you through life.

Physiologically, cardiovascular exercise burns off **adrenaline**, associated with stress responses (see section above on handling stress), and helps to release **endorphins** which bring feelings of pleasure. Originally known as enkephalin, endorphins are **neurotransmitters** which have been described as the 'brain's own morphine' and as causing, among other things, the 'euphoria associated with exercise' (Pert, 1999: 349).

The standard advice is to build up slowly if you are unused to vigorous exercise. If you have health problems it is wise to consult your doctor, who will be able to advise you.

Team sports are an obvious choice for some but if you are not the team sport type you might also consider racket sports such as tennis, squash or badminton, where getting your cardiovascular exercise can also be fun.

Walking is perhaps the simplest form of cardiovascular exercise and, if you do it regularly enough, it can be all you need to keep your heart in shape. Walking round town can be good exercise, but getting out to the hills and vales at the weekend can also be a rewarding hobby. Walking with others can be a good and sociable activity, but walking alone also provides a good time to think and reflect. Even if you have a car, you don't have to drive everywhere. Do consider the park and walk option which will both give you exercise and save you money, as will walking in preference to taking the bus.

Running is an excellent form of cardiovascular exercise but can be very hard on the joints, especially if you are road running. Investing in the right footwear can really help to overcome the tendency to develop joint problems. If you have problems in this area, swimming is a clear alternative as it also provides excellent cardiovascular exercise but takes the weight off your joints. Swimming is usually a cheaper option than many other sports, needs little equipment and local pools will often have a discounted student rate.

Joining university sports groups can be a very good way of committing yourself to regular exercise and of making new and perhaps healthier friends. Alternatively, finding a training partner or buddy can also help, as there is a feeling of letting someone else down if you don't turn up. However, please remember when you don't take sufficient exercise to maintain your body you are always letting someone down – and that is you!

 Activity: How fit are you?

1. Take a minute to reflect upon your own level of fitness. Here are a few questions to help you:
   - Are you currently getting more fit, staying about the same, or becoming less fit?
   - Do you get more or less puffed out than friends when walking up a hill?
   - On a scale of 1 to 10, how would you rate yourself if 1 was a couch potato and 10 was an Olympic athlete?
   - Where would you like to be on that scale and where could you realistically expect to get to in, say, the next six months?

2. Make an action plan to improve your level of fitness, deciding:
   - what you want to achieve;
   - how you will go about it;
   - how you will measure your improvement;
   - when and how you will review it.

(See also Chapter 2 on planning your continuing personal development.)

Drugs, alcohol and smoking

The first thing we are going to say on this is:

we are not going to say don't!

Oedipal rebellion – tendency for the child to rebel against the parent.

The reason for this is that we believe that it would clearly be counterproductive. We recognise the phenomenon of **oedipal rebellion** – rebelling against the parent, so we are definitely not going to get parental with you. However, we know that many students do have problems in these areas, so we are going to discuss them and then allow you to decide what you want to do.

Even the most rudimentary study of anatomy and physiology reveals the human body to be an amazing machine, capable of achieving great physical and mental feats. It has immense power to maintain and even repair itself, given the right encouragement in terms of environment, sleep, diet, exercise, etc. You may perhaps see 'your body as a temple' yet some students choose to adopt destructive behaviour patterns as represented by smoking, excessive drinking and drug abuse. Why should this be so?

We want to suggest to you that people adopt destructive behaviour patterns because they are unhappy with themselves as they are. Drugs (including nicotine and alcohol) offer the promise of escape from ourselves, making us something else – more than we otherwise would be – and also perhaps suggest social acceptability and being 'one of the gang'. So what is cool about being 'off your face' or reeking of nicotine?

Excessive alcohol intake is sometimes seen as the undergraduates' birthright, and one of the authors of this book was a willing and guilty victim of that particular mythology. However, let's examine the evidence. Alcohol is frequently associated with having a good time in pubs, clubs, at parties and so on. However, it is neither the same as pleasure nor does it assure pleasure, because physiologically it actually depresses the central nervous system.

In many ways alcohol is the drug of denial because it helps us to avoid thinking about our problems, hence expressions such as 'drown your sorrows' or being 'off your face' or 'out of your head'.

Habitualised – a behaviour pattern normalised through repetition.

While moderate drinking may form part of a normal social life, persistent **habitualised** heavy drinking may lead to alcoholism, which in turn will cause major damage to the liver and other vital organs together with cognitive degeneration. Walking through most city centres, it is all too easy to see the results of alcoholism laid bare before our eyes. We are not saying don't drink, just suggesting being careful.

Smoking is probably the worst thing you can do to your lungs, heart and circulatory system but, again, one of the authors of this book used to do that too. It is clearly a very expensive hobby and increasingly socially unaccept-able. However, once you start, that nicotine addiction is an itch you just have to scratch. This was recognised by Carr (1995). He also recognised the asso-ciation between the act of smoking and acts of pleasure, such as smoking after food or after sex. Carr offers an effective non-medical route to giving up, but there are also the well-tried patches and gums which can be obtained commercially from chemists and sometimes on free prescription from health advisers and primary care providers.

Non-prescription narcotic drugs are, by definition, mind affecting. They variously offer a 'heightened sense of reality', the ability to dance all night or to simply 'chill out'. Many students experiment with non-prescription drugs. There is a perceived glamour but we need to recognise the existence of a well-developed commercial market, in which some students are not only users but also dealers. They may appear as friends offering a service, but rather it is an exploitative commercial transaction offered by those who at that point in time need a fix more than you do. Most students who experi-ment do not get addicted but some do and, like Russian roulette, that is the risk you take.

 Activity: Are my behaviour patterns destructive?

1. Take a minute to consider your own behaviour. In particular:

   - Do you drink excessively? If you answered yes, why do you think this is? What is the payoff for you from doing this?

   - Do you smoke? If you said yes, can you say why you started? Would you like to stop?

   - Do you use non-prescription narcotic drugs, occasionally or regularly? Can you say why? What is the payoff for you in doing this?

   - Do you have any other problematic behaviour patterns such as an eating disorder?

2. If you have identified any areas where you feel you need help, please read the following section and the end of chapter material, where you will find sources of help.

A student told us ...

A student who was six months into his course told us that he was having problems with coursework because he was using drugs, drinking too much alcohol and in financial diffi-culties. He said he was so confused he couldn't think any more or do his work. We referred him to our student services department which arranged long-term counselling and other support. He stuck at it and, although it took him longer than the rest of his cohort, he even-tually graduated successfully.

Dealing with health problems

The incidence of health problems can clearly be minimised by looking after yourself as we have suggested in this chapter. Your accommodation, manag-ing your money and your stress, together with a good diet and exercise all help – but we are only human.

Many complaints are stress related, and it is no coincidence that the word disease is formed of 'dis' and 'ease'. If we are **dis-eased** we are likely to become **diseased**, so dealing with stress, anxiety, fear, phobias and depres-sion is important. In general, dealing with health worries promptly will help to avoid further stress. If you have health worries, an early trip to the uni-versity or college medical centre is clearly advisable.

Sexual health is a particular area of concern for many students, because this is a time when a lot of people begin to explore their sexuality and/or experi-ment with sex. The use of condoms can significantly help to reduce both the likelihood of catching sexually transmitted diseases (STDs) – including HIV – and the incidence of unwanted or unplanned pregnancies, which could seri-ously affect your studies. You may find that sexual health advice and condoms are available for free from your university or college medical centre and/or from a university/college or public health project.

Problems and fears in the area of sexual health should not be ignored, but embarrassment is a big factor here. However, the staff who work in university medical centres and the STD clinics of local hospitals will be especially used to dealing with patients in this area. If you have any doubts or concerns you should talk these over with them as soon as possible. Failing to treat STDs can not only mean you pass them on to others but can also lead to long-term health problems.

Accessing help and support

The first port of call for many problems will be your personal tutor or course leader. They will most likely be quite experienced in many of the problems which regularly occur in student lives. They will often be able to refer you to the most appropriate source of help. It is also important for them to know about what is happening to you as personal problems tend to impinge upon studies and they may have to argue your case in examination boards if your performance suffers.

For accommodation and financial problems contact:

- the Student Services Department;
- the Students' Union's welfare adviser or debt counsellor;
- the local Citizens' Advice Bureau.

For health problems contact:

- your Student Medical Centre or the general practitioner with whom you are registered;
- the local STD clinic for help with sexual health.

Overall, there is a lot of help on offer, but you have to be prepared to access it. Pride can sometimes be a barrier but there is no shame in asking for help. We all need support at times and it is sometimes the mark of the successful student that he or she can seek help and guidance when it is needed.

Follow-up activities

Time for action – Checklist

Have you:

- considered what you need to do to upgrade your self-nurturing skills?
- thought through the transition to living independently?
- made plans for managing your time effectively so as to achieve your goals?
- calculated a budget to help you with managing your money?
- learnt methods for handling stress and developed relaxation techniques?
- developed techniques for getting to sleep and sleeping soundly?
- given sufficient attention to your health, including diet, exercise and health problems?
- considered the impact of any destructive behaviour patterns you may have adopted and what you might do to change these?
- made yourself aware of sources of help and support?

Further reading

Bird, J. and Pinch, C. (2002) *Autogenic Therapy*. Dublin: Newleaf.

Cameron, S. (2009) *The Business Student's Handbook*, 5th edn. Harlow: Pearson.

Carr, A. (2013) *The Easy Way to Stop Smoking: Be a Happy Non-smoker for the Rest of Your Life*, 5th edn. London: Penguin Books.

Chopra, D. (2001) *Perfect Health*. London: Bantam.

Cottrell, S. (2013) *The Study Skills Handbook*, 4th edn. Basingtoke: Palgrave Macmillan.

Kermani, K. (1996) *Autogenic Training*. London: Souvenir Press.

Lee-Davies, L. (2007) *Developing Work and Study Skills*. London: Thomson.

Pert, C. (1999) *Molecules of Emotion*. London: Pocket Books.

Pert, C. (2007) *Everything You Need To Know To Feel Good*. London: Hay House UK Ltd.

Smith, H. W. (1998) *The 10 Natural Laws of Time and Life Management*. London: Nicholas Brealey Publishing.

Thompson, M. (2013) *Winning Strategies for Sport and Life*. London: Gabrielle Lea Publishing.

Websites to look up

- For help with money/student finances, health, drugs, etc.:
  www.nus.org.uk/en/lifestyle
- For help with financial support from the student support in the UK:
  www.gov.uk/student-finance/overview
- For information on health, including mental health issues:
  www.nhs.uk/Pages/HomePage.aspx
  www.studenthealth.co.uk

Time for review and reflection

This is your space to log your reflections on this chapter, to think about what you have learnt, how you will use it and what else you need to find out.

What were the key learning points of this chapter?
What are your strengths in the areas covered by this chapter?
What areas did you identify for development?
What have you learnt about yourself?
How will you use this knowledge?
What else do you need to learn or find out about in relation to this chapter?

PART II

How to Develop Your Academic Skills

5

How Do You Learn and How Do You Know What is Required of You?

Overview – what's in this chapter?

- Why do you need to upgrade your learning skills?
- Understanding how you learn and your own learning styles
- Recognising why reflection is important to learning
- Developing critical thinking skills
- Using mapping and brainstorming techniques for study and creativity
- Understanding assessment
- Completing group assignments successfully
- Follow-up activities, further reading and websites to look up
- Time for review and reflection

Why do you need to upgrade your learning skills?

Try completing the short self-scoring test overleaf, to assess your own level of confidence in relation to developing your learning skills to help you complete your course successfully.

✎ **Activity: Why do you need to read this chapter?**	
You need to self score each question on a scale from 0 to 10, where 0 is low and 10 is high.	
1. How good do you consider you are at learning?	
2. How often do you take time to reflect upon what you have learnt?	
3. How often do you take time to reflect upon how you learn?	
4. How good are you at developing critical arguments and not just taking things you read or hear at face value?	
5. How good are you at taking notes?	
6. How good are you at analysing a problem you are given?	
7. How good are you at thinking creatively?	
8. How likely are you to do exactly what an assignment asks you to do?	
9. How good are you at completing assignments on time?	
10. How confident do you feel about leading or participating in a team in order to complete a group assignment successfully?	
Total score	

Interpretation

What did you score?

- Less than 50%   You definitely will find a lot of help in this chapter.
- 50%–75%   There is still plenty to learn in this chapter.
- 75%–100%   You are very confident – read on to confirm your understanding.

We all learn, not only in education but throughout our lives, but our time is valuable and sometimes pressured, especially when we have deadlines to meet, so it is important to learn how to learn more efficiently and more effectively. In higher education it is going to be important that you learn effectively if you are going to achieve your goals. Your time is valuable, so learning efficiently makes sense.

Good academic work is largely about understanding certain conventions that operate. Imagine trying to play football or tennis if no one ever told you the rules. We do not believe that the processes of learning and assessment should be a guessing game and so part of our aim is to demystify the process for you.

In this chapter we will look at how we learn, how we can improve our learning skills and, in particular, why reflection is important to learning, developing critical thinking skills, note taking, mind mapping, brainstorming and creativity. We will also explore the problems of understanding assessment and of working in, or leading, teams in order to complete group assignments successfully. Finally there are some follow-up activities, some suggested further reading, websites to look up, and some space for review and reflection.

Understanding how you learn and your own learning styles

To understand how we learn, it is useful to see learning as a process. As with any other process it can be broken down into stages. Understanding each stage and our relevant strengths and identifying areas for development can really help us to develop our own learning.

> **Learning cycle** – developed by Kolb and Fry, sees learning as a circular process with a number of stages we pass through.

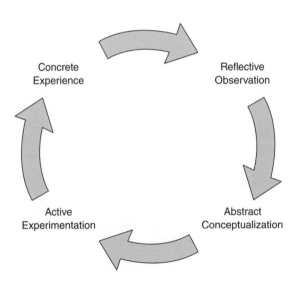

FIGURE 5.1 Kolb learning cycle

Source: Kolb and Fry, 1975

Kolb and Fry (1975; Kolb, 1984) have suggested that there is a **learning cycle** (see Figure 5.1). Learning can occur at any point in the cycle and there is, therefore, no 'right way' of learning. Newton was supposedly hit by a falling apple and through reflection developed the theory of gravity, which can be tested by **active experimentation**. However, he might have started the process by reflecting upon what would happen if an apple fell, formulating a theory as to why it would happen and then testing it in an experiment which would then lead to a **concrete experience**.

> **Learning styles** – as developed by Honey and Mumford, recognise that individuals learn in different ways and may employ one or more learning styles.

We don't all learn in the same way. Honey and Mumford (1982) developed four **learning styles** which can be plotted against the stages of the learning cycle as shown below (see Table 5.1).

TABLE 5.1   Comparison of Kolb learning cycle and Honey and Mumford learning styles

Kolb learning cycle	Honey and Mumford learning styles
1. Concrete Experience	Activists
2. Reflective Observation	Reflectors
3. Abstract Conceptualisation	Theorists
4. Active Experimentation	Pragmatists

Honey and Mumford (1982) also suggest that we may favour particular learning styles and that our learning styles may develop over time as a result of our experience of learning.

✍ Activity: How do you learn?

1.   Consider the learning styles introduced by Honey and Mumford (1982) in terms of how you learn:

Activists involve themselves fully without bias in new experiences and revel in new challenges.	**Reflectors** stand back and observe new experiences from different angles. They collect data, reflect on it, and then come to a conclusion.
Theorists adapt and apply their observations in the form of logical theories. They tend to be perfectionists.	**Pragmatists** are keen to try out new ideas, approaches and concepts to see if they work.

2. Try to allocate one of the following statements to each of the descriptors above. You can give more than one of the descriptors to the same statement if that seems right for you.

    - Most like me

    - Fairly like me

    - A bit like me

    - Nothing like me.

3. Consider what impact this knowledge will have for your studies. There are two potential outcomes:

    - You may decide that knowing how you learn, you will try to 'play to your strengths', using those methods which come most naturally to you.

    - Alternatively, you may decide to try and develop those methods of learning which you are least likely to use at the moment.

Understanding and developing your learning styles is an important step towards becoming an effective student, but it is quite likely that your learning styles will change and develop during your life and especially so while you are in higher education.

A student told us...

A student told us after completing the Honey and Mumford learning styles questionnaire that he had done the same test two years earlier at college but that his learning styles had changed. Through discussion we established that it was his experience of education that had encouraged this development.

What is your attitude to study? In Chapter 1 we asked you to think about your motivation to learn (see the section on recognising your own motivation to learn, grow and develop). If you can't remember what you said, it might be helpful to refer back to what you wrote there. We believe that your motivation will tend to condition everything else you do in education as well as in life in general.

We see that students fall into two broad categories:

- **Optimistic learners** – who tend to see learning as an opportunity to learn, grow and develop. They often see learning as fun, an adventure or a positive experience.
- **Pessimistic learners** – who tend to see learning as a requirement which must be fulfilled. They often see it as a chore, a bore and a generally negative experience and frequently look to do the minimum required.

Activity: Are you an optimistic or pessimistic learner?

1. Consider your previous experience of education. Were you more of an optimistic learner or a pessimistic learner?
2. What is your attitude to your current studies?
3. Does your attitude need to change? If so, how?

Recognising why reflection is important to learning

Reflection can be seen as an essential part of the learning process (as identified in the previous section of this chapter). The reasons for reflection include:

- Making sense of what we have studied – in other words, what does it mean?
- Considering what we think about what we have learned – in other words, is it any use and what do we feel about it emotionally?
- Seeing how what we have learned fits together with other knowledge and ideas.

Reflection is a recurring theme in this book, but what is the point of reflection? According to Moon (1999), reflection is linked with the process of learning:

> Reflection is a form of mental processing that we use to fulfil a purpose or achieve some anticipated outcome. It is applied to gain better understanding of relatively complicated or unstructured ideas and is largely based on the reprocessing of knowledge, understanding and possibly emotions that we already process.

Reflection – the conscious act of mental re-processing in order to make sense of past learning or events.

Within the context of higher education, reflection can be viewed as fitting into a three-stage model (see Figure 5.2).

As a student you may often feel bombarded with inputs and unable to make sense of them in your outputs, be it in reports, presentations or in the examination hall. It is easy to spend too much time at stage one, and not to take the time to think about and reflect upon what you have learnt. The journey that you are asked to make in higher education is that from **surface learning** to **deep learning**. Completing the next activity will clarify what we mean by these terms.

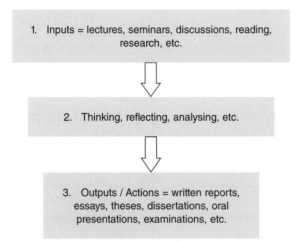

FIGURE 5.2   Three stage model of reflection

✎ Activity: Are you a deep or surface learner?

1.   Have a look at the levels of learning below, suggested by Moon (1999).

2.   Where do you feel that you are in the hierarchy?

Transformational learning ⇧		Meaningful, reflective, restructured by the learner, creative
Work with the meaning ⇧	Deep learning	Meaningful, reflective, well structured
Making meaning ⇧		Meaningful, well integrated, ideas linked
Making sense ⇧	Surface learning	Reproduction of ideas, ideas not well linked
Noticing ⇧		Memorising, representation

(Continued)

(Continued)

3. Now have a look at the following distinctions (adapted from Entwistle and Marton, 1984).	
Surface approach to learning	**Deep approach to learning**
• Intention simply to reproduce parts of the content. • Accepting ideas and information passively. • Concentrating only on assessment requirements. • Not reflecting on purpose or strategy. • Memorising facts and procedures routinely. • Failing to distinguish guiding principles or patterns.	• Intention to understand material for oneself. • Interacting vigorously and critically with the content. • Relating ideas to previous knowledge and experience. • Using organising principles to integrate ideas. • Relating evidence to conclusions. • Examining the logic of the argument.
4. What could you do to deepen your learning?	

Understanding how you learn, and deepening your learning, will be a major determinant of how you develop in higher education and beyond. Reflection is not only a key part of the learning process but also a key element in the developmental process. Learning and development are clearly interrelated. How could we develop without learning in the process, and how could we learn without developing in that process?

Because we tend to learn in small bite-sized chunks, there is the question of how it all fits together. Imagine standing really close to a brick wall so that you could only see a few bricks right in front of your face. What you are looking at may be hard to determine, but by standing back you may see that it's a house or a hotel or another type of construction.

Gestalt – psychological concept relating to structure or form and how things fit together into a whole.

The concept of **Gestalt** comes from the German word that corresponds, approximately, to structure or pattern. The concept was first developed in Germany during the early twentieth century by the so-called **Berlin School** of writers. Later Perls (1951), who was born in Berlin but later moved to the United States, developed Gestalt as a form of therapy focusing on the 'here and now'.

In Gestalt, the structure or pattern is explained by the **SOR model**:

S = Stimulus pattern	What affects me
O = Perceptual organisation	How I deal with it
R = Response based upon perception	What I do about it

Gestalt psychology recognises **insight** as its central concept. We see the example of Archimedes discovering his famous principle of the displacement of water when sitting in the bath. 'Eureka!', he supposedly cried in a flash of insight. This is, potentially, where Gestalt leads us to – by seeing how the evidence links and connects, we come to a Eureka moment. **Mind mapping** (see section below on mind mapping and brainstorming) can be a useful tool both for reflecting upon our studies and revealing the picture as suggested in Gestalt psychology.

 Activity: Reflecting upon your studies?

1. Try drawing a mind map or diagram which expresses the following steps:

   - Take an idea, theory or concept from your studies and try to link it first to the topic it forms a part of.
   - Next draw a link to the topic of the module it comes from.
   - Now link the module to the rest of your course.
   - Finally link your course to your own life as expressed in your personal development plan (see Chapter 2).

2. Sit back and have a look at your diagram. What sense does the original idea, theory or concept make in the context of your studies?

Developing critical thinking skills

Handling the intellectual argument

In higher education it is particularly important to question everything you read, are told or discover and not to take anything at face value, but rather to deal with all knowledge critically. The golden rule is that **all knowledge is provisional** and can be overtaken by both new discoveries and advances in thinking.

There is an old joke which suggests that an expert is someone who understands all the latest misconceptions. The trap is to fall into believing that the latest knowledge is probably correct, when history clearly shows that most accepted knowledge is overturned eventually. Therefore, good academic work is objective, critical and supported either by established theory and/or by evidence that has been collected, but does not claim to be true or that anything has been proved conclusively.

A student told us…

A student complained after a lecture which had been both full of theories and systematic in its criticism of each of them, 'Why do you teach us all these old theories if they are all wrong?' This is a good question and one which deserved a good answer. The answer was that each theory showed the development of thinking in that field and that understanding the development of theory and critique was to understand where we are now – and why.

The science of knowledge

In order to handle intellectual arguments successfully in your academic work, it is important for you to have an appreciation of a number of critical concepts. **Epistemology** is the science of knowledge which looks at how knowledge is constructed and asks us to consider two critical questions:

- How do I know what I know?
- How do I know that what I know is true?

Epistemology – the science of knowledge which questions the construction and validity of knowledge.

These questions are perhaps at first sight simple and you may feel them unworthy of consideration, but consider for example quoting a simple statistic in your work. How do you know it is true? Perhaps you found it in a book, an article or website, but does that make it true? If it was taken from British Government data, does that make it true? How was the data collected, analysed and presented? How could you validate the work? The questions are potentially endless and may sometimes seem quite pointless, but understanding why they need to be asked is the key.

Handling the intellectual arguments successfully, therefore, starts with the proposition that knowledge is not necessarily truth. This is because a proposition only holds until it is disproved. For example, the earth is flat and the sun goes round it – or does it? There was a time when that was the perceived wisdom, but now we know better. The implication is, as stated earlier, that **all knowledge is provisional**.

We need to clearly distinguish between two types of statement which you will definitely be making in your academic work:

- **Positive statements** are those supported by evidence or examples. A positive statement supported by evidence is one which can be defended on that basis.
- **Normative statements** are statements which offer no evidence and are merely thought to be true. A normative statement can be protected from the criticism that it is not necessarily true by the use of a **caveat**, one of those small words such as 'perhaps', 'might' or 'maybe'.

Positive statement – statement supported by evidence or examples which can be defended on that basis.

Normative statement – a statement which offers no evidence and is merely thought to be true.

Caveat – words used as a warning or a proviso as to the uncertain status of the statement being made.

 Activity: Writing positive and normative statements

1. Try to write a positive statement.

2. How can your positive statement be supported, i.e. with evidence?

3. Try to write a normative statement.

4. Have you covered yourself by the use of a suitable caveat?

This leads to the question, is a positive statement ultimately possible? When we talk of knowledge about markets, we must bear in mind that we find it hard both to define a market and to predict its behaviour. Thus, is our knowledge merely belief?

Objectivity – requires the exclusion of all opinions and biases.

Subjectivity – allows for the inclusion of opinions.

Value judgement – a statement which embodies our own opinions.

Deduction – involves taking a theory and testing it empirically to verify or refute it.

Conjecture and refutation – doctrine developed by Karl Popper, arguing that a thesis becomes more certain with each positive replication, but when successfully refuted it must be abandoned or refined.

Induction – accumulating evidence in support of a proposition in order to produce a generalised formula.

This in turn leads to another important distinction:

- **Objectivity** – to be objective requires us to exclude all of our own opinions and biases.
- **Subjectivity** – allows for opinion. For example, take the statement: 'it was a good film'. In this case 'good' is a value judgement.

A **value judgement** embodies our opinions and there is limited scope for them in academic work. If you were writing a lab report on a chemical reaction there would clearly be little value in saying how you felt about it. However, if you were asked to write a critique of a film, it might be valid to include your subjective opinions towards the end of an otherwise objective analysis. However, when including our own value judgements we must always make it absolutely clear that is what they are.

The question then is, can knowledge ever be completely **value free** and, therefore, totally objective? The point of this question is exemplified by the problem of collecting social data through questionnaires when the questions may embody the values of the designer. See also Chapter 6 on conducting primary source research.

Knowledge can be seen to advance as a result of two alternative processes:

- **Deductive logic** or **deduction** involves taking a theory and testing it empirically to verify or refute it. We may start by deciding what we expect to discover, but the danger is that we may exclude evidence which does not fit our hypothesis. Popper (1989) introduced the idea of **conjecture and refutation**. He argues that a **thesis** is postulated and becomes more certain with each positive replication. When it is successfully refuted, it must be either abandoned or refined. For example Newton's law of gravity was reinforced by each incidence of something falling to earth, but had to be refined with the discovery of gases that are lighter than air. A helium balloon clearly does not fall to earth like an apple falling from a tree.
- **Inductive logic** or **induction** involves accumulating evidence in support of a proposition, i.e. arguing from specific

116

instances to produce a generalised formula. However, the proposition is never proved because of the possibility of finding other, opposing, evidence. For example smoking is generally accepted as a major cause of lung cancer, because of the strong statistical correlation between smoking and the incidence of lung cancer. However, not all smokers develop the disease and not all sufferers smoke. While the proposition may be broadly accepted as correct, it is clear that there are other factors at work. Arguing from a single instance to make a generalised formula is never acceptable in academic work because, as Popper (1989) has suggested, it is by repetition that we gain certainty and by refutation that we lose it.

How knowledge is acquired or developed can be seen to derive from three processes:

Empiricism – belief that the only valid source of knowledge is that which can be experienced.

- **Empiricism** – empiricists hold that the only valid source of knowledge is that which can be experienced. Knowledge is, therefore, knowable and the world discoverable. However, for empiricists no hypothesis is effectively possible and thus nothing can be known unless it can be experienced.

Rationalism – belief that knowledge can be gained through reasoning.

- **Rationalism** – rationalists reject empiricism in favour of either inductive or deductive logic. Rationalism involves reasoning and may therefore include assumptions which might be wrong and also the possibility is that it may lead to value-laden theory.

Dialectics – belief that knowledge can be gained through a process of argument or conversation involving thesis (argument) and antithesis (counter argument).

- **Dialectics** – date back as far as the ancient Greek philosophers, whose preferred form of the dialectic was literally an argument or conversation. All dialectics involve a process of **thesis** (argument) and **antithesis** (counter argument). In the nineteenth century a dialectical approach was adopted by Marx and Engels (1967). In Marx's materialist conception of the history of western civilization, he argues that society developed by stages as a result of its contradictions. Class against class, conflict leading to development and further contradiction.

Epistemology – the science of knowledge which questions the construction and validity of knowledge.

Paradigm – an internally consistent set of ideas or beliefs which purport to offer a reliable explanation.

An important advance in the development of **epistemology** has been the idea of **paradigms** developed by Kuhn (1970). A paradigm is a set of ideas which is internally consistent and can make real sense when you study it. However, a problem arises where there are competing paradigms or idea sets, such as in religion or politics, where we are offered alternative versions of the truth by advocates of different paradigms. Some examples of competing paradigms within fields of study or belief are:

- **Politics**: conservatism, liberalism, socialism, communism, anarchism, environmentalism, etc.
- **Psychology**: behavioural and cognitive psychology.
- **Economics**: Keynesianism, Monetarism and Marxism.
- **Religion/belief systems**: Buddhism, Christianity, Hinduism, Islam, Judaism, Sikhism, Humanism, etc.

Kuhn (1970) argues that revolutions in science occur when a number of anomalies challenge an idea set. The great 'scientific revolution' occurred in the seventeenth century. Copernicus had theorised in the 1540s that the sun did not revolve around the earth but that the reverse was true. After almost two centuries and the work of Kepler, Galileo and Newton, the theory became generally accepted. This acceptance was slow in coming as the theory challenged not only conventional scientific wisdom, such as it was, but also the ideas of the church.

Evaluating what you read

Thesis – an intellectual argument. The term is also used for an extended piece of academic work.

Antithesis – a counterargument.

Synthesis – the merging or combining of arguments.

The clear message of this section is to be critical, recognise how the knowledge was acquired and perhaps to challenge it. Some terms which will be useful to you in recognising what you are reading include:

- **Thesis** – this is an intellectual argument, although the term is used more often for a long piece of work which would contain your argument or arguments.
- **Antithesis** – this is the counter argument to a thesis.
- **Synthesis** – this is a combining of arguments.

In higher education we don't expect you to just take what you read at face value but to treat it critically, remembering the earlier point that all knowledge is provisional. Some of the critical questions that you might want to ask are:

1. What is the main area under review or discussion?
2. What are the main findings?
3. Where does the author's data and evidence come from, and are they appropriate and sufficient for the purpose of their argument?

4. What are the main issues raised by the author?
5. What questions are raised and how well are these questions addressed?
6. What are the major points/interpretations made by the author in terms of the issues raised?
7. Is the text balanced? Is it fair or biased and, if the latter, how is it biased?
8. How does all this relate and compare to other literature on this topic, your own experience, ideas and views?
9. How can you summarise all of the above points?
10. What are your conclusions about the literature?

(Adapted from: CAPLITS Centre for Professional Literacies)

 Activity: Reviewing literature from your course

- Start this activity by identifying an item of reading for your course.

- Read and review this critically, using the ten questions in the critical questions list above as a basis for your analysis.

- How does the work look to you after this critical review?

- Try to make this critical approach the way that you normally approach academic literature, developing a 'critical eye' in the process.

Using mind mapping and brainstorming techniques for study and creativity

Our amazing brains

In developing a sound study technique it is useful to consider how your brain works. We normally have 10,000,000,000 brain cells at our disposal. These cells or **neurons** are connected by **synapses** or **boutons** (buttons) which are the product of our life experiences which have been processed and encoded by our brains as we make new connections. Whilst we never forget what has been memorised, our practical problem as students is recalling information as and when we want it.

In recent years the concept of **neuroplasticity** has been developed, which recognises the ability of our brains to develop neural connections and which has displaced the old idea of the brain as a fixed and static

> **Synapses or boutons** – connect neurons in the brain in order to encode and store memories.

> **Neuroplasticity** – the concept that brains develop by making new neural connections.

119

organ. Seminal work on monkeys by Nobel Prize-winning neuroscientists Hubel and Weisel (Hubel, Weisel and Levay, 1977) recognised the extent to which we build our own brains through a process of pruning. For example, a child learning the piano will develop those parts of the brain controlling motor drive to the fingers, whereas a child concentrating on football will develop other parts controlling foot and head movement. The exciting implication of the neuroplasticity concept is the recognition that we literally build our own brains based on our life experiences. More recently work by neuroscientists has shown that our bodies also have a molecular informational system which challenges the idea of an electrical synapse model (Pert, 1999: 138).

Autonomic nervous system – that part of the body's peripheral nervous system that operates subconsciously to keep body systems running.

We all have an amazing piece of equipment at our disposal – a sort of super computer – which can analyse and store a range of information and direct complex motor skills such as playing sports or musical instruments, while at one and the same time monitoring and controlling our body functions though the **autonomic nervous system,** whilst growing and developing in the process. We don't have to remember to breathe, digest food or even to repair a cut finger. Our brains just take care of that, leaving us free to think and grow.

However, when we are in education we can often feel overwhelmed and overloaded with cognitive inputs, including those from lectures, seminars, reading and discussions. This is why it is important for us to develop techniques to help us develop our brains if we are to achieve our goals in education and beyond.

Mind mapping – technique developed by Tony Buzan, to plot ideas graphically avoiding linear techniques.

Using mind mapping for note taking, creativity and examination preparation

The idea of **mind mapping** was introduced by Buzan (1974) and avoids the standard **linear** technique of note taking in favour of concentrating on the quality of our encoding of information. This involves drawing mind maps, in which we put the topic at the centre of our notes rather than at the top, and then work outwards from the centre in expanding branches, using **key words** to summarise each body of knowledge.

Key words – words used in mind mapping to summarise a body of knowledge which can be recalled by reference to the keyword.

As we identify key words we make a connection not only on the paper, but also in our brain. As we make these connections we are inserting psychological triggers, which can be pulled when we want to recall not only the key words, but also other information that is filed away with them. We can see the brain as being similar to a computer or filing cabinet – if files are clearly named and filed away in a logical sequence, the process of retrieving information becomes much easier. Similarly, we use keywords in the index of a book, in order to find the content we want.

The power of keywords is demonstrated when you are in conversation with a friend who mentions somewhere that you have both been at different times. Although you may not have thought of this place for a very long time, mention of the name, a key word, brings a host of memories flooding back, and you will probably remember what you did, who you were with, what the weather was like, where you stayed and what you ate.

When taking notes in lectures and seminars, you can try using a mind mapping technique for note taking, or you can use it to summarise your notes or handouts and other materials after the session. Doing this systematically will help you store ideas away in your brain for later use when writing up your work. Looking at your mind maps will help refresh your memory and you can always go back and add to them if there is more to say, perhaps from your reading around the subject.

Mind mapping can also be used to enhance your powers of creativity. Try putting a problem at the centre of a piece of paper and then working out from it in different directions. This helps us to expand our **lateral thinking** and again gets away from the **linear thinking** which is associated with making lists, taking notes and writing formal reports.

Lateral thinking – thinking may go in different directions to look at problems from different angles.

When writing up a formal report or essay, try to **brainstorm** all the main points first. Then order your points into a logical sequence and write around them. Your key words may become your subheadings. Similarly, you can use a mind map to structure the content for an oral presentation (see also Chapter 7 on writing up reports and essays, on structuring material and constructing your arguments, and on giving effective presentations).

Linear thinking – going through accepted steps or stages to follow an obvious line of linear thought.

When revising for examinations, try reducing all your topics to mind maps. If you use these for revision you can improve your recall in the examination. Brainstorm your key words in the examination, not only will they give your essays structure but you will also avoid the tendency to dry up (see also Chapter 8, How to develop successful examination techniques).

Brainstorming – method of problem-solving or of collecting knowledge or ideas often associated with mind mapping.

Activity: Making mind maps work for you

- Identify a topic from your course and reduce your notes to a mind map. Use colour, highlighting, drawings or diagrams to make it really memorable.

- File your mind map away for a couple of days and then try to re-draw it from memory. You may be surprised at how much you remember.

- Consider how you can use this technique in your studies.

Understanding assessment

Why do we have assessment?

If you are struggling to complete a piece of work by the deadline or revising for a dreaded examination, you may well be asking, 'why do we have to have assessments?' Here are a few suggestions:

- To monitor your progress and development.
- To measure your own performance.
- To show what you have learnt.
- To get feedback on your ability.
- To allow for progression through your course.
- To acknowledge your achievement (as at a graduation ceremony).
- To give access to higher qualifications.
- To get a good job or move into the area of employment you want.
- To allow you to progress in life.

It is important to see that, although the process may feel somewhat painful at times, there are positive reasons for going through it, plus positive outcomes to focus upon. This clearly links back to what you said about your motivation in the activity in Chapter 1 and helps in planning your continuing personal development, which was covered in Chapter 2.

Assessment can either be formative or summative, as outlined below:

Formative assessment – provides feedback on progress within a module or course.

- **Formative assessment** can take place at any time during your course and its purpose is to provide you with feedback about how well you are progressing in your studies and also to provide you with guidance as to topics that you may need to focus on before the summative assessment takes place.

- **Summative assessment** occurs at the end of a module or a course and this assessment will result in the final mark awarded for your work. It is important to seek formative assessment/feedback if you need help to ensure that your work is of the appropriate standard before summative assessment takes place.

> **Summative assessment** – provides final assessment of work completed in a module or course.

What do degree classifications mean?

If you are new to higher education you may be unsure as to what your marks mean. Table 5.2 can be used as a guide to what your tutors are trying to tell you.

TABLE 5.2   What do degree classifications mean?

Mark	Degree class	Your work is
70+	First class	Excellent
60–69	Second class (division 1) more commonly known as 2.1	Good
50–59	Second class (division 2) more commonly known as 2.2	Fair
40–49	Third class (3rd)	Passable
0–39	Fail or refer	Poor

In Britain it has been less common to mark into the upper end of the percentage range. Although there has been some movement away from this tradition in recent years, not employing the full range of marks available may still occur and can often confuse new students, and especially international students, if they are used to assessments being marked up to 100%.

 Activity: What sort of grades do you want?

- Take a few minutes to consider what sort of grades or degree class you realistically think you could achieve.
- What do you need to do to get the grades you want?
- Is this part of your personal development plan?

Building grade achievements into your personal development plan can bring real dividends (see Chapter 2 on planning your continuing personal development), particularly if you set realistic grade outcomes, detail what you need to do to achieve them, and set regular times for review. Setting a single review date after grades are issued will be too late, because it is what you do day-by-day and week-by-week which ultimately will determine your success.

Understanding what you have to do to complete your assessments successfully

Content words – words used in assignments and essay questions to indicate the subject area covered.

It may sound too obvious to say, but being absolutely clear about what you have to do is essential to completing your assessments successfully. Don't be surprised if you find your assessments hard; in higher education the work is meant to be difficult in order to stretch you, but not impossibly so.

There should always be a written assignment brief and this should be clear. If you don't understand what you have to do just ask your tutors. Beware of relying on your peers' interpretation of the assignment brief. Many a myth has been fostered within a group of students who didn't like to ask and marks have suffered as a consequence. Similarly, do stick to what you were asked to do. It is all too easy to go off at a tangent, particularly if what you discover starts to seem more interesting than what you were asked to do.

Action words – words used in assignments and essay questions to tell you what you are expected to do.

A good approach is to break assignment tasks or essay questions into key words. These tend to fall into two categories:

1. **Content words** which indicate the subject area covered.
2. **Action words** which tell you what you are expected to do.

For example, say you were set a question such as:

'Analyse the causes of fluctuations in London share prices over the last ten years.'

Here the content words are: **causes, fluctuations, London, share prices** and **last ten years**. The topic is clearly bound both geographically and chronologically. **Analyse** is the only action word, and this indicates that you have to do more than simply report what has been happening.

The golden rules for completing your assessment successfully are: follow the assignment brief, do just what it calls for and, if you don't understand, ask for guidance. It is as simple as that and will lead to disappointment if you waste a lot of your valuable time doing the wrong thing.

✍️ **Activity: Understanding action words in your assessment task**

- Try to match the following action words with the appropriate meaning.
- Next check your answers against those given at the end of this chapter.

1. Analyse		a.	Describe and distinguish similarities and differences.
2. Clarify		b.	Give reasons why or how; clarify, justify and illustrate.
3. Compare and contrast		c.	Describe or summarise, often with an evaluation.
4. Discuss		d.	Examine and break into component parts.
5. Evaluate		e.	Provide a framework or explanation – usually in narrative form – of a concept, idea, event or phenomenon.
6. Explain		f.	Show how things fit together; provide analogies.
7. Illustrate		g.	Provide pros and cons of something; provide an opinion and justify it.
8. Justify		h.	Explain, review and consider.
9. Outline		i.	Provide examples; show instances.
10. Relate		j.	Provide a condensed, precise list or narrative.
11. Review		k.	Explain with significant detail.
12. Summarise		l.	Explain why a concept can be supported, typically by using examples and other types of support.

(Adapted from Feldman, 2000: 152)

Getting feedback on your work

There are three potential sources of feedback on your assignment work:

- self-assessment;
- peer-assessment;
- tutor-assessment.

Self-assessment –
your own assessment
of your work.

Peer-assessment –
assessment of your
work conducted by
your peers, i.e. fellow
students.

Tutor-assessment –
assessment of your
work by your tutor.

Self- and **peer-assessment** can be used to obtain valuable feedback before you hand in your work. If you are very lucky your tutor may also be willing to look over a draft, but you can't expect this. For more ideas on how to obtain and use all three sources, see Chapter 7 on improving your grades through feedback from self-, peer- and **tutor-assessment**.

Your tutor should provide you with feedback on your assignment work, which may be some combination of written feedback, audio feedback or a marking grid as well as a specific mark or grade. This will give you valuable information on what you are doing right and what you need to work on. Even if you get good grades, it is important to keep taking the feedback on board if you want to progress successfully.

A critical question to ask is, 'does this feedback tell me why I didn't get 100% on this assessment?' If you are unhappy with grades or don't understand how the grade was arrived at, it is very useful to look at the written feedback you received. If you are still unsure, or didn't get sufficient written comments, don't be afraid to ask your tutor to go through the assessment with you (see also Chapter 3 on giving and receiving feedback).

For a detailed summary of how assessment is dealt with at your institution, refer either to documentation you were given at induction or on your institution's website or intranet.

Completing group assignments successfully

Group dynamics –
the interactions
between group
members and the
implications of these
for group behaviour.

Working in and perhaps leading a group or team brings more complications and challenges through the increased complexity of interactions between people – known as **group dynamics**. When completing group assignments, there may be no formal leader and so you might have to take the lead in order to ensure a successful outcome.

Activity: What makes a good team?

Think about the qualities of a good group or team that you have been a member of and consider the following questions.

- What was good about the team?
- What areas could be improved?
- What did you learn from the experience?

Group formation

Tuckman and Jensen (1977: 419–27) suggest that groups may go through five stages, namely:

- **Forming** – when a group is formed.
- **Storming** – when the group culture is established.
- **Norming** – when the group culture is accepted.
- **Performing** – when the group performs successfully.
- **Adjourning** – when the group breaks up.

Through this process the culture of the group is established. Culture may in turn be seen to comprise the roles which people take on within the group, the rules which are set up, the norms of behaviour which are established and the values which the members have accepted. The theory was first developed by Tuckman in a clinical environment but also seems to work well in the context of project teams, which are put together for a particular purpose and have a definite life. It is not perhaps so convincing for ongoing operations or 'business as usual' where there is a gradual turnover of staff over time, with people joining and leaving at regular intervals.

Group formation – the process by which groups are formed and group culture is established.

In terms of completing a group assignment we can perhaps see that the situation is very much that of a project team, which has a clear goal to complete the work by a deadline and, therefore, has a fixed term of life. In the early stages, meeting, talking, organising and – perhaps most of all – bonding will all be more important than doing any of the work. Some ideas for fostering the process of group development include:

- Suggesting an early meeting to elect a leader, to look critically at the assignment brief, to discuss what has to be done, to agree who will do it and by when.
- Exchanging email addresses and mobile numbers so you can keep in touch between meetings and perhaps forming a social networking group.

> **Gantt chart** – type of bar chart used to schedule work and monitor progress towards completion of a project.

- Writing down everything that was agreed and circulating it to the group by email or perhaps making a **Gantt chart** in order to plan and track progress towards your objective.
- Doing something of a social nature together which is unrelated to the task, such as a quiz night or bowling, in order to help the team to bond.
- Arranging regular follow-up meetings to review progress at intervals until the deadline.

Team roles

> **Team roles** – concept developed by Meredith Belbin which identifies a finite set of team role behaviours.

The concept of **team roles** has been developed by Belbin (1993, 2000, 2010). In the extensive use of syndicated teaching (group work) at Henley Management College, staff noticed that while some groups gelled well, others did not. Thus began the work on team roles, in an effort to explain the relative good and bad chemistry of teams. He draws a clear distinction between **team roles** and **functional roles** and argues that while the type of behaviour evident in groups is infinite, the range of behaviours which make a useful contribution to a group is finite and that these behaviours can be grouped into team roles. He suggests that within any team, the member who is strongest in a particular team role will tend to take on that role.

 Activity: What are your team roles?

1. Visit: www.belbin.com/rte.asp?id=8 and download the team role descriptors.
2. Consider which are your strongest and weakest team roles.
3. Consider how you might develop these.

When participating in group assignments it may take some time for the team to shake down into clear team roles and you may find you have a mix of team roles which is less than ideal for the task. In the latter case flexibility may be the key to getting things done and this may mean you filling gaps in your team and taking roles you would not normally choose to do. This can be a developmental experience in itself.

Leadership styles

Leading an assignment group can be a good developmental experience and valuable preparation for taking on leadership roles in your professional career. If you become the leader of your group, it will be useful to consider what style you will adopt and what competences you will need.

Leadership styles – types of approaches to leading their followers adopted by individual leaders.

Tannenbaum and Schmidt (1973) have suggested that there are four major stages on a continuum of **leadership styles** ranging from boss centred to subordinate centred:

Tells ⟷ **Sells** ⟷ **Consults** ⟷ **Joins**

Clearly at the 'tells' end of the continuum the style is dictatorial which can be effective for getting things done but can quickly alienate the team members. At the other end of the scale, 'joins' really means to abdicate leadership responsibility. In between are the ideas of selling and consulting, which have to do with gaining people's consent to work for you and trust you as a leader.

Emotional intelligence competencies – discrete aspects of emotional intelligence which we may have to a greater or lesser extent.

Research by consultants Hey/McBer (reported by Bloisi et al., 2007: 586–7) found that managers typically used six leadership styles based upon **emotional intelligence competencies**. They found that the best performing managers used most of them every week, depending upon the situation they encountered. The six emotional intelligence leadership styles are:

- **Coercive** – demand immediate compliance in crisis.
- **Authoritative** – mobilise employees towards a vision.
- **Affiliate** – skilled at creating emotional bonds and harmony.
- **Democratic** – build consensus through participation.
- **Pace-setting** – set high performance standards and expect self direction from others.
- **Coaching** – help others improve performance.

A useful analogy is with a golfer. Imagine a golfer who has only one club and you can perhaps see that a round of golf would be made unnecessarily difficult. With six assorted clubs in the golfer's bag the task would potentially be a lot easier. However, it's not enough to have six clubs, you also have to know when and how to use each of them.

Leading a group of student peers is in reality little different from leading a work team. Although the context may be different, you will find that developing your skills in the emotional intelligence competencies will make you more effective in the role and your task much easier.

 Activity: Leading a team

1. Consider, if you were leading a team, what would be the likely problems and what would be the likely rewards?
2. Which leadership style(s) would you want to adopt?
3. Would the style you adopt need to be contingent upon the situation and the people involved?
4. Which emotional intelligence competencies would you need to develop and which ones do you already have?

Follow-up activities

Time for action – Checklist

Have you:

- considered what you need to do to upgrade your learning skills?
- identified how you learn and your own learning styles?
- recognised the role of reflection in your learning?
- considered how you need to develop your critical thinking skills?
- developed your note taking, mind mapping and brainstorming skills?
- appreciated what you need to do to understand your assessments?
- identified what grade or grades you hope to get and included this in your personal development planning?
- recognised the special problems of working in a team completing group assignments successfully?
- considered what leadership style you might adopt and what leadership skills you might need to develop, in order to lead a course work group successfully?

Further reading

Belbin, M. (2010) *Team Roles at Work*, 2nd edn. Oxford: Butterworth Heinemann.
Belbin, M. (2000) *Beyond the Team*. Oxford: Butterworth Heinemann.
Burns, T. and Sinfield, S. (2012) *Essential Study Skills: The Complete Guide to Success at University*, 3rd edn. London: Sage.
Buzan, T. and Buzan, B. (2010) *The Mind Map Book*. London: BBC Books.

Buzan, T. (2006) *Use Your Head*, 3rd edn. London: BBC Books.

Cameron, S. (2009) *The Business Student's Handbook*, 5th edn. Harlow: Pearson.

Cottrell, S. (2013) *The Study Skills Handbook*, 4th edn. Basingstoke: Palgrave Macmillan.

Honey, P. (1994) *Learning Logs – A Way to Enhance Learning from Experience*. Maidenhead: Peter Honey Publications.

Lee-Davies, L. (2007) *Developing Work and Study Skills*. London: Thomson.

Moon, J. (1999) *Reflection in Learning and Professional Development*. London: Kogan Page.

Moon, J. (2006) *Learning Journals: A Handbook of Reflective Practice and Professional Development*, 2nd edn. Abingdon: Routledge.

Race, P. (1995) *Who Learns Wins*. London: Penguin.

Race, P. (2007) *How to Get a Good Degree: Making the Most of your Time at University*. Buckingham: Open University Press.

Ridley, D. (2008) *The Literature Review: A Step-by-Step Guide for Students*. London: Sage.

Russell, T. (1998) *Effective Feedback Skills*, 2nd edn. London: Kogan Page.

Websites to look up

- For further information on learning styles:
  www.peterhoney.com
- For further information on the Kolb learning cycle and reflection:
  www.ldu.leeds.ac.uk/ldu/sddu_multimedia/kolb/static_version.php
- For further information on reflection:
  www.learningandteaching.info/learning/reflecti.htm
- For further information on critical thinking in relation to what you have read:
  www2.open.ac.uk/students/skillsforstudy/critically-processing-what-you-read.php
- For further information on mind mapping:
  www.tonybuzan.com
  www.mind-mapping.co.uk
- For further information on team roles:
  www.belbin.com

Answers to the 'Understanding action words' activity (p. 25)

1.	Analyse	b.	Examine and break into component parts.
2.	Clarify	c.	Explain with significant detail.
3.	Compare and contrast	j.	Describe and distinguish similarities and differences.
4.	Discuss	a.	Explain, review and consider.
5.	Evaluate	e.	Provide pros and cons of something; provide an opinion and justify it.

6. Explain	f.	Give reasons why or how; clarify, justify and illustrate.
7. Illustrate	d.	Provide examples; show instances.
8. Justify	k.	Explain why a concept can be supported, typically by using examples and other types of support.
9. Outline	g.	Provide a framework or explanation – usually in narrative form – of a concept, idea, event or phenomenon.
10. Relate	i.	Show how things fit together; provide analogies.
11. Review	h.	Describe or summarise, often with an evaluation.
12. Summarise	l.	Provide a condensed, precise list or narrative.

Time for review and reflection

This is your space to log your reflections on this chapter, to think about what you have learnt, how you will use it and what else you need to find out.

What were the key learning points of this chapter?
What are your strengths in the areas covered by this chapter?
What areas did you identify for development?
What have you learnt about yourself?
How will you use this knowledge?
What else do you need to learn or find out about in relation to this chapter?

6

How to Plan, Conduct and Review Your Research

Overview – what's in this chapter?

- Why do you need to upgrade your research skills?
- Designing your methodology
- Conducting primary source research
- Using secondary source material
- Recognising the purposes of a literature review
- Developing skills for research interviews and recording the outcome
- Reviewing and evaluating your research findings
- Follow-up activities, further reading and websites to look up
- Time for review and reflection

Why do you need to upgrade your research skills?

Try completing the short self-scoring test overleaf, to assess your own level of confidence in relation to developing your research skills in order to complete your course successfully.

Activity: Why do you need to read this chapter?

You need to self score each question on a scale from 0 to 10, where 0 is low and 10 is high.

1. How much do you know about methodology?	
2. How confident would you feel about writing a research proposal?	
3. How confident do you feel about achieving academic rigour?	
4. How confident do you feel about conducting your own research?	
5. How much do you know about designing questionnaires and surveys?	
6. How confident do you feel about completing a literature review?	
7. How confident do you feel about finding and using academic library resources such as books and journals?	
8. How confident do you feel about using online library facilities, online reading lists and databases to access academic journal articles?	
9. How confident do you feel about looking for other sources of data/information?	
10. How confident do you feel about reviewing and evaluating your findings?	
Total score	

Interpretation

What did you score?

- Less than 50%   You definitely will find a lot of help in this chapter.
- 50%–75%   There is still plenty to learn in this chapter.
- 75%–100%   You are very confident – read on to confirm your understanding.

Whether you are writing a short essay, extended essay, dissertation or thesis, you will need to research the content, either by reading other people's work or by doing your own. These two basic categories of research sources can be explained as follows:

Primary source – data which you have collected yourself.

- **Primary source research** means finding out for yourself, at first hand. This could include using methods such as experiments, interviews, focus groups, questionnaires, surveys or participant observation.

- **Secondary source research** means reading other people's work and ideas in academic books, journals and any other publications, including '**grey materials**'; whether you read the hard copies or access material through websites.

> **Secondary source –** other people's work as reported in books and journals, etc.

Good research requires you to learn an appropriate range of skills and mastering these will go a long way to determining the quality of your output in terms of assessment work, together with your analytical and presentational abilities.

> **Grey materials –** material such as company or public data which may be appropriate to cite in your work.

In this chapter we will first look at designing your methodology, together with some basic research methods, completing a literature review, conducting research interviews and reviewing and evaluating your findings. Finally there are some follow-up activities, some suggested further reading, websites to look up, and some space for review and reflection.

Designing your methodology

> **Methodology –** systematic development of method or methods used in research work.

Methodology refers to the systematic development of method or methods that are to be used in order to research your work. If you are doing primary source research it is essential that you can describe your methodology before you start your research work to ensure it is **rigorous**.

> **Academic rigour –** strict adherence to normal rules and procedures for conducting academic research.

Academic rigour has to do with strict adherence to normal rules or procedure both in the conduct of research and in the analysis and reporting of results. For example, interviewing only people you think might support your views, out sorting questionnaires that don't fit your contention, or ignoring lab results which produce inconvenient results are all clearly unacceptable.

> **Research question –** the question which your research will seek to answer.

Good research starts with a clear **research question** to be answered or a **hypothesis** which is to be examined. Having a good question or hypothesis will be your guiding light and will condition how you research. It is all too easy to get sidetracked and lose sight of your objective. Taking some time to refine your question or hypothesis will be important.

> **Hypothesis –** a proposed explanation for something which may be proved or disproved.

135

Research proposal – explains what you are proposing to research, how you will do it and may include a preliminary literature review.

Running your ideas past your tutor will also usually pay dividends in the long term. See also Chapter 7 on understanding what else you need to know to write an extended essay, dissertation or thesis.

A **research proposal** or proposition must explain what you hope to find out, what research you will need to undertake, and how you will go about doing it – i.e. your methodology. You may also be required to submit a preliminary literature review. See 'What is a literature review' section below.

In order to write up your methodology, you will have to choose your research method or methods. Conducting **primary source** research will involve finding out new information for yourself and this could involve experiments, interviews, questionnaires, surveys or other methods. The key point here is that it is your data which you have collected. In contrast, secondary source research will require you to read other people's work and ideas in books, journals or on websites, etc. Frequently your work will involve you using a combination of primary and secondary sources, with the secondary source material providing a theoretical framework through which you can interpret your own results.

Research ethics – includes consideration of risk assessment, data security, confidentiality and anonymity and informed consent.

Your methodology will be more convincing if you can justify the methods that you utilised in preference to other methods that you might have reasonably used. For example, you may have collected questionnaire data in preference to data from focus groups because of the difficulty of gathering individuals from remote locations together in groups.

Risk assessment – relates to the probability and extent of risk experienced in the proposed research activity.

You should also give consideration to **research ethics** when devising and writing up your methodology. This is an area of developing importance and is to some extent related to the sensitivity of the subject of your research. Key questions to consider include:

- What risks are there in conducting the research and what is the extent of any risks? If any risk is perceived, there should be a **risk assessment** covering both you as the researcher and the participants.

Data security – relates to the storage and restriction of access to paper-based and electronic data.

- How will data be stored and disposed of after the research is completed, and will access to the data be restricted in order to provide for **data security**? This will include both written and electronic data which you collect.

- Will the **anonymity** of individuals be preserved in your written output, i.e. your report, essay, dissertation or thesis? In this case you will need to explain how this was achieved. For example you might state that questionnaires were completed anonymously and returned online or in a prepaid envelope.

Anonymity – relates to protecting the identity of research participants when reporting data.

- Will you be maintaining **confidentiality**? This might include a discussion of if and how individuals are identified in the research, what data is reported and with whom it might be shared. There is an important difference between confidentiality and anonymity. Take for example the reporting of a unique case disclosed to you in confidence. Even reporting this anonymously would be a breach of confidence.

Confidentiality – relates to the level of secrecy to be observed when collecting data.

- How will you be obtaining the **informed consent** of participants? For example, for consent to be informed, it would not be enough merely to get written permission from people that you interviewed, but rather you would need to explain how they were informed about the project and how their responses might be used.

Informed consent – research participants give agreement on the basis of an informed appreciation of the implications of participation and how the data will be used.

In general, it is essential that you can describe your methodology clearly before you start researching. If you cannot do so you may waste a great deal of time exploring 'false trails' and – worse still – your results may lack sufficient academic rigour.

A student told us ...

A student told us that he wanted to conduct his research on nightclub bouncers and that this would take place in the late evening and early morning when they were on duty. We had some concern about his personal safety until we found out that he was himself working as a licensed nightclub bouncer. We therefore concluded that he was at no greater risk when conducting the research than he would be in his normal employment.

Conducting primary source research

As stated previously, primary source research means finding out for yourself at first hand. In certain disciplines, especially the natural sciences, this could involve experiments which may be designed or may be prescribed by your tutor. However, in most cases it will be down to you to determine your methodology; see the section above on designing your methodology.

Activity: Defining your research question and identifying your methodology

1. Before starting your research try to write a clear question. Then look critically at your question and ask yourself:

   - Can this question be answered?
   - What would you need to do or know to answer it?
   - What methods could you use to investigate the question, i.e. your methodology?
   - Have you given appropriate consideration to research ethics and how you will obtain the informed consent of participants?
   - What criticisms could be made of your methodology?

2. Now try writing up your methodology. If you can, run it past your tutor for feedback.

Conducting **interviews** for research has the potential advantage of getting into greater depth with interviewees but the disadvantage is that the process can be time-consuming, not only in terms of the time taken conducting the interviews and in travelling to locations to meet people face-to-face but also because of the problem of recording or transcribing notes from interviews (see the section below on skills required for interviewing and recording outcomes). **Telephone interviews** can sometimes be a compromise solution because travel time is removed and you can jot down notes as you go, but there is always some loss of the feedback we get from reading one another's body language. However, using **Skype** for interviews does to some extent restore your ability to read your interviewees body language.

Interviews may be **structured**, **semi-structured** or **unstructured** and this requires another choice from the researcher. To conduct effective interviews you will need a good range of interpersonal skills. See Chapter 3, How to improve your people skills, particularly the sections on questioning and listening skills and preparing for formal interviews.

Structured interview – interview based upon a predetermined list of questions.

Semi-structured interview – interview guided by a predetermined list of questions or agenda.

Unstructured interview – free-flowing interview not bounded by predetermined questions or agenda.

Focus groups have become a popular research method in recent years and can be seen as a sort of group interview, in which questions are asked by a facilitator of a number of participants who meet together. This has the advantage of being less time-consuming than conducting individual interviews and also that ideas may emerge during the course of the session. However, there is a danger of cross contamination, in that individuals may frame their answers based upon what they have already heard from other participants and so the output might be somewhat different from that collected from either a series of discrete interviews or from individual questionnaire responses.

> **Focus group** – qualitative research collecting data from a group of participants in response to questions from a facilitator.

Questionnaires have certain advantages over interviews as it may be possible to collect more data from more people and in a more structured way, potentially making the data more easily analysed and reported, especially where the questions are of a quantitative nature. Quantitative questions normally ask respondents to tick boxes or circle options, perhaps using a **Likert scale.** A Likert scale typically offers a range of responses to a question or statement e.g. 'most like me', 'something like me', etc. Qualitative questions ask for a narrative response and can also be categorised and quantified by using a system of **coding**. Data can be analysed using specialised software such as SPSS, which should be available through your institution, but this does require some investment of time to learn how to use it. For small samples, we have used highlighter pens to colour code textual responses for 'quick and easy' quantitative analysis. Coding can also be used for **content analysis** of the responses from interviews, focus groups and any other research method which produces textual responses.

> **Questionnaire** – standardised method of collecting data from individual respondents, using a paper-based or online questionnaire.

> **Likert scale** – method of scaling responses to questions.

> **Coding** – system of categorising qualitative responses.

> **Content analysis** – analysis of textual or verbal research data.

Because questions are prescribed in a questionnaire, it makes them inflexible when compared to a free-flowing or semi-structured interview. Questions may even be misunderstood as there is no possibility of judging the response as in a face-to-face interview, where body language can be assessed and alternative or supplementary questions asked to clarify points.

Normative assumption – assumption of what is thought to be as opposed to what is.

When writing a questionnaire, it is easy for the designer unintentionally to embody his or her own ideas or **normative assumptions**. When phrasing questions it is important not to lead the respondents by asking loaded questions such as: 'Don't you think it's a bad idea that...?' Similarly, imagine a question such as: 'How serious do you consider the problem of immigration to be?' This question starts from the position that there is a problem and therefore effectively excludes anyone from responding who thinks either that it is not a problem or that immigration is a good thing. In other words it embodies a normative assumption of the designer.

With a 'tick box' type of questionnaire you should mix up the questions so that there is no discernable pattern to the answers which might lead the respondent to think that, say, column three was the correct answer. Even with simple questions that require only yes or no answers, there should be no chance of the respondent becoming 'tick happy' or the point of the research will be lost.

In designing a questionnaire it is helpful to start by asking fairly easy questions, leaving the challenging content until later on when the respondent is more relaxed and 'warmed up'. For example, if you were researching alcohol abuse, you might hide your 'real' questions among others in a general questionnaire about lifestyle. The worst idea would probably be to head it up: 'Do you have a drink problem?'

When giving respondents options to tick, it can also be very helpful to give them an option which avoids them having to tick an option that they don't agree with. Examples include 'rather not say', 'none of these', and 'other', etc. Where offering an 'other' option, it can be really helpful to provide a space for qualitative comments. This can help you collect unexpected data which you hadn't considered likely when designing the questionnaire.

An important decision to make will be about how your questionnaire is to be distributed to potential respondents. Consideration must be given as to how and where data is collected. Standing around with a clip board and asking the questions yourself may produce very different results to those from either an online or postal questionnaire that is to be completed anonymously (see also the 'Hawthorne effect' later in this section).

A further issue with questionnaires relates to the size and composition of the **sample**, and how representative it is of the population you wish to survey. In general a larger sample might be expected to be more representative, but as a student there are also issues about how you will handle the data and you will almost certainly want to restrict the size to make it manageable.

Sample – the total number of respondents to your questionnaire.

There is also the question of which '**population**' you identify. For example, distributing a question- naire on smoking only to smokers might be expected to give very different results from distributing it to the wider population. Both might provide interest- ing data, but you would need to consider this matter very carefully when designing your methodology and again your research question should be your guiding light (see the section above on designing your methodology).

Population – the total number of people who might have responded to your questionnaire.

The question then arises, 'a sample of what?' It could be of the population of a country, the staff of an organisation, or of some particular group such as fell walkers or asthma sufferers. The group being sampled must be clearly identifiable and the sam- ple should be a **representative sample** of it. Collecting some **demographic data** as part of your questionnaire – such as age, gender and ethnicity, etc. – will allow you to compare the profile of your sample with that of the group it represents and in turn allow you to draw some conclusions as to just how representative it is.

Representative sample – a sample deemed to be broadly representative of the population concerned.

Demographic data – data relating to the composition of a population.

Increasingly questionnaires are being designed and distributed using online facilities in preference to traditional paper-based methods. You should have access to appropriate software for doing this through your institution. Alternatively, Survey Monkey offers a commercial service, although smaller surveys are currently free. Online systems offer signifi- cant advantages in terms of design, distribution by means of a link, which can for example be communicated through email databases or social networking contacts, and also in relation to data collection and calculation of statisti- cal output.

A final consideration will be to **pilot** your draft questionnaires with a small sample – maybe even made up of friends – who will give you feedback on the content and construction and allow you to put things right before you start in earnest.

Pilot – a small survey conducted to test out your questionnaire or other research methods.

As with questionnaires, **surveys** are to a large extent dependent for their success upon covering a representative sample of what is being surveyed. Types of survey are many and various and include

Survey – systematic collection of data by observation.

UNIVERSITY OF WINCHESTER
LIBRARY

such diverse activities as counting customer footfall, i.e. people passing a site in market research, to examining aerial pictures for signs of lost buildings in archaeology.

Simple **observation** might seem to be a fairly obvious method of researching human behaviour. However, the effect of the researcher upon the research must always be acknowledged. The so-called **Hawthorne effect** refers to the tendency of people to behave differently when being observed (Mullins, 2013). This holds implications not only for observation but also for the design of all social research methodology, in terms of the impact of researchers upon their results. For example, responses to a questionnaire of a personal nature, such as illegal drug use or safer sex practice, might be quite different where the forms are returned anonymously in a plain brown envelope or online, rather than being taken down in person by an interviewer with a clipboard.

Hawthorne effect – tendency of people to behave differently when being observed.

Participant observation – research conducted undercover by a researcher who poses as one of the group being observed.

To avoid problems created by the Hawthorne effect, some researchers developed **participant observation**, which required the researcher to work 'undercover'. However, this might now be considered as unethical, because of the problem of not being able to obtain the informed consent of participants (see earlier discussion in this chapter on designing your methodology). **Action research** is an alternative approach, which addresses real life problems in a collaborative venture between researchers, participants and practitioners. Its success can be measured according to whether the actions solve the problems and realise change (Blumberg et al., 2005).

Action research – addresses real life problems as collaborative venture between researchers, participants and practitioners.

There is also the possibility of using some combination of two-way mirrors, hidden microphones and cameras for remote observation. However, the use of such technologies again raises ethical issues in relation to the difficulty of obtaining the informed consent of participants. Also the problem of maintaining secrecy remains and, once discovered, we can expect that people will behave differently, just as drivers slow down when they see a speed camera.

Activity: Selecting your primary source methods

When you are selecting which primary source method(s) to use for your research, consider the following points and questions.

- Review your assignment carefully. What are you being asked to do?
- Develop a clear research question or hypothesis to guide your work.
- Consider which method(s) would be most appropriate, most practical, and most reliable in order to complete your work successfully.
- Try to think what problems you might encounter.
- Try to foresee what criticisms might be made of your methods and how you might counter these.
- Be prepared to ask your tutor for feedback on your methodology before you commence researching.

Using secondary source material

Researching through secondary sources inevitably involves reading other people's work and ideas. Secondary sources are clearly very extensive, but can be seen to include:

- **Books** – which either may be authored or edited books of readings by other writers.
- **Academic journals** – which contain **refereed** articles, which means that submissions have passed successfully through a process of **peer review**.
- **Other journals, magazines and periodicals** – these may have useful articles but do not have the status of refereed journals.
- **Websites** – where online material can be downloaded. These require special consideration and we should ask, 'What is the source of the material and can it be trusted?' A key question may be, 'Who is moderating the site?'
- **Local and national government publications** – including the Public Record Office and other sections of the National Archives, etc.
- **Organisational data** – including internal publications from companies and other organisations. These are sometimes known as **grey materials**.

> **Peer review** – process by which academic materials are critically reviewed by academic referees.

> **Grey materials** – material such as company or public data which may be appropriate to cite in your work.

Online library – facility which allows direct access to digitalised library resources and to check the availability of 'shelved' materials.

Academic libraries normally hold much of the sort of secondary source material you will need, and you will usually find that your own institution's library will be geared to the needs of your course. Increasingly, library resources can be accessed online and it would be helpful to your studies to make sure that you have a good working knowledge of your university's **online library** facilities.

If you are doing project work you may need access to other academic or specialised libraries. Local libraries can be very helpful, as for example when conducting a local history project. Similarly, many organisations will have their own libraries and may welcome student researchers even if they are not open to the general public, although you may need an introduction from your own institution's library.

Visiting reader facility – allows the researcher to use a library other than that of their own institution.

Visiting reader facilities allow you to use libraries which might otherwise be closed to the general public, while **inter-library loans** allow you to read work from other locations without the need to travel there, which can be a very useful and time-saving option. Your own institution's library staff should be able to advise you on such things as inter-library loans and reader facilities for other libraries.

Inter-library loan – facility allowing the researcher to borrow material from a library other than that of their own institution.

When using secondary source materials it is all too easy to read and collect too much information and end up with a big pile of notes and no idea what to write about (see Chapter 7 on writing up reports and essays, and on structuring material and constructing your arguments). Be guided all the time by your research question (refer back to the section on designing your methodology). This can be used as a filter when looking for materials and when examining contents and index pages in order to make sure you read just what you need to. Using your time and energy effectively is essential if you are to achieve your goals. A good distinction here is between reading that which you **need to know** as opposed to that which is **nice to know**.

When using books and journals be aware that they also provide you with other sources. You may find that the references they give you to other works are worth exploring further. Similarly, websites provide you with useful links to other sites which can be explored.

Sometimes a number of works will all refer back to the same source and what you may have found here is reference to the **seminal work** – i.e. the first piece written in a particular area, often highly original and influential. Ideally we would all go back to seminal works, but that is not always a practical possibility, so be guided by your lecturers as to what to read. In many disciplines textbooks are quite acceptable and offer you a distilled account of many other works.

Seminal work – first piece written on a particular subject, often highly original and influential.

When you take notes from books and journals make sure that you collect all the details you will need for your **reference list** or **bibliography** (and store them carefully). For books this will include the author, year of publication of the edition you used, plus the title, edition, place of publication and publisher. Page numbers should also be noted so you can find the source material again and because you may need them when source referencing (see Chapter 7 on plagiarism and source referencing).

Reference list – lists secondary source material cited in your work.

Bibliography – lists secondary source material cited in your work and/or additional secondary source material not cited in your work.

 Activity: Identifying your secondary source material

When you are identifying secondary sources for your research consider taking the following steps.

- Ask your tutor or supervisor for any suggestions as a starting point, together with any other staff or students who have an interest in the subject area.

- Make internet searches using your institution's online library and/or academic search engines such as Emerald or Google Scholar.

- Use textbooks to get an overview of the subject area, noting which sources they quote. These may be seminal works which you can go back to.

- Talk to the subject librarian at your institution's library to establish what they know or are aware of that could help you.

- Talk to specialist people at other universities or in external organisations in the field.

When using **internet sources** it is important to record the date you visited the site together with the full URL. The easiest way to capture the full URL is to cut and paste it directly into your reference list or bibliography (see Chapter 7 on source referencing). However, it can be a good idea to check the URL, by re-pasting into your web browser to ensure it works.

Academic articles published in print journals which are accessed online are not currently classed as internet source material and are normally referenced as if you had read them in the print journal. If you access academic articles online, it may not be immediately obvious as to whether they are from a print or electronic journal. A useful tip is to check whether the article has page numbers – print journal articles will always have these, where as electronic journals will tend not to.

Recognising the purposes of a literature review

Literature review – a critical review of relevant literature within a defined subject or topic area.

A **literature review** is an appraisal of the available academic work within a particular field of study. We find that students often make the mistake of simply reporting the literature rather than reviewing it, and slip into the trap of what we call 're-writing the textbook'. So the key word here is **review,** and depending upon what you are being asked to do, this could mean doing a combination of the following things (following Blumberg et al., 2005: 154):

- Establish the context of the problem or topic by reference to previous work.
- Understand the structure of the problem.
- Relate theories and ideas to the problem.
- Identify the relative variables and relations.
- Show the reader what has been done previously.
- Show which theories have been applied to the problems.
- Show which research design and methods have been applied to the problems.
- Show which research designs and methods have been chosen.
- Rationalise the significance of the problem and the study presented, synthesise and gain a new perspective on the problem.
- Show what further work needs to be done in the light of existing knowledge.

A literature review may be an assignment in its own right, but will often be an essential component of a longer work such as an extended essay, dissertation or thesis. In this case the purpose of the literature review is to lay out the theoretical background or framework for the entire work (see also Chapter 7, on understanding what else you need to know to write an extended essay, dissertation or thesis).

In some academic work literature is **embedded** into an intellectual discussion, rather than there being a discrete literature review section or chapter. Be guided by your assignment requirements and your tutors in determining how to use literature in your academic work.

> **Embedded literature** – literature is embedded into an intellectual discussion rather than a discreet literature review.

 Activity: Completing your literature review successfully

1. When you are asked to complete a literature review, take a close look at your assessment brief. What exactly are you being asked to do and why? If this is not clear, go back to your tutor and ask!

2. Consider which of the points in the bullet list provided above you might want to achieve in your literature review.

3. Try to read and take notes critically in order to extract what you need from the work in hand. You will not only need to note down quotations but also what points of analysis strike you as you read the text.

4. Review all your notes critically (see Chapter 5 on developing critical thinking skills), before making a plan and writing up your review.

5. Take a good look at your final draft. The key question for you to consider is: 'Have I provided a critical review of the literature required or simply a report of it?'

Developing skills for research interviews and recording the outcome

As suggested earlier, one of the decisions you need to make when establishing your methodology is whether to use interviews and, if so, of what type. Interviews can be structured, i.e. based around a list of scripted questions, semi-structured or unstructured (see also Chapter 3 on developing your questioning and listening skills, and on preparing for formal interviews). Some of the most productive interviews can be free-flowing but the open format also means it is easy to miss something, so a semi-structured interview – maybe with a checklist of things to cover – can be a useful compromise.

Recording the outcome also requires some methodological decisions. There are two basic options:

Verbatim – findings are reported word for word as opposed to being summarised.

Informed consent – research participants give agreement on the basis of an informed appreciation of the implications of participation and how the data will be used.

- Taking notes is the obvious solution but it can seriously interrupt the flow of your interview. If you can manage with key words or a mind map, this will help immensely. You don't always need to report what people say **verbatim**; for most purposes it will be acceptable to summarise what they say, as long as you get the import correct.
- Using recording devices saves a lot of time in the interview but may affect your interviewees' propensity to be honest with you. You will need to ask participants if they mind you recording the interview and this will need to be included in the **informed consent** which they give. Afterwards you have the problem of transcribing the recording and this can be very time-consuming, although you may be able to use voice recognition software if this is available to you.

Interviewees will sometimes ask you for a copy of your notes or even a copy of the recording and this is something that may have to be discussed or even negotiated. If you are going to quote them, they might want to be sure of what they said. However, in our experience most interviewees are very helpful and forthcoming, with the right encouragement. If you are taking a research degree, then you will probably be required to get the content of the transcripts of interviews confirmed by interviewees as part of achieving the informed consent of the participants to use the output in your work.

Reviewing and evaluating your research findings

When you have completed your research, and perhaps during the process, there comes a point when you will need to start reviewing what may be a number of disparate pieces of evidence or findings from a variety of sources. It is important to look at your own findings from primary sources as critically as you would those you read in secondary sources. See also Chapter 5 on developing critical thinking skills – especially the part on handling the intellectual argument.

Making sense of what you have found out can be a major problem and writing up your findings as you go along really helps, even if it means some extra cutting and pasting later on. If you have written up your findings it can be very useful to print off a copy at this stage to review; drawing lines, highlighting things, numbering points or whatever else helps you to review your research, before making a plan to write up your work for presentation (see Chapter 7 on writing up your work).

Both quantitative and qualitative data can be coded for efficient analysis. A simple and effective way to do this is to type responses into the columns of a spreadsheet and then to sort the data by different criteria. Where you have collected a mass of qualitative data,

Coding – system of categorising qualitative responses.

perhaps from questionnaires, it will be necessary to look for themes and then to categorise responses through a system of **coding**. This will ultimately allow you to report results such as 'while 87 per cent of respondents mentioned X only 12 per cent mentioned Y; however, some 6 per cent mention both X and Y'.

If there were shortcomings in your research it is better for you to draw attention to them than be criticised at assessment. Similarly, be prepared to highlight anything that you didn't or couldn't find out and why this was. It isn't always possible to do what you planned, so it is better to say so; for example an organisation can withdraw cooperation or restrict access to certain data.

A student told us ...

A student told us that she was planning to conduct her research at the headquarters of a well-known retail store. She had conducted an initial interview with the HR manager, but when she returned some months later asking her for permission to distribute a questionnaire to the staff, she was told that they were now too busy to cooperate. Given the shortness of time available, we allowed her to complete a project based only on the initial interview and secondary source material.

Triangulation is the process of comparing the data from the various primary research methods employed, to see if they support each other. For example, you might have your own primary source data from interviews and questionnaires, plus earlier research conducted by other people that you have read in secondary sources. How do these data

Triangulation – process of comparing the data collected from different primary research methods.

sets compare? Clearly if all the results are consistent it is relatively easy to draw firm conclusions with a level of certainty about the reliability of your work. If they do not, this may require explanation and perhaps further research.

Follow-up activities

Time for action – Checklist

Have you:

- clearly identified your research question or working hypothesis?
- designed your methodology, giving due consideration to research ethics and how you will obtain the informed consent of participants?
- written up your proposal?
- considered how you will conduct primary source research?
- identified how you will use secondary source material?
- recognised what is required for a literature review?
- developed skills for research interviews and recording the outcome?
- thought about how you will review and evaluate your research findings?

Further reading

Bell, J. (2010) *Doing Your Research Project: A Guide for First-Time Researchers in Education, Health and Social Science,* 5th edn. Maidenhead: McGraw Hill.

Blumberg, B., Cooper, D. and Schindler, P. (2005) *Business Research Methods.* Maidenhead: McGraw-Hill.

Bryman, A. and Bell, E. (2011) *Business Research Methods*, 3rd edn. Oxford: Oxford University Press.

Bryman, A. and Buchanan D. A. (2009) *The Sage Handbook of Organisational Research Methods.* London: Sage.

Burns, T. and Sinfield, S. (2012) *Essential Study Skills: The Complete Guide to Success at University,* 3rd edn. London: Sage.

Cameron, S. (2009) *The Business Student's Handbook*, 5th edn. Harlow: Pearson.

Churchill, H. and Sanders, T. (2007) *Getting Your PhD: A Practical Insider's Guide.* London: Sage.

Cottrell, S. (2011) *Critical Thinking Skills: Developing Effective Analysis and Argument,* 2nd edn. Basingstoke: Palgrave Macmillan.

Cottrell, S. (2013) *The Study Skills Handbook*, 4th edn. Basingstoke: Palgrave Macmillan.

David, M. and Sutton, C. D. (2011) *Social Research: An Introduction*, 2nd edn. London: Sage.

Gill, J. and Johnson, P. (2010) *Research Methods for Managers*, 4th edn. London: Sage.

Kumar, R. (2014) Research Methodology: A Step-by-Step Guide for Beginners, 4th edn. London: Sage.

Oliver, P. (2013) *Writing your Thesis*, 3rd edn. London: Sage.

Ridley, D. (2012) *The Literature Review: A Step-by-Step Guide for Students,* 2nd edn. London: Sage.

Saunders, M., Thornhill, A. and Lewis, P (2012) *Research Methods for Business Students*, 6th edn. Harlow: Pearson.

Thomas, G. (2013) *How to do your Research Project: A Guide for Students in Education and Applied Social Sciences,* 2nd edn. London: Sage.

Walliman, N. (2014) *The Undergraduate Dissertation: The Essential Guide for Success,* 2nd edn. London: Sage.

Wellington, J. (2010) *Making Supervision Work for You: A Student's Guide*. London: Sage.

Whisker, J. (2009) *The Undergraduate Research Handbook*. Basingstoke: Palgrave Macmillan.

Wilson, J. (2010) *Essentials of Business Research: A Guide to Doing Your Research Project*. London: Sage.

Websites to look up

- For further information on primary and secondary source research:
  www.ithacalibrary.com/sp/subjects/primary
- For further information on developing your research methodology:
  www.socscidiss.bham.ac.uk/methodologies.html
- For further help with interviewing:
  www.public.asu.edu/~kroel/www500/Interview%20Fri.pd
- For further help with designing questionnaires:
  www.bath.ac.uk/students/support/academic/projects/Questionnaire.pdf
- For further help with setting up focus groups:
  www.sru.soc.surrey.ac.uk/SRU19.html
- For further help with writing your literature review:
  www.library.bcu.ac.uk/learner/writingguides/1.04.htm

Time for review and reflection

This is your space to log your reflections on this chapter, to think about what you have learnt, how you will use it and what else you need to find out.

What were the key learning points of this chapter?
What are your strengths in the areas covered by this chapter?
What areas did you identify for development?
What have you learnt about yourself?
How will you use this knowledge?
What else do you need to learn or find out about in relation to this chapter?

7

How to Write Up and Present Your Work in Order to Get Better Results

Overview – what's in this chapter?

- Why do you need to upgrade your written and presentational skills?
- Writing up reports and essays
- Structuring material and constructing your arguments
- Plagiarism, source referencing and bibliographies
- Improving graphic presentation
- Improving your grades through feedback from self-, peer- and tutor- assessment
- Understanding what else you need to know to write an extended essay, dissertation or thesis
- Giving effective presentations
- Follow-up activities, further reading and websites to look up
- Time for review and reflection

Why do you need to upgrade your written and presentational skills?

Try completing the short self-scoring test overleaf, to assess your own level of confidence in relation to developing your written and presentational skills in order to complete your course successfully.

✍ Activity: Why do you need to read this chapter?

You need to self score each question on a scale from 0 to 10, where 0 is low and 10 is high.

1. How good are you at writing up essays and reports?	
2. How good are you at introducing your work?	
3. How competent are you in terms of structuring material?	
4. How confident are you about handling intellectual arguments?	
5. How good are you at summarising your arguments in your conclusions?	
6. How important to you are the visual aspects of presenting your work?	
7. How confident are you that you can source reference correctly in your reports and essays?	
8. How confident are you about writing up longer works such as extended essays, theses and dissertations?	
9. How good are you at oral presentations/public speaking?	
10. How concerned are you about improving your grades?	
Total score	

Interpretation

What did you score?

- Less than 50%   You definitely will find a lot of help in this chapter.
- 50%–75%   There is still plenty to learn in this chapter.
- 75%–100%   You are very confident – read on to confirm your understanding.

Transferable skills – skills learnt in one context which can be applied in another.

A large part of your work as a student will require you to write up work, whether it is in the form of reports, essays, dissertations or theses. The quality of your writing will go a long way to determining your grades. It is also likely that you will have to make oral presentations. These are all essential academic skills to develop if you are going to achieve your goals at university or college, but they also provide **transferable skills** such as giving presentations and writing formal reports, which you will almost certainly use in your professional career.

In the course of developing your skills you need to find your own voice (also discussed later in this chapter), otherwise your work is going to sound like a boring repetition of your textbooks. Conducting good research (as outlined in Chapter 6) will help you do this, but you also have to be prepared to analyse what you have found out and to bring your own analysis and ideas into your writing. You will also need to develop a style which is your own. In doing this, you will no doubt be influenced by what you read and by what your tutors say.

In this chapter we are going to look at written work, including some stylistic conventions for academic writing, some ideas for constructing academic arguments, and at how your work looks. We also look at avoiding plagiarism by source referencing correctly in the text and by constructing appropriate reference lists and/or bibliographies. We then look at how you can get better grades by using self-, peer- and tutor- feedback; and the problems experienced in writing longer works such as dissertations and theses, together with the skills needed for giving oral presentations. Finally there are some follow-up activities, some suggested further reading, websites to look up, and some space for review and reflection.

Writing up reports and essays

Stylistic conventions for academic writing

When writing up academic work you will be expected to learn to follow some basic conventions. You will no doubt notice some of these when you are reading academic books and articles, but the following conventions will give you some idea of what is generally considered good practice (following Cottrell, 1999: 166–7).

- **Use formal English** – academic English avoids slang and expressions such as 'These findings need to be *taken with a pinch of salt*', or 'the argument was *a bit over the top*'.
- **Avoid abbreviations and contractions** – words should be written out in full: 'didn't' as 'did not', 'dept.' as 'department', 'isn't' as 'is not'. If you feel that you have to use abbreviations such as 'OPEC' or 'ACAS', a list should be supplied at the start of the work.
- **Be impersonal** – in most disciplines they will prefer you to avoid using personal pronouns such as 'I', 'we' and 'you'. If this is the case in your discipline, you can begin sentences with phases such as:

It can be seen that…

There are a number of…

It has been found that…

> **Reflective statement** – narrative written to reflect upon your own experiences, thoughts and feelings.

If you do need to refer to yourself, you can describe yourself as the 'researcher' or the 'writer', but aim to use these terms sparingly.

- However, when writing **reflective statements** it is quite in order to use personal pronouns such as 'I'. It would clearly be ridiculous to describe yourself as 'the student'.
- **Be cautious** – to protect yourself from criticism because nothing is ever completely certain. Insert **caveats** such as: 'perhaps', 'maybe', 'appears to', 'seems to', 'tends to', 'may', 'might', 'possibly', 'generally' (see also Chapter 5, Developing critical thinking skills).

> **Caveat** – words used as a warning or a proviso as to the uncertain status of the statement being made.

- **Avoid conjunctions** – such as starting sentences with 'or', 'and', 'but', or 'yet'.
- **Be objective** – avoid subjective words such as 'nice', 'wonderful', 'natural', 'usual'.
- **Be concise** – edit out unnecessary words, for example: '...in a book called *The Undergraduate Dissertation: The Essential Guide for Success* by a man called Walliman...' can be reduced to a simple source reference such as 'Walliman (2014), states that...' (see the section below on source referencing).
- **Use continuous prose** – write in full sentences grouped together into clearly thematic paragraphs.

Writing developed introductions

How you start your report will tend to condition the reader's view of the whole piece of work, so it is important to get off to a good start. In particular your introduction should try to:

- **tell the reader what your work is about and what you are going to cover** – make sure your introduction actually does this and remember that your introduction sets up the whole report or essay;
- **attract the reader's attention** – you can start with an 'attention grabber' such as a pertinent quotation, an interesting statistic or a question that you will try to answer;
- **explain your aims and objectives** – these relate to what you are aiming to achieve in the piece of work and how you will know that you have done this;
- **explain your methodology** – this explains how you researched your work (see Chapter 6, How to plan, conduct and review your research) and should be a separate section in a longer report, dissertation or thesis;
- **give direction to your report** – there is often a final 'directional paragraph' in an introduction which starts 'The report will first' and then goes on, 'it will next turn to the question of...' and later says '...and finally it will...' or something similar. What you are doing here is giving the reader a short itinerary or route map to follow when reading your work (see the next section on structuring material and constructing your arguments).

Your introduction in a work of any length should be more than one paragraph and should be developed into several *thematic* paragraphs. Students coming from school or college sometimes find this hard as they are used to writing only a one paragraph introduction, but it's just a case of breaking down what you have to say and developing it. For example, you could follow the above bullet points, which would give you at least four paragraphs, but it's also useful to check with your tutors for any specific guidelines they have.

Developing your argument in the main body of your work

What goes between your introduction and conclusion is often referred to as the **main body** of the work or text but please note, this term is **never** used in the work. In order to produce a cogent argument you should consider the following points:

- **Organising your content**. Organise content into a logical sequence following the directions given in your introduction (see the following section on structuring material and constructing your arguments).
- **Writing thematically**. Organise the content according to specific themes in your work. In a report you can use sub-headings to help you do this.
- **Knowing what to include**. Include *need to know* and exclude *nice to know* information. Avoid waffle but explain all points clearly.
- **Avoid normative statements**. Distinguish **positive** and normative statements (see Chapter 5 on developing critical thinking skills).

> **Normative statements –** statements of what is thought to be.

- **Avoid unsupported arguments**. Say why and support your arguments with references to source material where appropriate (see Chapter 5 on developing critical thinking skills, and the content later in this chapter on plagiarism and source referencing).

> **Positive statements –** statements supported by evidence or reference to authoritative literature.

- **Link the parts of your work together**. Write linking sentences or paragraphs to link and connect the parts of your work. For example, you might say, 'Having discussed X the report will now turn to look at Y'. Also you might want to make a brief summary at the end of each section, which will then be collected and condensed in your 'summary conclusion'.
- **Make a logical argument**. Try to make an argument or arguments which will lead logically to your **summary conclusion**. Argue from point to point. There should never be a missing step in your analysis, nor should you jump to a conclusion which is not supported by earlier discussion, analysis and findings, etc.

> **Unsupported arguments –** arguments offering no evidence or reference to authoritative literature.

Writing summary conclusions

As with your introduction, your conclusions will tend to condition your reader's view of the whole work. It is your chance to really convince the reader that you know what you are writing about, so we suggest that you consider the following systematic approach:

- **Summarise your findings and analysis**. Go back through your report and pick out all the main points of analysis which can then be summarised in your conclusion. If it is a longer document, it might be useful to print off a draft and go through it with a highlighter pen, perhaps also jotting key words in the margin.
- **Conclude your report**. What does your analysis mean? Can you draw together all the strands and make sense of them? Have you achieved the aims and objectives you set out in your introduction – and, if not, why not?
- **Make recommendations – if appropriate**. This will depend upon the nature of your work and the discipline. For example, if you are analysing a business problem-solving case study, it may be quite important to say what you think should happen next. Alternatively, if your task is to analyse two competing views of history, then clearly such a recommendation would be inappropriate. In a longer piece of work your recommendations will form a separate section after your conclusions and should flow logically from them.
- **Never introduce new material in your conclusion**. The reason for this is that your conclusions are the summary of your earlier analysis and as such they cannot include anything that was not part of that earlier work. While there may be a temptation to hold back some startling revelation, as in the final scene of a murder mystery, it is not appropriate in academic work.

It can be very useful to write a preliminary conclusion before you start to write up the rest of your report. You can look at your report as taking your reader on a journey, so knowing your final destination before you start can help you to avoid taking the reader on a mystery tour and focus your writing towards the point of your conclusion.

Structuring material and constructing your arguments

When writing up your work you will need to develop a clear structure. You could start by imagining that you are taking the reader on a journey, which has a beginning, a middle and an end. The beginning is your introduction, the middle or main body is your findings and discussion, and the end is your conclusion. The more clearly you can explain that journey, the more likely it is that the reader will engage with your work.

Essay – a short intellectual discussion on a given subject.

An **essay** can be described as a short intellectual discussion. Typically you will not use sub-headings, but will be expected to introduce your essay, discuss the topic or essay question, and then bring your work to a justified conclusion. Your conclusion should follow from your analysis and answer the question you posed in the introduction. You will also be expected to use source references throughout the essay and to provide a corresponding **reference list** or **bibliography.**

A **formal report** will tend to look different to an essay but will again require you to make an intellectual argument, but within a more rigid formant. A formal report will typically be structured as follows:

- Title page.
- Contents page.
- List of any abbreviations and any acknowledgements (if appropriate).
- A well-developed introduction, i.e. more than just one paragraph.
- Methodology – which will form part of your introduction in shorter reports.
- Findings and analysis reported under appropriate sub-headings.
- Well-developed summary conclusions, i.e. more than just one paragraph.
- Recommendations if appropriate.
- A full list of references and/or bibliography.
- Any relevant appendices.

Reference list – lists secondary source material cited in your work.

Bibliography – lists secondary source material cited in your work and/or additional secondary source material not cited in your work.

Formal report – a structured narrative based upon specific terms of reference.

If you have collected a lot of material it can be quite difficult to construct a cogent essay or report. In fact a large pile of notes can seem quite intimidating. The problems include what to mention, what to leave out and how to structure the content so as to reach your conclusion. It can really help to adopt the following systematic approach:

- Start by reviewing all your notes, page by page, making a mind map to identify key points/headings that you might want to include (see Chapter 5 on using mapping and brainstorming techniques for study and creativity).
- Now review your mind map and highlight those points you really want in your work. Exclude anything which is peripheral or tangential.
- Then number points or headings in a logical sequence that makes sense to you. Be prepared to change the sequence until you are happy with it.
- Next number your notes from your mind map in the left-hand margin and perhaps using a different colour for each reference number.
- Open a computer file and enter in your headings or key points from your mind map first.
- Now you can write around headings or key points, inserting quotations or points where appropriate from your notes. It is useful to tick off points as you include them to avoid using the same one twice in the same piece of work.

- Use 'cut and paste' if necessary, to revise your sequence.
- Use 'word count' regularly to check length. This will help you achieve something close to the required word length.

On this last point, writing to the required length is a skill with which many students struggle. We find many students worry about not being able to write enough, but also that many students actually overshoot the total – perhaps as a result of worrying about not writing enough. Here are a few more tips that might help you avoid this:

- Take your essay or report plan and try to estimate how many words there might be in each section. Then you can check your word count, by section, as you write. You might find it doesn't quite work out how you planned but at least you have a chance to adjust as you go along.
- For longer works such as extended essays, dissertations and theses, it can be useful to set up a spreadsheet in which you have the projected word count for each section in one column and the actual amount you have written to date in the next. When you summate the columns, you can clearly see how close you are getting to your final overall word count and adjust your writing style as you go along.
- If you undershoot, try to look back and expand on what you wrote, adding anything you missed and explaining things in more detail.
- If you overshoot, look through and try to edit out anything which is unnecessary to your argument. Try to reduce the overall word counts by using fewer words to say the same thing and by summarising direct quotations in your own words. Any content which is relevant but not vital can be placed in an appendix that can then be referred to in the report.

 Activity: Structuring your written work

- Try making a mind map to help you structure your next piece of work.
- Use the systematic approach outlined in this section to structure your work.
- When you have completed your work, think about how useful you found this approach and what you have learnt.

In writing up reports and essays, you should also try to develop your own voice. This is that part of what you write which is in your own words and may also embody your own thoughts. The balance between your voice and citation of other people's work will depend both upon the academic discipline within which you are writing and the assessment you are completing.

Similarly the use of **personal pronouns** such as 'I' and 'my' will be looked upon very differently in different disciplines. As suggested earlier in this chapter, the tendency in academic work is towards the impersonal, but you should be guided by your tutors on this point.

> **Personal pronouns** – nouns used to describe the individual e.g. I, you, we, my, he, she.

Plagiarism, source referencing and bibliographies

What is plagiarism and how can you avoid it?

Plagiarism is the act of copying the words, the ideas or even the structure of the work of another writer or writers, without giving them due credit. It is seen as an act of dishonesty or intellectual theft and cases of plagiarism are taken very seriously in higher education. If your work is found to include copied work, including cut and pasted elements from the internet, you will be penalised and your work could be awarded zero. You may also face disciplinary action and might even be asked to leave your institution.

> **Plagiarism** – copying the words, ideas or structure of another writer or writers, without giving due credit.

If your institution has adopted an online system for submission of your work, you may be able to use the system to check your work for **originality**. This is not the same as plagiarism, but simply indicates that some or all of your text also appears somewhere else. This could be because of coincidence, especially with short phrases, it could be because of your own work being saved somewhere or it might be plagiarism. However, it does provide an opportunity for you to review what you have written and to ensure that everything is source referenced correctly.

> **Originality Report** – tells you that some or all of your text appears elsewhere.

The good news is that it is considered excellent academic practice to refer to, summarise or use direct quotations from published authors to support your own work, provided you give them due credit by **citing** your sources. In order to do this correctly and to avoid committing acts of plagiarism it is important to adopt a recognised system of source referencing for all quotations and ideas drawn from your reading.

> **Citation** – entry in the text of academic work from which the original source can be traced in your reference list or bibliography.

Activity: What does your institution say about plagiarism?

Review the materials that you were supplied with as part of your induction and also search for anything relevant to plagiarism on your institution's website. In particular try to find out:

- What does your institution say about plagiarism?
- What penalties might plagiarism incur?
- What can you do to avoid this?
- Is there a recommended or preferred system of source referencing?

Source referencing your work correctly

Source referencing – process of citing secondary sources in the text of academic work so that they can be traced to a reference list or bibliography and potentially to the original source.

Harvard convention – also known as author-date style, a system of source referencing giving limited details in the text of academic work and full details in an alphabetical reference list or bibliography.

Reference numbers – numbers used in the text of academic work to identify citations which can then be traced to a numerical reference list.

There are various systems for **source referencing**, and you should be guided by your institution as to which you should use, for while some have adopted a particular system others are more liberal. The two basic systems are:

- **Harvard convention** (also known as author-date style) – this involves you inserting limited details in the text of your academic work, so that the reader can trace the full details of each source in your reference list or bibliography (an alphabetical list, by author, of books and other sources that you have used). Sometimes this is divided into two separate lists: a list of *references* used in the text and a *bibliography* of other relevant material you may have looked at.
- **Reference numbers** – this requires you to place a unique reference number against each quotation or citation in the text of your report, which can then be traced by the reader to a single numerical list of references.

In each case the system should be operated in such a way as to allow the reader to trace the source from the text back to the original work, creating something akin to what accountants call an 'audit trail'.

If you make an honest but incorrect attempt to source reference correctly, this will not be considered as plagiarism. However, you may find that you lose marks, so it's a good idea to learn the skills you are going to need as soon as possible after starting your course and before you submit your first piece of work. Losing a few marks in every piece of work will tend to affect your overall degree result, so it really is worthwhile investing time in learning how to do this properly.

> **Reference list** – lists secondary source material cited in work.

A colleague told us...

A senior colleague told us that he had attended an American university. Having worked hard on his first piece of work, he was surprised to find that he had been awarded zero per cent! Upon enquiring he was told that he had failed to reference his sources. He never made that mistake again and went on to have a long and successful academic career.

Making Harvard convention citations in your text

In the Harvard convention, citations in the text for references drawn from books you have used are made using the author's surname, followed by the year of the publication and for direct quotations, the page number or numbers. Unfortunately, there is no single agreed format for making Harvard citations, but the examples given here and those used for citing secondary sources in this book are fairly typical. For example, if you are using the author's name in the sentence it would tend to appear like this:

> **Bibliography** – lists secondary source material cited in your work and/or additional secondary source material not cited in your work.

> According to Smale and Fowlie (2015: 54), '...'

If you are not mentioning the author's name in your discussion then it can go inside the brackets like this:

> (Smale and Fowlie, 2015: 127–8)

Notice in the above example that a range of pages has been referred to, rather than a single page. This can be particularly useful when referring to or paraphrasing an idea or concept rather than a quotation, although a quotation may also go over more than one page.

Where writers have more than one publication in the same year, a suffix letter is placed after the year, both in the in-text citation, as shown in the following example, and in the bibliography or list of references.

> (Bryman, 2007a)

'Cited in' reference – citation in which you cite an author or authors referred to in the work of another author or authors.

There are extra considerations when referencing a source that is quoted in another work, as for example where you use a core textbook which enables you to read about a variety of ideas and concepts from many authors in one book. If you are citing a work from another writer, you need to give a **'cited in' reference,** giving the details of both works and to add the words 'cited in', as shown in the following two examples:

Belbin (1997: 13, cited in Mullins 2013: 340)

(Belbin, 1997: 13, cited in Mullins 2013: 340)

Corporate author – organisation responsible for an online or printed publication where no author is stated.

When citing an internet source, you should give the **corporate author** and the year in the text of your academic work, saving the URL and date accessed for use in your reference list or bibliography. For example:

(Marks & Spencer, 2015)

You will probably now find a referencing facility on the toolbar of your computer and there are also referencing programmes such as Endnote. These do require some investment of time in learning how to use them, but this can prove worthwhile in the long run and especially when you are completing longer pieces of work. However, you need to ensure that the format of citations and reference lists or bibliographies complies with the requirements of your institution.

 Activity: Inserting a Harvard citation in the text

1. Write a sentence in this box, including a 'Harvard' citation, drawn from your notes, which might appear in your work.

2. Check that the style is consistent with the examples we have given.

Making a Harvard convention reference list or bibliography

If using the Harvard convention your work should include a reference list and/or bibliography. A reference list should only contain sources that you have cited whereas a bibliography may contain additional sources that you have used but not cited in the text of your work. If you are asked to submit both a reference list and a bibliography, then the former should contain only sources that you have cited in the text of your work, whilst the latter should contain only additional sources that you did not cite.

A reference list or bibliography should be a list ordered alphabetically by author/editor generally, where the format for entries is generally as shown in the following examples.

For books you should give the author (s), year (in brackets), title (in italics), edition (if not first), place of publication and publisher. For example:

Burns, T. and Sinfield, S. (2012) *Essential Study Skills: The Complete Guide to Success at University*, 3rd edn. London: Sage.

If you have cited an author or authors referred to in the work of another author or authors, you need to use a **cited in reference** and the entry will follow the style in this example:

Belbin, R. M. (1997) *Changing the Way We Work*. Oxford: Butterworth-Heinemann, cited in Mullins, L. J. (2013) *Management and Organisational Behaviour*, 10th edn. Harlow: Pearson.

For journals you should give the author(s), year of publication (in brackets), title of article (in inverted commas), together with the journal title (in italics), volume, issue and page numbers (beginning and ending). For example:

Dennett, A. Cameron, D. Bamford, C. Jenkins, A. (2014) 'An investigation into hospitality cruise ship work through the exploration of metaphors', *Employee Relations*, 36(5): 480–95.

When you read academic journal articles from print journals online, it is currently the practice to source reference these as if you had read the printed version and therefore not to give an internet source. However, conventions are liable to change over time as more journals become available only in electronic form.

Corporate author – organisation responsible for an online or printed publication where no author is stated.

When you reference internet sources it is important to give the **corporate author** and year, as well as the URL and date accessed. For example:

> **Marks & Spencer (2015) [online]. Available from: www.marksandspencer.com [Accessed 27 January 2015].**

While we normally cite published sources in our work which can be traced back to their source, there may be times when other so-called **grey material** might be acceptable. For example, if you were researching absenteeism at a particular company as part of a module in Human Resource Management, you might want to cite the company's internal procedures which had been issued to staff as a pamphlet. However, it is increasing likely that you will find this type of material on the company website, which offers an alternative method of citation as an internet source.

Grey material – material not published formally in the public domain e.g. internal organisational reports, etc.

 Activity: Making a Harvard reference in your reference list or bibliography

1. Make a reference list/bibliography entry in this box, which refers to the 'Harvard' reference you cited in the previous activity.

2. Check that the style is consistent with the examples we have given.

This concludes a brief description of Harvard convention referencing system, which we believe is the easiest system to use. However, you may prefer or be required to use the alternative reference number system.

Using the reference number system of referencing

The main alternative to using the Harvard convention is to adopt a system of reference numbers. This involves inserting sequential numbers, usually in superscript form, from one onwards, against all your references to source material in the text of your work. Thus a reference might appear as follows:

According to Smale and Fowlie[1] "..........."

Where there is no mention of the author's name, as for example where quoting statistics, the number might simply appear after the source material:

Their 2014 annual report also shows that they made a group profit before tax of 580.4 million pounds sterling.[2]

Making a list of references when using the numbered style

Your list of references will be similar to that of a Harvard convention list of references or bibliography, except that you must list all your sources against numbers from one onwards, as for example:

1. Smale, B. and Fowlie, J. (2015) *How to Succeed at University*, 2nd edn. London: Sage.

2. Marks and Spencer Annual Report (2014) [online]. Available from: http://annualreport.marksandspencer.com/ [Accessed 27th June 2014].

If you have a further reference from the same work on the next line of your list you can use the abbreviation **ibid.**, meaning 'as previously'. This would appear as follows:

> **Ibid** – abbreviation used in reference list to mean 'as previously'.

3. Ibid.

If you have made further citations to a work listed earlier in your list of references, you can use the abbreviation **op. cit.**, meaning 'in a work already cited'. This might appear as follows:

> **Op. cit.** – abbreviation used in reference list to mean 'in a work already cited'.

7. Smale, B. and Fowlie, J. (2015), op. cit.

Harvard or reference numbers?

While the reference number system is somewhat easier to explain than the Harvard system, each does have its own advantages. Here are some of the advantages of each as we see them:

Advantages of Harvard Convention	Advantages of Reference Numbers
You get some limited details in the text which might obviate the need to always consult the list of references or bibliography.	You only have to put a number in the text, so less information to clutter it up and interfere with the flow.
You only need to list sources once in the list of references or bibliography, no matter how many times you cite them.	You can see sequentially how all the sources appear in the text and how many citations were used.
You can trace sources alphabetically in your list of references or bibliography.	You can trace sources numerically in your list of references.

Including sources not cited in your text

One question that arises with both systems is, 'what if I consulted sources but did not cite them in the text?' There is a strong argument for listing these, first because it shows the breadth of your reading and second because they may have influenced your thinking without you realising it. If so you will have a partial defence against any claim of plagiarism. In both systems it is easy enough to include additional sources in a separate bibliography, after your reference list.

Constructing your reference list or bibliography

When constructing your reference list or bibliography, your task can be made much easier by inserting the entries electronically into a table. This allows you to add entries from time to time, when you are researching your work, as and when the information becomes available. Then before you complete your work you can sort the entries alphabetically, which potentially will be much quicker and more accurate than doing this manually.

Improving graphic presentation

Graphic presentation – refers to the appearance of your work, i.e. how it looks.

Your academic work will not only be judged by its intellectual content, but also by how it looks. Good layout gives your work visual impact. A key question here is, how attractive does your report look before you start reading the content? Some key points to consider here are:

- **Title page** – this will normally be the first thing the reader sees. It should be well laid out and as a minimum should include your report title, name, course, and perhaps seminar group and word count.
- **Contents page** – this should list all the sections, sub-sections and appendices, which should be *left justified*, with page numbers on the right-hand side. If you are unsure, please refer to the format of the contents page of this book.

- **Sub-headings** – these should be used throughout the body of your report, including your introduction and conclusion. Sub-headings should be thematic, indicating to the reader the content of the sub-section.
- **Paragraph formation** – link sentences into clear thematic paragraphs. Consider linking very short paragraphs and breaking longer ones up.
- **Spacing** – sections and paragraphs should be spaced consistently throughout your report. Good use of space gives your report visual impact and appeal.
- **Widows and orphans** – try to avoid both 'widows' (where an odd word or line, often part of a sub-heading, appears at the top of a page) and 'orphans' (where the first line of a paragraph is left separated at the bottom of a page). Space the text over the pages so as to link it together.
- **Font sizes** – keep these consistent throughout your report, although you can use different font sizes for headings to good graphic effect.
- **In-text citations, reference list and/or bibliography** – use the correct format advised by your institution and/or tutors. See also the section above on avoiding plagiarism and source referencing correctly.
- **Appendices** – these should be identified by a number or letter in the top right-hand corner and should be listed at the end of your contents page. They will always be the last part of your report or portfolio.

 Activity: Improving the graphic impact of your work

- Review the bullet list above and then note down anything that you need to do from it to improve your graphic presentation skills.
- Spend some time looking over your next piece of work, asking yourself how it looks and whether you have taken all the points you identified on board?

Improving your grades through feedback from self-, peer- and tutor-assessment

Self-assessment

You can significantly improve your chances of getting good grades by taking a little time to check over your work. The most widely-used definition of self-assessment has been provided by Boud (1986: 1):

> **Self-assessment –** making an assessment of your own work.

> Self-assessment involves students taking responsibility for monitoring and making judgements about aspects of their own learning.

Self-assessment is often used prior to tutor assessment and to make this process really effective, we suggest that you use a systematic approach.

The self-assessment sheet included in the next activity was compiled after we recorded the errors made by over one hundred undergraduates submitting work for tutor assessment. The idea is that if you self-assess your own work and correct as many errors as possible before handing it in, then you can avoid losing marks in those areas.

✍ Activity: Self-assessing your work to improve your grades

Try using this tick sheet to self-assess your work before handing it in.

Have you: **Tick**

In general

- Followed the assignment brief you were given in completing your work?   ☐
- Completed all the tasks that were set?   ☐

Construction

- Given your work a title and created a title page?   ☐
- Created a contents page showing page numbers on the right-hand side?   ☐
- Written a well-developed introduction?   ☐
- Used sub-headings to group your ideas thematically within the main body of your report?   ☐
- Written a well-developed summary conclusion and remembered not to introduce new material in it?   ☐
- Given attention to the visual presentation including fonts, font sizes, spacing and layout?   ☐
- Submitted other documents required as appendices to your report?   ☐

Intellectual argument

- Avoided normative statements that do not offer any evidence?   ☐
- Supported positive statements with examples drawn from your experience or evidence from your reading?   ☐
- Provided clear and logical arguments?   ☐
- Structured your arguments so as to reach your conclusion?   ☐

Source material

- Used appropriate source material (books, journals, etc.) to support your arguments? ☐

- Used an acceptable system of source referencing in the text of your work? ☐

- Ensured that all references in your text can be traced directly to your bibliography or reference list? ☐

Submission

- Put your name on your work? ☐

- Included all that was asked for? ☐

- Submitted your work within the deadline set? ☐

Your comments on your work

What were your strengths in completing the work and what areas for development did you identify?

Your self-assessed grade

What degree classification, grade or percentage do you think your work deserves?

Review of self-assessment

How useful did you find the self-assessment process?

Some of the advantages of self-assessment can be seen to include:

- It is a developmental experience for you in terms of learning to be reflective, self-critical, constructive, and to learn from the experience in order to inform future practice.
- To engage you more fully in the assessment process rather than being a passive recipient of it. To help you see yourself as an 'active partner' in the assessment processes.
- To encourage a climate of self-criticism in which you might perhaps be both more open to and less reliant upon the feedback you receive from your tutors.
- To help you develop realistic expectations about your work, and thus to help avoid surprise and/or disappointment with final marks, grades or comments.

A student told us ...

A final year student told us that he had photocopied a stack of our self-assessment sheets in year one and then used them in all his modules throughout his course. By doing this he had picked up a lot of errors and was convinced that he had increased his marks overall.

Peer-assessment

Peer-assessment can be defined as an arrangement for peers to consider the level, value, worth, quality or successfulness of the products or outcomes of learning of others of similar status. (Topping et al., 2000: 149)

Peer-assessment – assessment of your work by your fellow students or your assessing their work.

In addition to self-assessing your own work it can be very useful to get someone else – a peer – to look over your work and to give you feedback. Your peer can use the same categories as used in the previous self-assessment activity. However, it is important not to take comments on board if you don't agree with them because, in the end, it has to be your work.

Tutor-assessment

The ultimate assessment of your work will probably be by your tutor. We know that the most important thing for most of our students is the grade awarded, but we would ask you to look carefully at the comments your tutors have made, which may ultimately be the most valuable feedback that you get.

Taking some time to work though the comments, trying to work out what you did well and where there is room for improvement, will help you to grow and develop in your course and beyond. If you don't understand or agree with the comments you should find a time and place to discuss them with your tutor; tutors are usually happy to do this (see also Chapter 3 on giving and receiving feedback).

Understanding what else you need to know to write an extended essay, dissertation or thesis

At some time in your course it is likely that you will have to write an extended essay, dissertation or thesis. Many students panic at the thought of writing five, ten, fifteen or perhaps twenty thousand words, but we find that far more students overshoot the word count than undershoot it.

In order to complete your longer pieces of work successfully there are a number of areas to consider:

- **Topic** – finding something to explore, designing a research question, setting aims and objectives, and also setting the scope and limitations of your study.
- **Timescale** – establishing a time plan in order to complete your work by the deadline.
- **Methodology** – deciding how you will go about researching.
- **Literature review and/or theoretical framework** – critically reviewing existing literature and creating a theoretical framework for your work.
- **Reporting and analysing your findings** – developing your analysis into a cogent argument which leads logically to your conclusions.
- **Conclusions** – summarising your analysis, concluding your work and answering the question which you set or explaining why you couldn't do so.
- **Format** – making sure that you adopt an acceptable format to report your work including citation and source referencing.

However, the good news is that what you will have learnt about writing shorter essays and reports applies to longer works too.

Finding a topic to explore

You will probably have to select your own topic, probably agreeing a research question, proposal or outline with your tutor or supervisor at an early stage. The key question here is: is the project doable? You may have a brilliant idea, but if it would take a team of skilled researchers five years working flat out to complete, forget it.

The most common problem we find is that students pick too big a topic, perhaps because they fear not having enough to write about. They then find it too big and unmanageable, both to research and write up.

A student told us ...

A student told us that he wanted to do a project on recruitment and selection, covering five companies in five different countries. We suggested to him that given the limitations of time and resources, that he stick to the company where he was working on a one-year industrial placement, in order to make the project doable.

Activity: What am I going to research for my extended essay, dissertation or thesis?

- Take some time out to think about what you would like to research. It is useful to look back over your course notes. What interested you and what would you like to know more about?

- Try making a mind map (see Chapter 5 on using mapping) to explore what you know already about your potential topic and what you think you might research.

- Try writing a 'research question', stating in one sentence what you hope to find out or explore. Time spent refining your question will help you to focus both your research and your writing.

- Ask critically whether the project is doable and, if you think it is, try running it past your tutor or supervisor.

Research question – the question to be investigated in a research project.

Hypothesis – a proposition which may be either proved or disproved.

Scope and limitations – setting the boundaries of what you will be researching.

It's very useful to reduce your ideas to a single **research question** which states succinctly what you are trying to find out, or a **hypothesis** which is to be either proved or disproved. Time spent refining and developing this question or hypothesis can pay great dividends over the life of your project. If you can't write a clear research question or hypothesis, then your ideas are still unfocused and you are likely to spend a lot of time collecting too much material (see also Chapter 6 on designing your methodology). You are also likely to have problems writing up your research and reaching a clear conclusion.

Your research question or hypothesis will be your 'guiding light', because it will guide both what you read in the way of secondary source material and also the primary source research you conduct. It may be well worth actually putting it up above your desk to keep it in your mind, to keep you on track and to help you avoid going off at tangents.

Setting the **scope and limitations** for your research is an essential step if your project is not going to grow too large and become unachievable. It's a question of narrowing down your work to manageable proportions to keep it doable. For example, parameters could include research into:

- **a particular topic**, such as 'a study into absenteeism among train drivers working on the London Underground System'.
- **a geographical area** such as 'a study of low pay among seasonal employees in Cardiff'.
- **a historical period** such as 'a study on the development of British Government policies promoting the development of the welfare state between 1945 and 1948'.

Setting **aims** and **objectives** can further help to clarify what you want to get out of the project. Students sometimes get confused about the difference between the two. The distinction is simply that aims are about what you expect to do whereas objectives are about outcomes that can be measured. A good analogy can be drawn with archery, where you take aim before you release your arrows. You aim to hit the very centre of the target, but only later inspection of it will tell you whether you achieved your objective or not.

> **Aims** – statements of intent, i.e. what you hope to do.

> **Objectives** – statements of measurable outcomes, i.e. what has been done.

 Activity: Establishing aims, objectives and parameters

In terms of your research question, try to establish:

- clear parameters for your study;
- aims which you hope to achieve;
- objectives against which you can assess your success in achieving your aims.

Establishing your timescale

Many students find that having a lot to do and being given a long timescale to do it in is a real problem. Effective time management will be essential to completing your work on time and to the standard you want to achieve (see also Chapter 4 on managing your time). Some good rules for completing longer works include:

- **Start early**. You might have got away with last minute panics on reports and essays in the past, but a longer work will definitely find you out. Trust us, you won't write 10,000 to 20,000 words on the night before the deadline!
- **Break down the task**. Breaking the work into manageable chunks means that you don't have to face something that feels akin to climbing Everest, but rather a series of small and manageable uphill steps.

- **Make a time plan**. Making a time plan which gives a deadline for completing each step or stage can really help you manage your time. It's no good having just one deadline – i.e. the hand-in date – you need a series of mini-deadlines along the way. Ticking things off as you go will give you a sense of achievement and that you are on the road.
- **Write up as you go**. There is no reason why you can't open files on day one and then start to write up material as you gather it from your research – and even record your thoughts as you go. It can either be cut and pasted into the final document or deleted if not required. Similarly, you can start building your reference list or bibliography right from the start, entering each source as you find it.
- **Don't wait to start writing up until you have got all your research done**. If you wait till you have everything you will never start, because there is always something else to find out. It is quite acceptable to leave some questions unanswered, as long as you make this clear in your conclusions.

Format

In terms of the format, you should get guidance as to what is required of you from your tutors, but typically the work will break down into sections such as:

- Cover and contents pages.
- An executive summary or abstract – this provides a short overview of the whole work.
- Acknowledgements to anybody who has helped you with the project. Your tutor or supervisor might be included here.
- Abbreviations – a list of all abbreviations used in the work.
- A well developed introduction which will introduce the work, explain why you are doing it and what you hope to find out. It may also include your research question or hypothesis, your aims or objectives together with the scope or limitations of the project. The scope and limitations are important in drawing lines around the project to mark out its extent. For instance you might be researching something between certain dates or within a geographical area.
- A theoretical chapter or literature review in which you critically review existing literature within the field of study. (See Chapter 6, on using secondary source material, and recognising the purposes of a literature review).
- Your methodology, which describes your methodological approach, how you will research the project and how you will report the data (see Chapter 6 on designing your methodology).
- A report and analysis of your findings and/or data. This may be more than one chapter, especially in a longer dissertation or thesis.
- A conclusion which summarises all the earlier analysis in your work and makes it clear whether you have answered your research question or not, or proved your hypothesis or not, whether your aims have been realised and your objectives met. Any unanswered or unresolved questions should be stated at this point and might be suggested as the subject of future research.
- Recommendations, if appropriate to the project, which should flow logically from your conclusions.

- A reference list and/or bibliography. See also the section above on plagiarism and source referencing.
- Any appendices. A good rule with appendices is to include only what is relevant and useful to the reader, not everything you collected during the life of the project. Remember it is an academic work and not a scrap book!

Developing your analysis

Make sure you report your findings systematically, step by step, in order to build a picture that can be summarised in your conclusions. In a longer piece of work you may find it useful to make a summary at the end of each chapter or section. Your final conclusions will then summarise the earlier summaries.

It is important to link your findings back to your literature review or theoretical framework, remembering that while they might be separate sections, they are not unrelated. We see too many dissertations where the literature is 'hermetically sealed' within the literature review section rather than forming a theoretical framework for the entire work.

You can be kind to your reader by telling a consistent story which makes sense as a whole, rather than by writing a series of discrete sections which don't link together. Try to take your reader on a journey from your introduction to your conclusion – one which they can understand. Link one section to another with linking paragraphs and phrases (see also the section above on writing up reports and essays). It is very hard to appreciate what a work is all about if you have to keep reading and re-reading it in order to see how it fits together.

Developing your conclusions

Remember that your conclusions are essentially a summary of earlier analysis and so you should never introduce anything new. Summarising longer pieces of work is a skill in itself. A good tip is to print off a draft and then to highlight all the key points of analysis you want to summarise. Your sections or chapters may already contain discrete summaries, as suggested earlier, which can be brought together in your final conclusions.

Make sure that your conclusions either show how you have answered the research question that you set out to answer or not, or proved your hypothesis or not, and whether your aims have been realised and your objectives met or explains why not. Remember that your objectives should be your measure of what you achieved. It is quite acceptable to highlight any unanswered questions, areas you could not complete or explore fully, and to suggest these as subjects for further research. If you didn't find what you expected, you may need to change the initial question, aims and objectives, your abstract or executive summary and your introduction. This may need to be negotiated with your academic supervisor.

It is good to be humble in your work and especially your conclusions. It is far better to say 'from the limited scope of the research, the evidence would seem to suggest that...' rather than 'it has been proven conclusively that...'. In academic work, to be overly bold is to lay yourself open to criticism. See also Chapter 5 on developing critical thinking.

A student told us ...

When a student told us about her research project it seemed to be covering too much. Her proposal included a rather longer list of objectives than we might have expected. When we read the final report we found that her conclusions followed the objectives and that point by point she had drawn together her findings and analysis to clearly show whether she had met her objective or not. Overall her dissertation was convincing and she received an excellent grade.

Giving effective presentations

Why do we need to develop our presentational skills?

As part of your course, it is very likely that you will have to present some of your work orally. The formal presentation has many purposes beyond your education including internal corporate briefings, the sales pitch to customers and the public relations address. In each case we are seeking to inform and influence, and in doing this we are primarily selling ourselves. If people believe in us, they will probably believe in our message.

If you have a presentation to deliver, you will need to think about what you want to say, who you want to say it to, and how. Knowing and understanding your message is clearly an essential starting point.

 Activity: Thinking about your experiences of presentations

Take a few minutes to think about the following questions.

- What have been your good and bad experiences of hearing other people make a presentation?
- What are your own good and bad experiences of making a presentation?
- What have you learnt from these experiences?

The audience

The first question to consider is, who are you trying to get your message across to? If you have the power to invite who you want to your presentation, then obviously some thought will have to be given to the guest list. Try inviting some people who might be expected to agree with you or who are generally receptive to new ideas, to help the balance of the audience. Think about how you invite them, what documentation you send out in advance, and what you ask them to do or prepare in anticipation.

If your audience is predetermined, try to find out what you can in advance by asking:

- What do they need to know?
- What do they know already?

This will help you to pace and pitch your presentation, neither insulting their intelligence nor assuming too much prior knowledge. If you are unsure, start with basics and build up your argument. It is wise to avoid technical terms and jargon which they don't understand – if it is necessary, explain the meanings.

 Activity: Identifying the audience

If you are planning a presentation, take a few minutes to consider the following issues.

- Who are your audience?
- What do they need to know?
- What will you expect them to know already?

Identifying and structuring content

Decide what you want to say and how you think you may say it to your audience. **Brainstorming** techniques (see Chapter 5 on using mapping and brainstorming techniques for study and creativity) are useful for working out what could be said, but beware of overloading your audience and losing your message in a morass of detail.

Brainstorming – method of problem-solving or of collecting knowledge or ideas often associated with mind mapping.

Attention span –
period during which an individual is able to maintain effective concentration on a task.

Magic three –
presentational technique which involves limiting content to three messages and repetition of messages three times with the aim that the audience will remember them.

Try to distinguish 'need to know' from 'nice to know' information and identify the key points you want to get across. Arrange key points in a logical sequence which makes sense. Points should follow on clearly from one to another. Try to start at a point with which people are already familiar and then draw linkages between points to create a thread which runs through your presentation.

Everybody in the audience will have a natural **attention span** after which they will tend to turn off and go into 'private circuits'. Remember looking out of the window at school! However, you can extend attention span by the use of good presentational techniques.

Three is considered by some to be a **magic number** in presentational skills. Our suggestion is:

- Don't expect to get more than three major points across in one presentation.
- Be prepared to repeat them all three times.

Sadly, people will forget most of what you say, however well you say it, so remembering the **magic three** can really help you to limit what you say and also to reinforce it by repetition.

Thinking about how you start

Entertainers talk about 'winning an audience', and a strong introduction will make this task much easier while a poor one can make it impossible. Therefore you should try to do three things:

- Get the audience's attention.
- Introduce yourself to them.
- Introduce your message and how you will deliver it.

Thinking about how you finish

Your conclusion is similarly important. Try to leave your audience on a positive note. Thank them for coming and for their attention, and ensure that you repeat and reinforce the key points of your message.

An old maxim is: 'Tell them what you are going to tell them, tell them, and then tell them what you told them' – that is introduction, body and conclusion. Again, it is the magic three!

Oral delivery

Your voice will be your most important piece of equipment when making a presentation and it deserves some consideration. The way we use our voices can be decisive in winning over our audience and getting our message across. We have the power to inspire people or send them to sleep!

If you were preparing to play sports you might reasonably expect that you would have to do some training. Similarly, singers and actors have to work hard to develop their voices. For some reason people who have to speak in public usually expect that it will just happen. A little work and practice in this area can pay great dividends. Some key ideas for improving your vocal projection include:

- **Breathe!** It may sound obvious, but learning to regulate your breathing is the most vital presentational skill. Like singers and actors, we should aim to breathe deeply from the abdomen in order to give us power and control over our voices. Breathe deeply to give yourself the power you need to present.
- **Practice** breathing slowly and regularly before you speak and it will help you to calm your nerves.
- **Volume** – aim to fill the room, reaching the furthest in your audience without blasting out those closest to you. Changes of volume can be very effective in making a key point, drawing the audience in by lowering your voice and reinforcing by raising it.
- **Pace your delivery** – too slow and you will bore them, too quick and you will lose them. Aim for a comfortable pace, but if you are nervous, slow down a little to avoid the natural tendency to speed up.
- **Pitch your voice** at a level which is comfortable to you. Again, if you are nervous, pitch down a little to avoid the natural tendency for it to rise.
- **Tone** – warm and friendly is usually best, but other tones may be appropriate in particular situations. Aggressive tones usually lead to further aggression and may risk alienating your audience.
- **Vary** pace, pitch and tone to accentuate points.
- **Drink water!** Make sure you drink plenty of water to avoid getting too dry and have some with you when presenting. It can be thirsty work!
- **Warm up your voice** beforehand if you can. Chatting with people will help.

Activity: Projecting your voice

If you have difficulty in speaking up and/or projecting your voice, this exercise will help you develop a stronger voice for presentations. Try doing this every day until your next presentation.

1. Place one hand on your chest and the other on your abdomen. Feel and be very sensitive to your breathing.

2. Start breathing more slowly and deeply and be very aware that your abdomen should now be moving in and out, far more than your chest.

3. Repeat your name, at first in your normal speaking voice and then a little louder each time until you have filled the room.

4. Make a note each day of how it went. You can score your own voice on a scale of 0 to 10, where 0 equals silence and 10 is enough to fill the room where you have to give a presentation.

Body language

Body language – non-verbal signals that we give to other people.

We can use **body language** to good effect if we stop repressing it. We shouldn't fear using facial expressions, hand and arm movements, etc. to reinforce our message.

It helps to start with a smile. Try looking around and smiling at everybody before you say your first word. It is also good to keep moving. Standing, sitting and walking around at different points in the presentation can help break it up and extend attention spans.

Maintain eye contact with your audience, looking around the room to keep everybody involved and watching for those drifting off into 'private circuits'. To do this you will need to learn to speak from headings rather than a script. This becomes easier once you get over the fear of drying up! If you are well prepared this is unlikely to happen. See also Chapter 3 on recognising non-verbal communication.

Audio-visual aids

Audio-visual aids – methods utilising sound and/or vision to deliver a message.

Your message may be enhanced by the use of appropriate **audio-visual aids**, so it is worth considering where you can show something more clearly than you can describe it. Methods include: 'PowerPoint', video clips and other computer-linked presentations, overhead projectors and 'OHP' slides, film and slide projectors, videos, closed-circuit television, maps, charts, posters, graphs and pre-prepared flip charts.

A good rule is never to use technical equipment you don't feel confident with. Many a presentation has been undermined by someone learning on the job! If possible, practice with the equipment beforehand, so you can feel confident on the day. Although often very busy, technicians can also be very helpful in showing you how to work equipment, particularly if you approach them politely and well before your presentation.

Handout materials

Handouts can be useful but please keep in mind that most will be either filed or thrown away, that few will actually be read, and that too many handouts can also be intimidating. Starting a presentation with a handout can also divert attention from the speaker or visual aids, so it

> **Handouts** – paper-based materials given out to an audience.

is worth considering if and when you give them out. Making your handouts interactive, by creating places for participants to write things down, can also help to make handouts more relevant to individual participants because, in a sense, they personalise what is otherwise a standard document.

Venue and layout

Not every **venue** is suitable for the presentation you are planning to give. Try to minimise problems by checking them out in advance, and arriving early on the day. Audio-visual aids need to be ordered, confirmed, and checked before use. Even a simple whiteboard quickly becomes

> **Venue** – the place where an event takes place.

useless without the correct pens and a suitable wiper!

Tables and desks, particularly in rows, form a barrier, so don't be afraid to rearrange the furniture into a friendlier format if you think that an alternative format might work better for your purposes. Some alternative layout options include:

- **Circle** – either with the presenter in the centre of the circle or taking one of the places on the circumference.
- **Horseshoe** – normally with tables around three sides and with the presenter at the open end.
- **Cabaret style** – involves grouping people around tables. This has the advantage of making it easier for participants to talk to each other, but the disadvantage that not everyone will be facing the presenter.

Dealing with problems

Getting started on time involves being assertive, raising your voice if necessary and 'stewarding' people if they won't sit down.

Giving an overview, being clear about what is going to happen and how long it will take helps to avoid some problems later on. Make clear your policy on questions, for example by saying early on either 'please feel free to stop me...' or 'all questions at the end please'.

> **Rapport** – developing a sense of connection with others.

Building **rapport** with the audience will help to minimise problems. You can use the tone of your voice, which can be both warm and reassuring, together with your body language – perhaps giving a smile or a nod as and when appropriate. You can also ask questions of the audience to help engage people.

Interruptions require a decision, either to allow or to postpone. Techniques for dealing with interruptions include:

- **Reframing** – difficult questions can be reframed, for example by asking 'so what do other people think about that?'
- **Reflection** – some questions can be 'reflected', i.e. repeated back to the questioner. You might say for example, 'That's a good question, but what would you want to say about it?'
- **Deflection** – some questions cannot be dealt with on the spot, so you might say, 'Could we talk about that after the session?' or, 'If you could drop me a line, I can look into that for you'.

However, it is not good to avoid questions, or to alter your vocal tone or body language as this will look defensive.

Overcoming anxiety about making presentations

> **Anxiety** – psychological state involving apprehension and uneasiness.

We know that many people get very anxious about making presentations but also that this will diminish over time if you learn to control your **anxiety** (see Chapter 4, Handling stress and developing relaxation techniques). Avoiding giving presentations will always bring greater anxiety, so it is always better to go and do it rather than to avoid it.

> **Reconceptualisation** – the act of changing the way we think about something.

Reconceptualisation involves changing what you think about something. Identifying positive thoughts and focusing on these can be a positive step in reconceptualisation.

A student told us ...

A student told us that he was so nervous that he couldn't do a five-minute presentation that was a required part of his course and that he was considering dropping out altogether. We persuaded him to stand up and do just one minute. After ten minutes we had to stop him, although he was only half way through what he had prepared! He had no idea where the time had gone, having forgotten all about his nerves once he got started.

Affirmations are statements that we choose to repeat in order to help us reconceptualise. For example: 'I am always calm and confident when giving a presentation'. There are three points to bear in mind when formulating your own affirmations:

Affirmations – statements we choose to make in order to reconceptualise.

- An affirmation is always a lie if we need to say it. When we don't, it is redundant!
- Affirmations should normally start with 'I' and should always be personal to ourselves – so they should never start with 'you' or 'we'.
- Affirmations should be positive and avoid negatives. For example 'I will speak confidently' rather than 'I won't be nervous'.

 Activity: Using affirmations to help overcome anxiety

1. Score your level of anxiety about making presentations.
2. Identify three positive affirmations about making presentations.
3. Repeat your affirmations at least twenty times a day.
4. After your next presentation, re-score your level of anxiety about making presentations.

Some top tips for overcoming presentation anxiety are:

- Prepare your presentation thoroughly, using the techniques outlined in this section. It may sound obvious, but knowing what you are talking about is a big confidence booster and not knowing can be truly terrifying.
- Practise your breathing and vocal projection at least once a day using the exercise in the projecting your voice activity above. As your voice gets stronger you will also feel more confident.
- Use affirmations to change the way you think (see previous activity).
- Visualise yourself being confident when you present your work (see Chapter 2 on visualising your success and putting the past behind you).
- Practise your presentational skills as often as you can, with or without an audience. Repetition will bring confidence in your own ability whereas avoidance will bring further anxiety.

Improving your presentational skills through feedback

Just as with your written work, you can get valuable feedback on your presentational skills from other people. In the following activity we suggest a systematic approach to gathering such feedback.

 ### Activity: Making your presentations really successful

1. To make your presentations really successful try working through this section, gradually taking everything on board in your preparations.

2. When making presentations, ask your peers to give you feedback using the presentation feedback sheet that follows this activity.

3. After your presentation reflect on how you thought it went and on the feedback sheets you have collected from your peers. Key questions here are:

   - What went well?

   - What could be improved?

   - What would you do differently next time?

Presentation Feedback Sheet

	Excellent	Good	Acceptable	Needs attention!
1. Impact of the introduction				
2. Clarity of the message				
3. Structuring of the content				
4. Relationship with the audience				
5. Vocal projection (too loud/soft?)				
6. Effectiveness of body language				
7. Maintenance of eye contact				
8. Pace of delivery (too fast/slow?)				
9. Pitch of delivery (too high/low?)				
10. Management of time (on time?)				
11. Closure of session				
12. Overall quality of session				

Other comments:

When evaluating feedback, make time to go over it and remember it does embody people's subjective opinions, so be prepared to ignore any one-off comments that don't make sense to you or fit in with the general view. For example, somebody might criticise your time management when actually you finished right on time. Conversely if nineteen out of twenty people said you spoke too quietly, it is very likely that you did. It is not personal, you don't need to get upset, you didn't fail, you just need to speak louder next time.

In the end there is no substitute for experience in developing your presentational skills, so it is good to take every opportunity to practise and to develop your skills. Avoidance will only increase your level of anxiety, so don't avoid. Remember that you don't have to be perfect, but learning good skills, practising them regularly and learning from feedback will help you to improve and become a really effective presenter.

Follow-up activities

Time for action – Checklist

Have you:

- recognised what stylistic conventions are important for writing up your work?
- thought about how to write developed introductions and summary conclusions?
- learnt how to structure your arguments in the main body of your report?
- recognised what you need to do to improve the graphic presentation of your work?
- appreciated the importance of avoiding plagiarism and of source referencing correctly?
- understood how you could improve your grades through feedback from tutor-, peer- and self-assessment?
- considered what else you need to know in order to write an extended essay, dissertation or thesis?
- thought about what is required to give really effective presentations and to overcome any anxiety about speaking in public?

Further reading

Blumberg, B., Copper, D. and Schindler, P. (2005) *Business Research Methods*. Maidenhead: McGraw-Hill.

Boud, D. (1995) *Enhancing Learning Through Self-assessment*. Abingdon: Routledge Falmer.

Burns, T. and Sinfield, S. (2012) *Essential Study Skills: The Complete Guide to Success at University*, 3rd edn. London: Sage.

Cameron, S. (2009) *The Business Student's Handbook*, 5th edn. Harlow: Pearson.

Cottrell, S. (2013) *The Study Skills Handbook*, 4th edn. Basingstoke: Palgrave Macmillan.

Churchill, H. and Sanders, T. (2007) *Getting Your PhD: A Practical Insider's Guide.* London: Sage Publications.

Cottrell, S. (2011) *Critical Thinking Skills: Developing Effective Analysis and Argument*, 2nd edn. Basingstoke: Palgrave Macmillan.

Lee-Davies, L. (2007) *Developing Work and Study Skills*. London: Thomson.

Mounsey, C. and Seeley, J. (2002) *Essays and Dissertations*. Oxford: Oxford University Press.

Pease, A. (2006) *The Definitive Book of Body Language*. New York: Bantam.

Ridley, D. (2008) *The Literature Review: A Step-by-Step Guide for Students*. London: Sage.

Russell, T. (1998) *Effective Feedback Skills*, 2nd edn. London: Kogan Page.

Saunders, M., Thornhill, A. and Lewis, P. (2012) *Research Methods for Business Students*, 6th edn. Harlow: Pearson.

Seeley, J. (2002) *Report Writing*. Oxford: Oxford University Press.

Topping, K. J., Smith, E. F., Swanson, I. and Elliot, A. (2000) 'Formative Peer Assessment Between Postgraduate Students', *Assessment and Evaluation in Higher Education*, 24(2).

Walliman, N. (2014) The *Undergraduate Dissertation: The Essential Guide for Success*, 2nd edn. London: Sage.

Websites to look up

- For further help with writing up reports and essays:
  www.unask.com/teaching/howto/essay
- For further help with source referencing and bibliographies:
  www.reading.ac.uk/internal/studyadvice/Studyresources/Reading/sta-references.aspx
- For further help with making presentations:
  www.kent.ac.uk/careers/presentationskills.htm

Time for review and reflection

This is your space to log your reflections on this chapter, to think about what you have learnt, how you will use it and what else you need to find out.

What were the key learning points of this chapter?
What are your strengths in the areas covered by this chapter?

188

What areas did you identify for development?
What have you learnt about yourself?
How will you use this knowledge?
What else do you need to learn or find out about in relation to this chapter?

8

How to Develop Successful Examination Techniques

Overview – what's in this chapter?

- Why do you need to upgrade your examination skills?
- Recognising why many students fear examinations and why some under-achieve
- Planning for success, including positive thinking and visualisation
- Organising your revision systematically
- Preparing yourself for examinations
- Remembering what to do in the examination hall
- Thinking about what to do afterwards
- Follow-up activities, further reading and websites to look up
- Time for review and reflection

Why do you need to upgrade your examination skills?

Try completing the short self-scoring test overleaf, to assess your own level of confidence in relation to improving your examination skills.

✎ Activity: Why do you need to read this chapter?

You need to self score each question on a scale from 0 to 10, where 0 is low and 10 is high.

1. How confident are you about taking examinations?	
2. How organised are you in terms of your revision?	
3. How good are you at managing your time in the revision period?	
4. How effective have your revision techniques proved to be in the past?	
5. How easy do you find it to visualise your own success in exams?	
6. How well do you pick the right question in the exam hall?	
7. How good are you at organising your thoughts into answers in the exam hall?	
8. How competent are you at developing your answers in the exam?	
9. How good are you at managing your time in the exam hall?	
10. How confident are you about getting the grades you want?	
Total score	

Interpretation

What did you score?

- Less than 50%   You will definitely find a lot of help in this chapter.
- 50%–75%   There is still plenty to learn in this chapter.
- 75%–100%   You are very confident – read on to confirm your understanding.

Many people find examinations difficult and some under-achieve. However, we believe that examination candidates can improve their performance by developing a range of appropriate techniques including not only systematic revision methods but also working on mental attitudes beforehand.

In this chapter therefore we first pose the question: 'Why do many people fear examinations and why do some people under-achieve?' We then turn to look at planning for success, including positive thinking and visualisation, organising your revision systematically, preparing yourself for examinations, what to do in the examination hall and what to do afterwards. Finally there are some follow-up activities, some suggested further reading, websites to look up, and some space for review and reflection.

Recognising why many students fear examinations and why some under-achieve

Burnout – complete psychological exhaustion.

Virtually all examination candidates admit to suffering from a certain level of anxiety and this is hardly surprising – sitting at a desk in a large room in complete silence is not, for most of us, a daily activity. Some candidates do too much work and suffer from **burnout**, while many arrive ill prepared and some do not arrive at all.

 Activity: Why do people fear examinations?

Try to answer the following questions:

- Why do you think that other people fear taking examinations?
- How many of these fears do you share?

Let us be clear, hardly anybody actually likes examinations, but to progress successfully through your course you will need to pass your exams. You don't want to become one of those students who has to take re-sits or repeat modules instead of progressing to the next year – or even to leave the course.

To succeed in examinations we suggest that you start from the position that you have the capability of passing, but doing this will require you to do three things:

- You will need to develop a positive psychological orientation, which we call **can do thinking**.
- You will need to have sufficient knowledge of your field of study and that will require **systematic revision** of course content.
- You need to develop your **study skills** in order to facilitate the first two points.

Developing your study skills will make the whole process a lot easier and less painful, because you will be more prepared psychologically, more efficient and thorough in your examination revision, and more effective in the examination hall. Therefore, we strongly recommend that you use the methods discussed in this chapter to develop your study skills and to support your preparation for all your exams.

Activity: Why do some students under-achieve in examinations?

1. Review the following list of potential answers to the above question:
   - Inadequate preparation.
   - Being overcome by anxiety either beforehand and/or in the exam hall.
   - Not being able to recall what they want to say.
   - Not reading the questions properly.
   - Answering the wrong questions.
   - Answering the question they wish had been asked.
   - Poor time management/spending too long on one or two questions to the exclusion of others.
   - Writing too little and/or leaving early, feeling that you have done enough.
2. Have any of these been a problem to you? If so, this chapter should help.

Planning for success, including positive thinking and visualisation

We are all to some extent conditioned by our past experiences, for good or ill, so it is good to start your preparation by thinking about what happened before.

 Activity: How are you with examinations?

Recall your previous experience of examinations and then answer the following three questions:

1. What went well?
2. What went badly or could have gone better?
3. What do you think you need to do differently next time?

What happened in the past does not necessarily determine the future. We can build upon the positives and overcome the negatives. In order to develop a positive approach to examinations we suggest that you consider taking the following steps:

> **Anxiety** – condition resulting from fears which may be to a greater or lesser extent rational or irrational.

- **Recognising anxiety is normal** – we need to recognise that a certain level of anxiety is quite normal in unfamiliar situations, but also that this anxiety can be controlled and it does not have to detract from our performance. See also Chapter 4 on handling stress and developing relaxation techniques.
- **Recognising your own motivation to succeed** – it is vitally important in the run up to examinations to remember why you are doing this course and to remember what your motivation is to succeed. We suggest that you review Chapter 1, Recognising your own motivation to learn, grow and develop. Recognising your motivation can really help you to overcome your anxieties.
- **Eliminating the 'can't do' psychology** – we must avoid saying anything negative such as 'I just can't do exams' because this establishes and reinforces a failure psychology. You may find that some of your peers start the 'can't do' chat in the run up to examinations, focusing on how difficult it will be. It is good either to challenge this, if you can, or avoid it as much as possible if you can't.
- **Developing a 'can do' psychology** – we must look positively at examinations, developing a view which recognises that success is mostly dependent upon our having mastered a set of techniques which work for us, which we can learn and develop, and is focused upon what needs to be done to ensure success. We need to reflect this in what we do and say. It's not just a case of talking 'can do' but backing this up with actually doing what needs to be done. If you don't, then it is just arrogance, and that won't ensure you pass!

> **Visualisation** – picturing and recording in our mind a future event to help us achieve a better outcome.

- **Visualising your success** – as well as talking, thinking, and acting positively, we can also practise a technique of positive visualisation. To do this we try mentally to picture ourselves revising systematically and then being relaxed and confident in an examination hall. Visualisation works by helping us to create some positive mental structures of an event before it happens, and thus we are more familiar with the situation when it arrives. See also Chapter 2 on visualising your success and putting the past behind you.
- **Learning to relax** – finding ways to relax and unwind during the examination period will be especially important. Maintaining normal social contact and exercise can be good. Eastern techniques such as meditation, yoga or tai chi are also beneficial and may be worthwhile learning, not just for examinations, but to help us deal with all other stressful situations in life. See also Chapter 4, Handling stress and developing relaxation techniques.
- **Dealing with severe anxiety problems and phobias** – in cases of severe anxiety or actual exam phobia, it may be appropriate to learn a **relaxation response technique** together with **progressive desensitisation**. This involves learning a relaxation method while gradually being exposed to a perceived threat. Taking mock examinations, working through past papers, and visiting the exam hall may all offer opportunities for desensitisation. See also Chapter 4, on handling stress and developing relaxation techniques.

Activity: What do you need to do to approach your examinations more positively?

Review the list of bullet points on the previous page and consider what you will do differently in order to approach your examinations more positively.

Organising your revision systematically

While many students spend a great deal of time revising, not all their valuable time is well directed. In order for you to revise really well we recommend that you consider the following systematic approach.

- **Know what you are going to be asked to do**. Attend any revision lectures or seminars that are available and take careful note of what your lecturers are saying. Ask questions if anything is unclear and, if you can't do this, send your lecturer an email or try calling in to see him or her.
- **Inspect past papers**. These will indicate the style of question which has been asked in the past, but do not assume that this will remain the same. Examiners change from time to time, and so does the syllabus and subject area as both modules and whole academic disciplines evolve.
- **Make a realistic revision schedule**. Once you have worked out what is expected of you and what you need to do to succeed, it's time to organise your revision by making a daily schedule. Make sure your plan is realistic in terms of what you can achieve in the time. You won't necessarily stick to your schedule exactly, but you will need to be firm with yourself, so that if you get behind one day, you ensure that you do more the next day to catch up.
- **Start revision early**. It is good to start as early as possible, firstly so you can use your valuable time productively. The old adage holds 'revision starts in September', the point being that you don't have to wait until teaching ends to start revising. Secondly, early revision is good because we learn best in bite-sized chunks – little by little, bit by bit. It takes us time to really absorb material and to get a firm grip on it rather than a superficial understanding.
- **Recognise attention spans**. We all have a natural attention span after which we tend to switch off and become less productive. Because we learn best in short bursts, it is good to break big blocks of time into many short periods of intense study. For example, a morning of study can be broken into several shorter periods. You can give yourself a little reward at the end of each period to help your motivation. See also Chapter 4 on managing your time.

  > **Attention span –** period during which an individual is able to maintain effective concentration on a task.

- **Review all your notes and handouts**. Re-read all material, making sure that you have a complete set of notes and that they are in a logical sequence. This will help you to remember the scope of the course you have taken, and thus make you aware of what might come up in the examination.

Key words – words used in conjunction with mind mapping to summarise a body of knowledge which can be recalled by reference to the keyword.

Mind mapping – technique developed by Tony Buzan, to plot ideas graphically avoiding linear techniques.

- **Reduce each topic to a series of key words or mind maps**. Remember that for the purpose of recall, your brain works much like a filing cabinet. By identifying key words you are attaching a **tag** and, from this, a whole file can potentially be recalled in the examination hall (see also Chapter 5 on using mapping and brainstorming techniques for study and creativity).
- **Memorise the key words or mind maps**. Try writing them out several times if necessary, to build confidence in your ability to recall them. Take them with you to look at on the bus or train, put them up over your desk, bed or in the bathroom. The more times you look at them, the more it will help you recall them later on.
- **Use tricks to help you to remember**. You can use acronyms, word association techniques, colour coding, diagrams, cartoons, music or whatever else you find useful. These tricks will help you remember what you want and also to overcome the fear of drying up in the examination.

A student told us…

One student reported that she played a different piece of music when revising each topic. In the examination hall she sang the appropriate tune to herself and then was able to recall the particular content that was associated with it. This is an association technique in action.

- **Test yourself**. Try to write up model answers to previous exam questions. At first you will probably need to refer to your mind maps or key words, but later you can start an answer by copying them out from memory. Try to keep to the timescale you will have in the exam hall, so that you will know how much you will be able to write on the day. You may even attempt a full mock exam. All this helps to desensitise you to the exam experience and to build confidence. As with everything, we tend to learn by repetition.
- **Set up a study circle**. If you can recruit a reliable group of your peers, it can be useful to meet up every so often to review your progress, discuss topics and perhaps to give each other feedback on model answers. However, it's not good to rely on a study circle to do your revision for you. In the end you have to learn the required material yourself.
- **Don't do too much!** A very few students burnout by doing too much, so make sure you take regular breaks when revising. Try to give attention to normal activities such as eating, sleeping, diet, exercise and having social contact. See also Chapter 4, How to look after yourself and upgrade your self-nurturing skills during the developmental process.

A student told us...

A final year student told us that she had worked night and day and tried to read everything in her discipline in the expectation of getting a first class honours degree. In the exam hall she felt totally confused and couldn't make sense of all the material. She came out with lower second and was very disappointed.

- **Don't do too little!** Far more students under-achieve through the lack of systematic revision than experience burnout by overdoing it. We don't want you to be one of them, so it is a question of getting the balance right – and that comes back to having a workable revision schedule and making sure you activate it.
- **Avoid all last minute revision and mugging up**. Anything you do learn at the last minute is likely to confuse you. You will tend to focus on what you read last when constructing your answers, rather than giving a balanced account.

 Activity: Organising your revision

- Review the bullet points in the previous section, making a note of all the suggestions you feel you need to pick up on.
- Find out exactly what will be expected of you in your examinations and what you will need to do to succeed.
- Make a realistic revision schedule for the period you have to revise, making sure you build in time for yourself.
- Turn your plans into actions and monitor your progress on a daily basis. Ticking off what you have done is a simple but effective way of both monitoring and recognising your achievement.

Preparing yourself for examinations

Once you have prepared yourself mentally for your exam and have your revision organised, it is also important to think about the practicalities. Check all your examination arrangements and make sure of everything beforehand. In particular you should check out:

- **Dates and times**. This might seem obvious, but check and re-check the dates and times of your examinations. It is not unknown for exam candidates to turn up at the wrong time and even on the wrong day.

- **Examination hall**. Do you know where the exam is being held? It may be in another building to the one where you normally study or even on a different site. We have even had students turn up on the wrong campus! If it is not a room familiar to you it would be useful to go and have a look beforehand, not only to avoid any last minute panic on the day, but also because it builds familiarity which helps to desensitise you.

A student told us...

A former student told us that as an undergraduate literature student, she ended up getting married in between the Milton to the Romantics and Shakespeare examination papers. They went on honeymoon for the three days between the two exams. They went to see a couple of plays and, on their return, she sat the exam and got a first, but says now, 'I wouldn't advise it'.

- **Travel and parking, etc**. It is also good to check your travel arrangements. If travelling by bus or train it may be safer to aim for the one *before* the one that would get you there on time, to give yourself some time in hand. If you are driving you will need to check out the parking arrangements and any restrictions. However you travel, be aware that if you have an early exam you may be caught in the morning rush – and you will need to allow for this too.
- **What you need to take with you**. What you need to take will vary considerably according to the discipline, but clearly pens will be required by virtually everyone plus pencils, rulers, etc. for many subjects. If it is an open book examination, be clear as to what you can take in. Does this include your file of notes? Can you take a dictionary into the exam?
- **The goodies you are allowed**. It is now common for students to take drinks, particularly water into exams. You may also be able to take sweets, chewing gum and perhaps a banana which can be useful for slow energy release. However, most institutions will draw the line at a packed lunch or a takeaway!

 Activity: Preparing for your exam

1. Review the bullet point list above, making note of all the suggestions you feel you need to pick up on.
2. Make sure you check out everything before the day of your examination.

Remembering what to do in the examination hall

Assuming that you have done all your revision and preparation, it is still important to think about what happens on the day, in the examination hall.

It's a question of translating all your hard work into the results that you deserve. It is rather like being an Olympic athlete: you have done all the training and now you want that gold medal. Here are some things to bear in mind:

- **Check that all is in order**. You don't want a wobbly table or to be sitting in a draft. Do not be frightened to draw any problems to the attention of the invigilators, either before the exam commences or during it, by raising your hand. You deserve and should have a fair chance to complete your examination under acceptable conditions.

A student told us…

During the course of an exam a student told us that she was being distracted by the smell of an over-ripe banana. We found that the student behind her had the offending item of fruit on her table and we managed to negotiate its immediate disposal.

- **Complete your documentation**. As soon as you are allowed, complete the documentation required by your institution before your examination takes place. This will normally be on the front cover of your answer book and perhaps an attendance slip or other document. You will probably need your student number which you should take with you. If you forget it, raise your hand as an invigilator may be able to get it for you.
- **Read the paper carefully**. When you are allowed to, read all the questions and all the instructions very closely. Be sure to select the questions which will give you the best chance to show your ability. While it is useful to look for **content words** in questions in order to help you identify the topic, it is also important to recognise **action words** which tell you what the questions are asking you to do. For example, 'compare and contrast' is not the same as 'analyse'. See also Chapter 5 on understanding what you have to do to complete your assessments successfully, and in particular the distinction between action words and content words in assessment questions.

> **Content words –** words used to indicate the subject area covered.

> **Action words –** words used to tell you what you are expected to do.

- **Know exactly what you have to do and do it!** Make sure that you know exactly what you are being asked to do. There are no extra marks for answering too many questions. You will lose marks by answering too few questions or indeed the wrong number from the various sections. So just do as you are asked!
- **Write essay plans**. Take a few minutes to write an essay plan for each question which you have selected, by recalling your lists of key words or mind maps. You may find that you know more than you think. Do not be afraid to use knowledge gained from other parts of your course, particularly if you can show how topics link and connect.
- **Answer the question on the paper**. You should not simply regurgitate the essay which you have planned, but rather you should marshal the evidence and arguments which you have recalled in support of the answer which is required.

- **Write a suitable introduction**. Make sure that your introduction tells the examiner that you have understood the question. If it is appropriate, define terms or concepts mentioned in the question. You can also describe how you will be answering the question. What you say here will signal to the examiner that you are a competent student, capable of answering the question.
- **Make points into paragraphs**. You can answer questions by writing paragraphs around points which you have listed or key words from your mind map.
- **Write suitable conclusions**. Make sure that your conclusion pulls everything together by summarising your arguments and makes it clear that you have understood and answered the question. Remember, do not introduce new material at this stage.
- **Write clearly and use space**. Try to write clearly so that your examiner can read your work and use space to present your work as clearly as possible. Start a new page for each answer and make it clear which question you are answering. Your examiner may have to read hundreds of exam scripts, so be kind to him or her.
- **Use all your time productively**. Make sure that you spend an equal amount of time on each question, assuming that they command equal marks. Avoid giving more time to your favourite topic or concentrating on earlier questions at the expense of later ones.

A student told us...

A student told us that upon reading his exam paper, he was pleased to see a question on the very subject of his recently completed dissertation. He started writing all he knew on the subject and completely lost track of time. When he completed the answer he realised that two and half of the three hours allowed had elapsed, but that he had only written one of the three required essays. He then quickly wrote up a couple of note form answers. Although he did pass the exam, it was with a grade far below his expectations.

- **Don't re-read or check over the paper unless you have spare time**. Many tutors will tell you to re-read or check over your paper before handing it in, but this may not be the most productive thing to do. If you still have things to say or work to do it may be better to keep working until the invigilators call time. The argument is that you will probably score more marks from the extra work than you would have lost by correcting the odd point here and there.

 Activity: Making your time in the exam hall really count

- Review all the bullet points in this section and make a note of what you think you need to do in the exam hall.
- If you have found exams difficult in the past, think carefully about what you need to do differently next time.

Thinking about what to do afterwards

Some students become unduly worried by what happened in the examination hall. It can be really useful to have a 'post mortem' with your peers in order to chat over how it went. However, the important thing to recognise is that there is nothing more you can do; you can't change a thing and it is now time for you to relax until you get the results.

Your tutors will not want to talk to you about your examination performance while they are marking and when examination boards are still in progress. Your work will normally be marked anonymously and your grade recorded by your student or examination number, so they won't know your grade at the marking stage nor will they be allowed to discuss it with you.

When you get your results you will hopefully be pleased. If you are disappointed it may be worth contacting your tutors. Even if they cannot talk specifically about your performance, you may be able to talk over with them how you think the exam went. If you have to re-take, it will clearly be important to understand where you may have gone wrong and you might get some pointers for the future.

Follow-up activities

Time for action – Checklist

Have you:

- checked out what you need to do to achieve the results that you want?
- made a realistic revision schedule and built in rewards for yourself?
- reviewed all your notes and handouts?
- made mind maps or other study aids?
- reviewed previous examination papers and given yourself mock attempts?
- checked out the venues, times and dates of your exam; made sure that you can find the venue and arrive in good time; and know what you need to take with you?
- done your best in the examination hall, selected the right questions and used all the time productively?
- remembered to relax afterwards?

Further reading

Burns, T. and Sinfield, S. (2012) *Essential Study Skills: The Complete Guide to Success at University*, 3rd edn. London: Sage.

Buzan, T. (2006) *Use Your Head*, 3rd edn. London: BBC Books.

Buzan, T. and Buzan, B. (2010) *The Mind Map Book*. London: BBC Books.
Cameron, S. (2009) *The Business Student's Handbook*, 5th edn. Harlow: Pearson.
Cottrell, S. (2013) *The Study Skills Handbook*, 4th edn. Basingstoke: Palgrave Macmillan.
Cottrell, S. (2012) *The Exam Skills Handbook,* 2nd edn. Basingstoke: Palgrave Macmillan.

Websites to look up

- For help and support in preparing for and taking examinations:
  www-users.york.ac.uk/~dajp1/Exam_Hints/Exams
  www.topuniversities.com/student-info/health-and-support/exam-preparation-ten-study-tips
  www.library.bcu.ac.uk/learner/Study%20Skills%20Guides/13%20Exam%20techniques.htm

Time for review and reflection

This is your space to log your reflections on this chapter, to think about what you have learnt, how you will use it and what else you need to find out.

What were the key learning points of this chapter?
What are your strengths in the areas covered by this chapter?
What areas did you identify for development?
What have you learnt about yourself?
How will you use this knowledge?
What else do you need to learn or find out about in relation to this chapter?

PART III
How to Develop Your Employability Skills

9

How to Understand What is Required for Your Success in Gaining Internships, Placements and Jobs

Overview – what's in this chapter?

- Why do you need to upgrade your employability skills in order to find an internship, placement or job?
- How to be a winner in the internship, placement or job selection process
- Finding an internship, placement or job
- Matching your skill set to the internship, placement or job you apply for
- Follow-up activities, further reading and websites to look up
- Time for review and reflection

Why do you need to upgrade your skills in order to find an internship, placement or job?

Try completing the short self-scoring test overleaf, to assess your own level of confidence in relation to the search for jobs and placements.

✍ Activity: Why do you need to read this chapter?

You need to self score each question on a scale from 0 to 10, where 0 is low and 10 is high.

1. How clear are you about what sort of internships, placements and jobs you will want to do?	
2. How confident are you in searching for internships, placements and jobs generally?	
3. How aware are you of where to look for internships, placements and jobs in your chosen field?	
4. How much do you know about graduate employment websites?	
5. How much do you know about the 'milk round'/employment fairs?	
6. How aware are you of what employers will be looking for from you?	
7. How good are you at identifying your own unique skill set?	
8. How good are you at analysing job advertisements to find out what employers are really looking for?	
9. How good are you at matching your skill set to internships, placements and jobs?	
10. How confident are you in your ability to get the kind of internships, placements and jobs you want?	
Total score	

Interpretation

What did you score?

- Less than 50%   You definitely will find a lot of help in this chapter.
- 50%–75%   There is still plenty to learn in this chapter.
- 75%–100%   You are very confident – read on to confirm your understanding.

There are winners in the employability process, so it is important to make sure that you get the best job you can and this means taking the sort of steps outlined in Chapters 9, 10 and 11. The steps outlined include:

- Correctly identifying your skill set and how it might be developed.
- Matching your skill set to job, internship or placement vacancies offered by potential employers.
- Presenting yourself in the best possible light at every stage in the process.

Feeling confident that you will have the skills to offer to a potential employer – whether for part-time employment to help with living expenses while you are studying, for an internship or placement, upon graduation, or for making progress in your career – can contribute to your motivation to do the necessary hard work to obtain good marks in all your assessments.

Placements form an essential component of some courses and if you have the option to take one we strongly recommend it. In our experience students who undertake a placement will be doing real jobs and applying theory to practice in the workplace. **Internships** tend to be shorter and often occur over the summer vacation, but still offer the opportunity of some real work experience. Short periods of **work shadowing** can also provide an opportunity to observe somebody doing a real job and offer you valuable insight.

Placement – extended period of work experience, normally paid.

Internship – shorter period of work experience, which may be paid or unpaid.

We have often been asked why we include employability in our year one undergraduate skills programme and it is suggested that this is really a final year concern. However, we see that early consideration of employability allows you to plan your path ahead, to review progress towards your goals at regular intervals and to change them if necessary. Your planning can also inform your choices of elective modules, placements or internships and the subject of dissertations.

Work shadowing – short period observing someone else doing a job.

Employability skills are not just for graduate employment, these skills can be developed and practised whilst you are in higher education, first in helping to obtain the part-time, weekend and summer employment which is often so vital in supporting your finances, second for gaining suitable placements and internships, third for graduate employment, and finally within your professional careers, where they may be used to facilitate both changes of employment and internal promotion.

In our experience, final year undergraduates are already busy making applications and frequently attending assessment centres as well as dealing with all the pressure of completing final year assignments and examinations. Therefore, the final year is too late. The idea of developing employability skills as an end of course activity misses the point and the opportunity for planning and preparation throughout your course.

In this chapter we will first look at how you might become a winner in the employability process, at the skill set you have and how this might be matched to job vacancies, and then at where you might find and how you might search for jobs, internships and placements. Finally there are some follow-up activities, suggested further reading, websites to look up, and some space for review and reflection.

How to be a winner in the internship, placement or job selection process

Although most graduates do get jobs, not all are equally successful in the employability process, not all get the jobs they want or deserve and not all are well matched to the jobs they get.

There are two parties to the recruitment and selection process. The employer should logically be trying to employ the best person for the job. Their task is to describe jobs accurately and then to organise the recruitment and selection process to recruit the best people for the jobs concerned. Similarly, you might logically want to find the job to which you are best suited and, if so, your task is to describe and present yourself both accurately and positively in order to secure such a position.

While selection decisions are ultimately down to employers, success in the employability process is partially within your control and this has implications for every stage in the process. In particular this will involve you in understanding:

- Who you are, what you have to offer and how you can match this to job vacancies, and internship and placement opportunities.
- How to describe and present yourself in application forms, your curriculum vitae (CV) and cover letters/emails – in order to make a positive impact upon the reader and to influence their decision to invite you to an interview or assessment centre.
- How to create a professional **digital identity** or **online presence** (see also Chapter 10 on developing your digital identity/ online presence).
- How to present yourself at an interview or at an assessment centre and what you can learn from unsuccessful applications (see Chapter 11, How to give yourself the best chance of success in the selection process, including the section on handling appointment or rejection).

Digital identity/online presence – your own profile on the internet utilising e-portfolios and/or professional networking websites.

It might be useful to regard the whole recruitment and selection process as a giant matching activity in which candidates are matched with jobs. Your responsibility as the applicant is to present yourself clearly and accurately whilst employers equally need to describe internships, placements and jobs clearly and accurately.

Activity: What are employers looking for?

- Imagine you are the administrator dealing with recruitment and selection in the human resource or personnel management department office of a large employer. You have 500 application forms or curriculum vitae on your desk/inbox and your task is to produce a shortlist of 20 candidates to invite for interview or assessment centre.

- What would you be looking for in order to pick the best people to invite? Try making a list of things that you would see as essential and desirable.

- When you have worked your way through Chapters 9, 10 and 11, review your list. How does what you have learnt affect how you would present yourself to employers?

Finding an internship, placement or job

Your chances of finding the job, placement or internship which is best suited to your skills and talents will be significantly enhanced by casting your net as widely as possible and perhaps outside of your home country. As suggested earlier, you are strongly advised to make a shortlist of possible jobs rather than relying on just one that you have set your heart on. To give yourself the best chance in the employability process we suggest that you consider looking at the following sources of information:

- **Internet sources** – today internet searches in one sense make the employability task a lot easier, although in another sense you may have more to choose from and it may prove quite time-consuming. Internet sites fall into two basic types:

  o **Recruitment sites** which offer jobs from a wide range of employers and within a range of specialisms. Several are aimed directly at graduate employment such as Prospects, Graduate Monster, etc. (for a selection of URLs, see the 'Websites to look up' section at the end of this chapter).

  o **Employer sites** which will often have a recruitment or vacancies link (for a selection of URLs see the 'Websites to look up' section of this chapter). If you have an idea about a company you might like to work for it's always worth making a search to see what they are offering. If you don't see anything, try making contact directly. They may be able to direct you to another source or put your details on file.

- **Professional networking** – many occupations have professional associations with many offering student membership with a low level of subscription. These are well worth joining if there is one appropriate to your discipline. It will probably give you access to local meetings, a professional journal and a dedicated website through which jobs may be advertised.

- **Professional networking sites** (such as LinkedIn) connect professionals across the globe and allow you to connect to other people and find out about jobs, news and access updates.
- **Newspapers** – tend to have different types of jobs on different days or in particular supplements such as 'education', 'public appointments' and 'scientific', etc. These often provide a useful snapshot of the employment situation within a particular sector of the labour market in terms of the jobs and salaries on offer.
- **Specific trade magazines and journals** – provide an invaluable source for jobs in sometimes highly specialised fields of employment. Again they provide a useful snapshot of a distinct sector of the labour market.
- **Recruitment agencies/recruitment consultants** – are common in certain industries not only for recruiting 'temps' but for many other positions. Head-hunting agencies specialise in recruiting people from other companies for particular jobs.
- **University careers office and departments** – will hold a lot of information but also should have a certain level of expertise in dealing with people from your course and in your specialism. You will probably be able to see a careers counsellor who can give you further help and guidance.
- **Alumni connections –** your university is likely to have an alumni network (former students), some of whom may already work in your preferred sector and who may be able to offer you valuable information and perhaps an introduction to a suitable employer.

> **Alumni** – the former students of a university, college or school.

In addition to exploring all of the recognised sources there is also merit in talking to your tutors, who will often have links with employers, and to your peers who will be going through the same sort of searches as you. Sharing ideas with your peers can save time and positions which they reject might be perfect for you; but you may also find yourself in competition with them for the same jobs.

 Activity: Finding positions to apply for

- Investigate all the sources listed earlier in this section.
- Identify a number of possible vacancies that could be the focus of your search.
- Think carefully about each vacancy. Ask yourself: Is this one I might reasonably expect to get? Is that one I might actually be interested in applying for in the future? Be prepared to focus your effort on a number of promising vacancies.
- Download the applications and any other available information on the jobs concerned and/or approach the organisations for recruitment application packs.
- See also Chapters 10 and 11 for help in completing the application requirements and selection procedures successfully.

Matching your skill set to the internship, placement or job you apply for

Understanding what you have to offer

The first stage in your employability process lies in understanding what you have to offer to employers and, in particular, what is special about you. Lumley and Wilkinson (2014: 3) talk about 'identifying and building **employability assets**'. These can then be matched against the requirements of specific jobs that you have identified.

There are many ways of identifying what you have to offer. A good starting point might be to think about your course: What aspects do you particularly like? What might you want to develop in your career? Internships and placements are an opportunity to put 'a toe in the water' before you commit yourself to a long-term career.

Undertaking **extra-curricular activities**, perhaps being an officer of a student society or doing voluntary work, can all provide useful experience, demonstrate your commitment, offer the opportunity to learn **transferable skills** and add to your stock of employability assets.

Throughout this book we have asked you to consider aspects of yourself, your skills and what you need to develop – particularly in the final sections of each chapter where we have invited you to review and reflect upon what you have learnt. Taking some time to review what you have written would also be a useful step in understanding what you have to offer employers.

In particular, it would be useful either to complete a new personal **SWOT Analysis** or to update the one you made previously, outlining your perceived strengths, areas for development or barriers you might face (refer back to Chapter 2 on recognising your own strengths and areas for development).

The next activity will help you identify your **skill set**, but the list is not exhaustive and you might want to add other skills that you have – especially

> **Employability assets** – what you have to offer potential employers.

> **Extra-curricular activities** – activities falling outside the normal curriculum of your course.

> **Transferable skills** – skills learnt in one situation which can be readily transferred to another, e.g. communication skills developed in social situations and then used in the workplace.

> **SWOT Analysis** – technique for analysing **s**trengths, areas for development (**w**eaknesses), **o**pportunities and **t**hreats.

Skill set – the particular set of skills which an individual has.

those which are particular to your discipline. We find students often forget very important skills for which they do not hold an academic qualification, such as speaking more than one language, being able to use various computer packages, together with other qualifications such as holding a driving licence, first aid certificate or sports coaching qualification.

 Activity: What skills do I have to offer?

Complete the **Personal Skills Inventory** below, by rating yourself out of 10 in the following categories (0 is low and 10 is high).

People		Activities	
Ability to get on with people from different backgrounds		Creativity, design and layout	
Ability to see and understand other people's points of view		Lateral thinking/thinking 'out of the box'	
Dealing with the general public		Ability to see the 'whole picture'	
Teamwork		Being good at argument and debate	
Managing other people		Making decisions	
Teaching or training others		Managing change and transition	
Negotiating		Setting priorities	
Helping others to arrive at decisions		Working out agendas	
Being sensitive to others' feelings		Organising work to meet deadlines	
Caring for others		Staying calm in a crisis	
Ability to read other people's body language		Problem solving	
Dealing with others by phone		Reading complex texts	
Ability to cope with 'difficult' people		Word-processing	
Speaking clearly and to the point		Computer literacy	
Being able to take direction from others		Working with numbers	
Courage to speak out against injustice		Analysing information/data	
Determination and perseverance		Classifying and organising information (e.g. filing)	

People		Activities	
Ability to set own goals		Facilitating meetings	
Maintaining a high level of motivation		Selling	
Ability to take responsibility for own actions		Interviewing	
Trust in my abilities		Listening and hearing	
Personal qualities		Asking questions	
Ability to recognise own needs and ask for help		Handling practical things	
Ability to learn from mistakes		Seeing how things work	
Stress management		Writing formal reports	
Willingness to take risks and experiment		Writing official letters/emails	
Assertiveness		Form filling/paperwork	

- Review the above scores.

- What did you learn from this exercise?

Understanding what the employer is looking for

A good employer will take time to conduct a thorough job analysis in order to know what they are looking for. Traditionally this was usually done by means of writing a job description which described the role and a person specification which described the person who might be expected to fill it. While some employers may still take this approach, the person specification is now seen to have potentially adverse implications for ensuring equality of opportunities and encouraging diversity among employees (Cornelius, 2001: 39–40). Therefore, many employers are now describing jobs in terms of **job competencies**, which are seen to avoid some of the potential problems of person specification.

> **Job competencies** – behaviours describing what an individual might be expected to do as part of a job.

Job competencies have been defined as:

> one of the sets of behaviours that the person must display in order to perform the tasks and functions of a job with competence. Each competency is a discrete dimension of behaviour. (Woodruffe, 2007: 87)

At root, a competency is something that someone could do, such as 'can work as part of a team' or 'can demonstrate analytical ability'. A competence can potentially be tested at various stages in the recruitment and selection process and in particular at assessment centres (see Chapter 11 on performing effectively at assessment centres).

Before advertising an internship, placement or job, an employer will normally analyse the role and decide the key competencies required. Internal reviews of the skill competencies being mentioned by employers offering year-long placements to Brighton Business School students in 2006 and 2011, revealed that they were asking for the following skill competencies (see Figure 9.1 below):

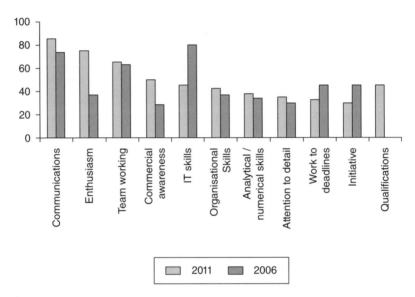

FIGURE 9.1   Skill competencies being mentioned by employers offering year-long placements

What becomes clear, both from our surveys and from casual observation of advertisements for graduate employment, is that there are a relatively small number of core competencies which many employers are looking for and that mastery of these will be very important both in gaining both internships, placements and in achieving successful graduate employment and careers.

Matching your skill set and aspirations with employer expectations

Once you have a clear idea of what you have to offer and what employers are looking for, it's time to try and match the two together. Your search should be as wide as is practical in order to try and identify your best chance of getting into something that you really want to do (see the earlier section on finding an internship, placement or job).

If you are going to make an application that will have a good chance of success it is important to have as much information as possible about the job and the organisation. If you have a job advertisement this is really a starting point and will give you only limited information. Some ideas for expanding your knowledge include the following:

- Look at the employer's website. They will probably have a recruitment or vacancies link and you may find much more information there – perhaps a job description or list of competencies.
- Contact the organisation and ask if there is a recruitment pack which they can send you. This will be quite normal for internship, placement, graduate entry level and higher positions.
- Ring the person dealing with the recruitment and selection for the position concerned to see if you can have a chat about what is involved. They may be very helpful, but avoid pressing them if they are not, as they might remember you as the awkward one on the phone!

If you are unable to get clear details of a job, it can also be useful to try to think yourself what might be involved and what might be required of you in terms of the competencies of the job concerned. Looking at similar jobs with other employers can sometimes throw some light upon what might be required.

It is good to aim high but applying for jobs which you have no realistic chance of getting or are ill matched for will not only waste your time, but also that of the employer. It is also good to make your own shortlist of the most suitable jobs for you and to pursue several applications at the same time. The one you set your heart on may not come up but another certainly will, if you are well organised and persistent.

 Activity: Matching jobs to your unique skills set

- Select and review details of an internship, placement or job you think you might be interested in.
- Are any job competencies listed? If not, identify what you think the employer might be looking for in a competent employee.
- How do these competencies match up against your skill set?
- Consider also which things would be hardest to demonstrate if you applied.

Follow-up activities

Time for action – Checklist

Have you:

- considered why you might need to upgrade skills in order to obtain a suitable internship, placement or job?

- explored a range of sources and identified a number of suitable positions to apply for?

- recognised what employers are looking for in the internship, placement or job selection process?

- reviewed what you have to offer to employers?

- matched your skill set to the internship, placement or job you are applying for?

Further reading

Byham, C. and Cox, J. (1998) *Zapp! The Lightning of Empowerment: How to Improve Productivity, Quality and Employee Satisfaction*. New York: Random House.

Cameron, S. (2009) *The Business Student's Handbook*, 5th edn. Harlow: Pearson.

Guirdham, M. (2002) *Interpersonal Skills at Work*, 3rd edn. Harlow: Pearson.

Herbert, I. and Rothwell, A. (2005) *Managing Your Placement: A Skills Based Approach*. Basingstoke: Palgrave.

Lumley, M and Wilkinson, J. (2014) *Developing Employability for Business*. Oxford: Oxford University Press.

Woodruffe, C. (2007) *Development and Assessment Centres*, 4th edn. London: CIPD.

Websites to look up

- For further information on careers and development:
  www.nus.org.uk/en/advice/careers

- For an example of a professional networking site:
  www.uk.linkedin.com

- Some graduate employability sites to explore:
  www.targetjobs.co.uk
  www.milkround.com
  www.graduate.monster.co.uk
  www.prospects.ac.uk

Time for review and reflection

This is your space to log your reflections on this chapter, to think about what you have learnt, how you will use it and what else you need to find out.

What were the key learning points of this chapter?
What are your strengths in the areas covered by this chapter?
What areas did you identify for development?
What have you learnt about yourself?
How will you use this knowledge?
What else do you need to learn or find out about in relation to this chapter?

10

How to Understand the Application Process in Order to Get Shortlisted

Overview – what's in this chapter?

- Why do you need to upgrade your application skills?
- Developing content for the application process that will attract a potential employer
- Completing application forms to present yourself in the best light
- Developing your CV in order to gain maximum impact
- Developing a digital identity/online presence
- Writing cover letters and emails that employers will want to read
- What to do if you don't get shortlisted for interview or assessment centre
- Follow-up activities, further reading and websites to look up
- Time for review and reflection

Why do you need to upgrade your application skills?

Try completing the short self-scoring test overleaf, to assess your own level of confidence in applying for jobs and placements.

✎ Activity: Why do you need to read this chapter?

You need to self score each question on a scale from 0 to 10, where 0 is low and 10 is high.

1. How successful have you been in making applications in the past?	
2. How accurate are you in describing yourself in the application process?	
3. How much attention have you given to developing a digital identity/online presence?	
4. How well compiled and presented is your curriculum vitae (CV)?	
5. How good are you at completing a convincing application form?	
6. How competent are you at writing effective cover letters/emails?	
7. How good are you at the graphic presentation of documents?	
8. How open are you to receiving feedback on your employability documents from a valued reader?	
9. How open are you to receiving feedback from employers on any unsuccessful applications?	
10. How confident are you in your ability to get the kind of internships, placements or jobs you want?	
Total score	

Interpretation

What did you score?

- Less than 50% You will definitely find a lot of help in this chapter.
- 50%–75% There is still plenty to learn in this chapter.
- 75%–100% You are very confident – read on to confirm your understanding.

You may feel that you don't need to give attention to this chapter because you have achieved success in job applications in the past or perhaps you just consider it to be form filling. However, when you apply for higher level jobs, the bar will be higher and so you will need to raise your game in order to succeed. The job market is very competitive and decisions between applicants are frequently very close, with many applicants having similar qualifications, so making sure you get the edge over someone else may come down to how well you present yourself and describe the skills and qualities you have to offer.

What you are doing is selling yourself in the labour market and, therefore, your application is effectively your advertising material. If someone gave you a poorly presented and uninformative leaflet advertising a company, you would no doubt be unimpressed. The analogy is clear; you have one chance to impress the employer and to get shortlisted for interview or assessment centre, so it is very important to present yourself in the best possible light.

In this chapter we look at what you can do to develop attractive application forms, curriculum vitae (CV) cover letters/emails and the developing concept of a **digital identity** or **online presence**. We also touch on what to do if you should make an unsuccessful application. Finally there are some follow-up activities, some suggested further reading, websites to look up, and some space for review and reflection.

> **Digital identity/online presence** – your profile on the internet utilising e-portfolios and/or professional networking sites

Developing content for the application process that will attract a potential employer

What you say about yourself will be very important in matching your skills and talent to the job concerned. In Chapter 9 you identified your key skills and these should definitely be part of what you say about yourself during the application process. However, your personal qualities are also part of what makes you special and in the following activity we ask you to identify them.

✎ Activity: What are my personal qualities?

Pick your top 10 personal qualities from the list overleaf and place them in order of preference.

1.	6. ....
2.	7. ....
3.	8. ....
4.	9. ....
5.	10. ....

Choose from these qualities:			
flexible	loyal	consistent	thoughtful
articulate	responsible	team player	cautious
calm	dedicated	independent	imaginative
organised	versatile	committed	patient
punctual	creative	careful	dependable
tactful	strong	dynamic	good under pressure
sensible	approachable	competent	friendly
alert	hard working	direct	methodical
quick	assertive	humorous	outgoing
reliable	capable	adaptable	self-motivated
practical	accurate	decisive	serious
thorough	enthusiastic	sensitive	cooperative
polite	perceptive	bright	trustworthy
likeable	analytical	innovative	able to work alone

If you already have a CV, check to see if your personal qualities are emphasised in it. If not, what are you saying about yourself?

Using active verbs

As well as describing your skills and qualities accurately in the employability process, it is also important to think about how you express yourself. Using active verbs in your employability documents and when you are talking about yourself at a face-to-face interview, during a telephone interview or at an assessment centre, will help you to project an image of an active, doing person. Some examples of active verbs include:

> **Active verbs –** used to describe yourself as an active 'doing' person.

coordinating	leading	handling	writing
growing	travelling	managing	planning
caring	developing	communicating	supervising
advising	diagnosing	training	driving
persuading	filing	researching	translating
recruiting	assessing	selling	selecting
establishing	sorting	teaching	enabling
performing	analysing	deciding	reading
serving	negotiating	compiling	drawing

Using the STAR technique to get your message across

STAR technique – technique for structuring answers to open-ended questions.

When describing the competencies employers require, it is very easy to ramble and not use the best example or include enough detail/information in the answer. The **STAR technique** (Byham and Cox, 1998) provides a framework to construct a relevant answer to open-ended questions asked during an interview or when completing an application form. The STAR technique enables you to structure what you have to say as follows:

- **S = Situation** – outlines a situation that demonstrates that you possess a personal quality or skill.
- **T = Task** – describes a task which you have completed.
- **A = Action** – explains what you actually did in this situation.
- **R = Result** – reports the result of your actions.

A STAR is really a little story, which you are proud of and which can be told to your advantage. The STAR technique gives you a format in which to tell stories about yourself. Some examples of the types of STARs which our students have reported include:

- You were the captain of a successful sports team or a key member of a team which succeeded in its endeavours.
- There was a crisis and you saved the day, as in someone drowning or needing the kiss of life.
- You were at work and there was a crisis which you managed to resolve.
- You found something personally very hard but overcame this in order to succeed.
- You achieved a personal goal. Perhaps you raised money for charity, made a presentation, acted in a play, played in a band, and so on.
- Through sheer hard work you got a place at university.

Many questions found in application forms and indeed asked at telephone/face-to-face interviews are actually quite predictable, as for example:

- What are your strengths?
- What are your weaknesses/areas for development?

- Describe a situation where you worked in a team
- What has been your greatest achievement?
- What do you think you could bring to the job/company?

When you prepare STARs ensure you include specific details which are relevant to your STARs and make them unique to you, e.g. the actual name of your college, school or part-time employer, the location, exactly how much money you raised. This will enable you to create colourful and memorable STARs.

> From a listener's perspective, this makes the story more interesting and they are more able to gauge your success. Nameless figures and undefined successes can make the answer less feel less convincing. ... [A]s there are likely to be many questions and interviewers have short attention spans, it's important to keep your answers concise: convey the maximum achievement in the minimum time. Finally, it's important to finish on a positive note so the overall impression is strong. (Higgins, 2014)

We also strongly advise you to prepare STARs to cover your weaknesses or areas for development. One way of handling such questions on these is to change the language and describe an area you needed to develop and what actions you took to develop it. For example, you might have found the quantitative aspects of your course very hard or were extremely nervous about making oral presentations. If you worked on an area for development and it then became a strength, you will have demonstrated some admirable qualities to the employer.

Sarah Cockburn, Head of Graduate Recruitment and Development at Barclays Wealth, has discussed using the STAR technique as a way of structuring and preparing answers to competency-based interview questions (see also Chapter 11 on competency-based interviews).

You can access this at: https://www.youtube.com/watch?v=0LpEKcFdcs4

Source: Cockburn (2011)

✎ **Activity: Making a STAR**

Try making a STAR for one or more of your top 10 personal qualities and another to cover an area for development.

- Situation or Task: _____

- Action: _____

- Result: _____

Completing application forms to present yourself in the best light

Planning your application form

Visual presentation will be the first thing which the reader sees, so your application must look good, but content, grammar, syntax and spelling are also very important.

Try following this systematic approach when completing your applications:

- Read and follow all the instructions.
- Analyse the job advertisement and any other information you have been sent about the organisation or job, doing further research and telephoning the company if this is appropriate.
- Organise your content before you start. As virtually all applications are now completed online, remember to have everything ready and to hand before you start.
- Give accurate information about yourself that is tailored to the job concerned, i.e. avoid *nice to know* in favour of *need to know*.
- Use the **STAR technique** to complete questions asking for examples.
- Demonstrate your ability to present yourself positively, avoiding negative statements, and making sure that you stress your **personal qualities**.
- Use **active verbs** in order to stress your positive abilities as a capable *doing* person.
- Include a link to your **digital identity/online presence**.
- Print off the application and fill in a draft before you complete the final version.
- Get someone else to read your draft as it is easy to read over your own mistakes.
- Check your spelling.
- Print off, and/or save the completed application form as you may be asked at interview for more information, or you may be able to use it as the basis for another application form.

Activity: Completing an application form

- Try completing a draft application form for an internship, placement or job you are interested in, using the systematic approach described in this section.
- Get a valued reader to proof-read your application form, as it is easy to read over and miss your own errors. It is also a good way to get positive feedback and constructive criticism. Be prepared to accept constructive criticism, but remember that at the end of the day it is your application form and should say what you want to say about yourself.
- Finally, write up your application form and post it or submit it online.

Developing your CV in order to gain maximum impact

What should my CV contain?

The content of a CV or curriculum vitae will vary from individual to individual and, while there are many suggested formats, you have to consider what is appropriate to our own situation and the positions you are applying for. We do not believe in providing a model CV which you might copy, but rather we want to make suggestions which might usefully inform your own design.

> **Curriculum vitae** – from the Latin meaning the course of life.

The following list provides an idea of the content of a typical CV:

- **Personal details**, including: name, address, telephone number, mobile number, email address (to make yourself easily contactable).
- A brief **personal profile** of yourself (see the section below, on what is a personal profile).
- **Education**, including schools, colleges, and universities attended, together with dates and qualifications obtained and something about your experience, including what you learnt, achieved and are most proud of.
- **Professional qualifications** held. Even if they are not relevant to the job you are applying for, they will show your achievement.
- **Any other qualifications** you hold (e.g. first aid certificate, driving licence or sports coaching qualification). These also show your achievement and may be relevant to the job concerned.
- Details of your **current or last job** and previous **employment history**, including: dates, job title, responsibilities, employer's name(s), any 'in-service' training and something about your experience in terms of what you learnt, achieved and are most proud of.

225

Extracurricular activities – activities falling outside the normal curriculum of your course.

Transferable skills – skills learnt in one situation which can be readily transferred to another, e.g. communication skills developed in social situations and then used in the workplace.

Digital identity/online presence – your own profile on the internet utilising e-portfolios and/or professional networking websites.

- **Extra-curricular activities** you have participated in, such as student societies, and voluntary work, which tend to show commitment and may provide you with **transferable skills**.
- **Personal interests** and any **other personal skills** or **talents** you think you have. These may again show commitment and demonstrate your **transferable skills**. Don't forget to mention skills for which you do not hold a qualification, such as the ability to speak languages or to speak in public.
- A link to your **digital identity/online presence**.
- **Referees** – give names, titles, addresses, telephone numbers and email if available/applicable.

 Activity: Deciding on content for your CV

- Review the typical CV content listed in this section and then brainstorm what particular content you will want to put in your own CV.
- What would be suitable sub-headings to use?
- When you have decided upon content, think about what sequence it should go in.
- When you have decided upon what you want to say about yourself, try to put your ideas under headings that are relevant to you and your life and experiences.

What is a personal profile?

Personal profile – short description of yourself towards the start of a CV.

A personal profile is a short description of yourself which helps the reader to come quickly to a view as to whether you might be suitable for the job. It is rather like visiting a book shop and just reading that small panel on the back of a book that describes the content. Though it may not instantly make up your mind to buy the book, it can prompt you to read further and look longer at the book, rather than returning it swiftly to the shelf.

Sadly, those who have the task of reading a great many CVs will not stop to read thoroughly all that is submitted. So the inclusion of a personal profile can help them match the right person with the right job more easily, and including such a short synopsis might just give you the edge. Consider bullet pointing your personal profile in order to maximise its impact.

 Activity: Completing a personal profile

- Draft a personal profile of 30–40 words (maximum).Try to include what is relevant to say about you.
- Now show your draft to a valued reader to get feedback.

CV construction

There is no 'correct' way to structure the material in your CV, but some formats may prove more effective than others in getting you a job. It is good to change the format of your CV when applying for different types of jobs, giving greater or lesser emphasis to various sections of your content, as appropriate to the job concerned.

Don't try to say everything you possibly could, because your CV will be too long and the reader will lose interest. Similarly, don't 'sell yourself short' by saying too little. Try to keep a balance. The 'normal' length of a CV in the UK is two sides, whereas in some other countries it is only one. However, for a senior post it might be much longer, where age is expected to have brought more experience which needs to be reported.

There is no need to put the words 'curriculum vitae' or CV at the top of the first page, because inevitably you will be sending it with a cover letter or email starting with something like 'Please find attached my curriculum vitae'. We don't head up letters with the word 'letter', so why do it to a CV? Instead, why not put your name in large print, to help reinforce your name and really sell yourself.

Try to think about the initial impact your CV will make. There is a sense in which the visual aspects of your CV may actually be more important than the content, simply because it is the first thing they will see. It is very important therefore to consider how it looks and to give attention to layout, spacing, indents, justification, fonts, etc. The more professional your CV looks, the more likely it is that the reader will take your application seriously and want to read the content.

The first page of many CVs is extremely boring, often containing only bare details such as name, contact information and qualifications, with nothing which is particularly influential in terms of getting a job. Including your personal profile after the name and contact details can help greatly, as will saying something more about your experiences, skills and personal qualities, rather than just listing schools, colleges and qualifications.

When listing jobs, courses attended or qualifications and so on it may be more useful to put the most recent information first. For example the placement or internship you did last year might be much more interesting and important than the holiday job you did three years ago. Similarly your university level qualifications will be much more important than those you achieved at school.

Make sure you include all the **personal qualities** which you think are important and use **active verbs** (see the earlier section of this chapter on developing content for the application process).

Finally, include the names and contact details of referees that you can rely upon at the end. You should include at least two referees; one should be an academic reference and another can be a current or past employer, if you have one. In general, try to avoid personal references. Some people put 'references supplied on application', which is simply a pointless irritation to a potential employer. Why not just put them in?

Make sure you update your CV for every new application. You will often be surprised how much has changed, even over a short period. It will also allow you to emphasise aspects that may be important for a particular job application. For example, if you are applying for a job with the sportswear manufacturer and were yourself a keen sports player, you might give this more emphasis than if you are applying to a financial institution.

 Activity: Completing your CV

- When you have completed the previous two activities, try to write up a draft CV, giving attention not only to the content but also to the layout.

- Next look at your CV from a distance, far enough away so that you can't read the actual words. How does it look? Try to visualise yourself as a potential employer, and consider what impression it gives and whether you would be encouraged to read the content.

- Get someone else to proof-read your CV, as it is easy to 'read over' or miss your own errors. This is also a good way to get positive feedback and constructive criticism. Be prepared to accept constructive criticism, but remember that at end of the day it is your CV, and should say what you want to say about yourself.

- Finally, write up your completed CV.

Developing a digital identity/online presence

The concept of developing a digital identity and maintaining an online presence in order to improve your chances of employability has developed in recent years. There are at present two main ways of doing this:

> **Digital identity/online presence –** your profile on the internet utilising e-portfolios and/or professional networking sites.

- **Professional networking sites –** perhaps the best-known being LinkedIn, which allows you to build a profile, access news and updates as well as networking with others. You will probably be used to using social networking sites such as Facebook, in which case you will find these relatively easy to use.
- **E-profile –** allows you to build a sort of online CV, but also to include photos and hyper-links. It will be based on software such as a Mahara platform, which may be available through your university or college. It will provide you with your own discrete URL, which can be inserted into application forms, CVs and cover letters/emails, in order to allow employers to access it.

We anticipate that the need to develop your digital identity and maintain an online presence will be likely to increase over the next few years, and so we would encourage you to start work on this as soon as possible in order to improve your employability.

Be aware that there is a potential danger in content that you may already have on social networking sites. Do you have embarrassing photographs or messages? Employers and employment agencies take a lot of time researching applicants and checking out everything they can about them, so it's important to delete anything that might undermine your chances of employability and/or review your security preferences.

Writing cover letters and emails that employers will want to read

Your cover letter/email is another opportunity to sell yourself in the application process and, as with your CV and application form, how it looks may be as important as what you say. Whilst emails tend to be less formal than business letters, when making your application by email, we suggest following the same conventions as for a business letter, to demonstrate that you know these.

In writing cover letters we suggest that you follow these conventions:

- Always use an acceptable and up-to-date business format for a cover letter.
- Address the letter correctly, quoting any name, department, etc.
- Quote any reference numbers that are given.
- Include a title or heading in bold, stating the position applied for and where it was sourced, after the salutation (e.g. Dear Mr Jones) and before your opening paragraph.
- State the purpose of the letter in the opening paragraph.
- Try to start the letter with something more creative than 'I am writing...'.
- Include only relevant details in the letter, rather than repeating items from the CV and application form.
- Include a link to your **digital identity/online presence** (see previous section).
- Where the salutation was **Dear Sir or Madam** close with **Yours faithfully**. Where it was addressed to a named individual such as **Dear Ms Shah**, close with **Yours sincerely**.
- Print and sign your name.

 ## Activity: Writing effective cover letters

1. Review the following letter in the light of the list of points above to see how many errors you can find.

2. What did you learn from reviewing this letter which might inform your own construction of cover letters/emails?

3. Try drafting your own cover letter/email and then get some feedback on it from a valued reader.

N. B. This is an example of poor letter writing, so not to be copied!
Flat 4,
147 Hanover Street
Brighton,
East Sussex,
BN2 4XX

11 July 2014

Miss S Wiseman,
Graduate Recruitment Officer,
Aviva,
PO Box 4
Surrey Street
Norwich
NR1 3NG

Dear Stephen Wiseman

Graduate Marketing Programme

Aviva is one of the largest companies in the UK. I am very interested in finding out more about the graduate marketing scheme that that you have available.

As an applicant who has a great understanding of the importance of branding and customer relations I believe that my skills and enthusiasm would be an asset to your company. I have a proven track record in the field of customer care in retail and service sector. I enjoy a challenge and as a graduate with a business and marketing degree I believe that I successfully meet your requirements.

Please find enclose my curriculum vitae, and above my contact details, including a link to my e-portfolio. I am available for interview at any time.

Yours faithfully,

B. Casselton (Student)

What to do if you don't get shortlisted for interview or assessment centre

If a job application is unsuccessful, don't be afraid to ask for feedback on your application as many employers are now very willing to give it. What you learn can be used to revise your employability documentation and, potentially, can help you to get the internship, placement or job you want next time. See also Chapter 11 on handling appointment or rejection.

Follow-up activities

Time for action – Checklist

Have you:

- considered why you need to upgrade your application skills?
- developed content for the application process that will attract a potential employer?
- recognised what is required in order to complete application forms that will present you in the best light?
- developed your CV in order to gain maximum impact?
- started to develop a digital identity in order to maintain an online presence?
- understood how to write cover letters/emails that employers will want to read?
- thought about what to do if you don't get shortlisted for interview or assessment centre?

Further reading

Byham, C. and Cox, J. (1998) *Zapp! The Lightning of Empowerment: How to improve Productivity, Quality and Employee Satisfaction*. New York: Random House.

Cameron, S. (2009) *The Business Student's Handbook*, 5th edn. Harlow: Pearson,

Herbert, I. and Rothwell, A. (2005) *Managing Your Placement: A Skills Based Approach*. Basingstoke: Palgrave.

Lee-Davies, L. (2007) *Developing Work and Study Skills*. London: Thomson.

Lumley, M and Wilkinson, J. (2014*) Developing Employability for Business*. Oxford: Oxford University Press.

Woodruffe, C. (2007) *Development and Assessment Centres*, 4th edn. London: CIPD.

Websites to look up

- Information on careers and development:
  www.nus.org.uk/en/advice/careers
- For further help with the STAR technique, CVs, cover letters and application forms:
  www.careers.theguardian.com/careers-blog/star-technique-competency-based-interview
  www2.open.ac.uk/students/careers/applying-for-jobs/pdp-star-technique
  www.gradjobs.co.uk/careers-advice/interview-advice/using-the-star-technique-to-succeed-at-interviews
- Some graduate employability sites to explore:
  www.prospects.ac.uk/cvs_and_cover_letters.htm
  www.grb.uk.com/making_applications0.0.html
  www.e4s.co.uk/graduate-jobs/free-application-form-tips.htm
  www.targetjobs.co.uk/careers-advice/applications-and-cvs

Time for review and reflection

This is your space to log your reflections on this chapter, to think about what you have learnt, how you will use it and what else you need to find out.

What were the key learning points of this chapter?
What are your strengths in the areas covered by this chapter?

What areas did you identify for development?
What have you learnt about yourself?
How will you use this knowledge?
What else do you need to learn or find out about in relation to this chapter?

11

How to Give Yourself the Best Chance of Success in the Selection Process

Overview – what's in this chapter?

- Why do you need to upgrade your skills for the selection process?
- Preparing for interview, including research and personal presentation
- Planning for success, including positive thinking and visualisation
- Developing your interview skills
- Performing effectively at assessment centres
- Handling appointment or rejection
- Follow-up activities, further reading and websites to look up
- Time for review and reflection

Why do you need to upgrade your skills for the selection process?

Try completing the short self-scoring test overleaf, to assess your own level of confidence in relation to the selection process for jobs and placements.

✎ **Activity: Why do you need to read this chapter?**

You need to self score each question on a scale from 0 to 10, where 0 is low and 10 is high.

1. How successful have you been in the past at interviews or assessment centres?	
2. How good are you at preparing for interviews?	
3. How important do you consider researching the employer to be?	
4. How important do you consider analysing the job to be?	
5. How good are you at answering questions about yourself?	
6. How good are you at formulating questions to ask at interview?	
7. How are your teamwork and leadership skills?	
8. How good are you at completing problem-solving activities?	
9. How likely are you to ask for feedback if you are unsuccessful?	
10. How confident are you in your ability to get the internship, placement or job you want?	
Total score	

Interpretation

What did you score?

- Less than 50%   You will definitely find a lot of help in this chapter.

- 50%–75%   There is still plenty to learn in this chapter.

- 75%–100%   You are very confident – read on to confirm your understanding.

Developing a clear understanding of the recruitment and selection processes, being well prepared and presenting yourself in a good light at interview or an assessment centre, will all help you to secure the position you want.

It is important to realise from the outset that when you submit your application, you are entering a competitive situation. This will perhaps become most obvious when you arrive to find a number of other people waiting for interview or when you are part of a group invited to an assessment centre. When you talk to the others you may find that they have similar backgrounds and qualifications to yourself, and then it may become really obvious that how good your preparation has been and how you perform on the day will tend to determine if you are successful or not.

The main purposes of this chapter are to help you prepare for interviews and to appreciate the special considerations for achieving success at assessment centres. As with many other things in life, good preparation will help you to achieve a good result. In particular you should consider what research you need to do, your analysis of the job, together with how you present yourself on the day.

The chapter will also look at how to handle success. What to do if you don't get the job – to help you handle rejection – is also discussed and includes getting feedback and learning from the experience. Finally there are some follow-up activities, some suggested further reading, websites to look up, and some space for review and reflection.

Preparing for interview, including research and personal presentation

Researching the organisation

It is important to make sure that you know as much as possible about the organisation and their business. Your research can include internal sources such as the information which they sent in an application pack, the company website and annual report. However, you should try to find out what is really happening with the organisation concerned rather than just relying on the organisation's own propaganda. Aim to access independent sources including newspaper and journal articles, in order to see what other people are saying about the organisation. It may also be interesting to see what the organisation's competitors are saying or doing and to look at the market in which they operate – to see what is happening and what is on the horizon.

Most employers will appreciate the time you have taken to find out about their business and will ask you if you want to ask them any questions. This is your chance to show that you know what you are talking about. They will expect you to have questions for them, so make sure that you have some prepared! See also the section below, on developing your interview skills, especially the part on formulating your own questions.

Analysing the job

A good employer will have broken down the job using a system of job analysis and perhaps created job competencies (see Chapter 9 on matching your skill set to the internship, placement or job you apply for, and especially the part on understanding what the employer is looking for). You may have been sent or downloaded a job description or list of job competencies. If so, it is worth taking some time to match this to your skill set and to ask yourself where your strengths and areas for development are. You can then be prepared to stress your strengths in relation to the job concerned and also ready to cover any areas for development. See also Chapter 10 on developing content for the application process and the discussion in this chapter on answering the question.

If no information is provided on the position concerned, it is very useful to do your own job analysis before the interview or assessment, in order to anticipate the type of questions you might be asked. If the job is particularly specialised or unusual, it may be appropriate to ring up beforehand and to try and get more information on what is required.

Personal presentation

Employers will not only judge you on what you say but also on how you look – and this includes physical appearance and body language. Appearance may well be as important as what is said, in respect of who gets a job. We strongly suggest you take note of the following in particular:

- **Think about how you dress**. Formality is the norm in most professions, so a smart and business-like appearance will be expected by most employers and they will appreciate the effort you have taken. Even where the normal dress code is more relaxed, try to be as smart as possible for interview.
- **Do not let minor details let you down**. For example dirty fingernails or chipped nail varnish may appear distasteful to your assessor or interviewer. If you have to eat on the way to the interview, take some chewing gum to clean your teeth and freshen your breath.
- **Be aware of your body language**. If you slump in the chair, you will appear sloppy to your interviewer. Crossed arms and legs can be a sign of defence and will give the impression that you are hiding something. Fidgeting and restlessness will make you look nervous (see also Chapter 3 on recognising non-verbal communication). This is also important even if you are interviewed on the telephone, as your body language can affect your voice!
- **Remember to maintain appropriate eye contact**. If you don't look your interviewer in the eye when answering a question, you will look dishonest and will be unlikely to secure a position. If you are facing an interview panel, it is best to look mostly at the person whose question you are answering, but also look at the other panel members from time to time to keep them interested in you and what you are saying.

In general, you should try to present yourself in the best light. Everyone else will probably be doing so, so why not give yourself the best chance of getting the job?

Activity: Preparing for interview or assessment centre

- Take a few minutes to review this section and then make a checklist of everything you need to do before your next interview or assessment centre.

- After an interview or assessment centre, take a few minutes to review how it went and to think how your preparation could be improved another time.

Planning for success, including positive thinking and visualisation

Being in the right frame of mind before arriving for a face-to-face interview or an assessment centre, or commencing a telephone or online interview is very important. Developing a positive mental attitude can really help you achieve a good result, but it doesn't happen automatically. There are a number of things which you can do to get in the right state of mind and be more successful. These include:

- **Good preparation** – as discussed earlier in this chapter. Doing thorough research and preparation will make you feel more confident, because you will have more to talk about in the interview and you will also be ready with your own questions.

> **Visualisation** – picturing and recording in our mind a future event to help us achieve a better outcome.

- **Positive thinking** – this involves spending time thinking positively about the job and **visualising** yourself doing it. You can also imagine yourself at the interview being positive and relaxed. Doing this will create positive connections in the brain, rather than the negative ones which build up when we are apprehensive. Try thinking **can do** rather than **can't do**. See also the section in Chapter 2 on visualising your success and putting the past behind you.

> **Stress** – physical or psychological pressure or tension.

- **Stress control and relaxation techniques** – giving attention to this area will mean that you will not arrive at the interview or assessment centre 'shaking like a jelly'. Learning to breathe and meditate will help you to stay focused in the interview and can be usefully combined with visualisation techniques. If necessary, you can learn a **relaxation technique**. See also Chapter 4 on handling stress and developing relaxation techniques.

- **Planning your journey** – this may sound obvious, but arriving late can be a wretched experience: it will give a bad impression and can definitely undermine your confidence, at least to start with. It is important to check whatever instructions you were sent, to print off maps and/or routes and study them, and to check train times. A good rule when taking trains is to take the train before the one which would get you there just in time.

- **Use your time before the interview or assessment centre productively** – once you have arrived, take some time to prepare yourself and focus your thoughts.

 Activity: Developing a positive mental attitude

- Take a few minutes to review this section.
- Make an action plan of what you need to do in order to develop a positive mental attitude towards an interview or assessment centre.

Developing your interview skills

At interview you have only a short time to impress the employer, so developing good interpersonal skills that are appropriate to the interview situation is essential. Key areas for consideration are developing your listening skills, answering questions effectively and formulating your own questions to ask.

Developing **active listening skills** involves learning to listen more and say less. The first step in answering questions successfully is to listen to what was asked. This may sound absolutely obvious but under the pressure of the interview it is all too easy to miss the point or to jump to conclusions. Listening is an important skill which can be developed with a little work. See Chapter 3 on developing your questioning and listening skills.

Learning to answer the question that was asked and not being evasive may be crucial to your success. This includes being honest and saying if you don't know the answer, if that is the case. Many interview questions are, however, quite predictable. The most commonly asked questions at interview tend to revolve around asking you what your strengths and areas for development are, although they may be disguised in various forms such as:

'What do you think you could bring the company?'

'What areas do you see as being most important to your future development?'

> **STAR technique –** technique for structuring answers to open-ended questions.

While it is important to answer the question that you were asked, it is also really useful to have developed some stock responses that can be adapted to the question. This preparation can help you avoid drying up and can give you more things to talk about. One way of structuring your answers is to use the STAR technique (see Chapter 10 on developing content for the application process that will attract a potential employer, and particularly the material on using the STAR technique to get your message across). A STAR is essentially a little story you tell about yourself and, in this context, STARs typically fall into two categories:

- **Achievements** – things you are proud of and want to relate. These can really help highlight your strengths.
- **Problems you have overcome** – these can help you express areas for development in the context of how you overcame them. You thus turn areas for development into strengths and so provide a positive way of answering a negative question.

Two students told us...

Two of our students told us the following stories as a result of preparing STARs:

'I was captain of football at school when we got to the final of the local cup competition. We were one goal down with ten minutes to go, but I managed to reorganise things and encourage the team. We scored a couple of quick goals to win the cup 2–1'.

'I found that I was struggling with maths when I got to university, but I went to the library and got more books to work through. I also saw my tutor and she went over the requirements with me. I talked to the best student in the group and she also helped me. In the end I passed all the quantitative tests and now I feel more confident about doing it'.

As part of your preparation for an interview it is useful to have prepared a number of STARs which you can pull out in response to appropriate questions. In Chapter 10 we invited you to make a couple of STARs and also suggested how you might deal with questions about your areas for development. In the following activity we invite you to prepare a couple more, but five or six might be a more realistic total to have prepared before attending an interview or assessment centre.

 Activity: Developing answers to standard interview questions

Try to develop answers to the following common interview questions, using the STAR technique:

1. What are your strengths/what might you bring to the job?
   - ○ Situation or Task: _____
   - ○ Action: _____
   - ○ Result: _____

2. What are your weaknesses? To avoid repeating the negative word 'weaknesses' we suggest that you change the language and start your answer with "An area I am currently aiming to develop is…".

  o Situation or Task: _____

  o Action: _____

  o Result: _____

Your answers during an interview should always be consistent with what you said in your application documents. Not telling a consistent story would be viewed with great suspicion by any prospective employer. The easiest story for you to tell will be the honest one and we strongly recommend that you don't act and that you don't lie at an interview or assessment centre. You are not trying to win an Oscar and it will surely show through at interview or assessment centre if you are trying to act a part. It is **you** that needs to shine through at interview. Similarly, lying will tend to show up and look very bad. No one wants a dishonest or untrustworthy employee on their payroll.

A manager told us…

A manager told us that if he suspected that an interview candidate was lying, he would ask more and more questions on the subject he was suspicious about. As he got into more depth he would tend to expose a liar because they either could not answer the question or would tend to make up further lies, or give more ridiculous answers.

Prospective employers will normally expect you to ask them questions at some stage in an interview and having some intelligent questions to ask will be essential if you are to make a good impression. This may also require you to improve your own question formulation skills by asking more **open-ended questions** in order to get them talking to you. See also Chapter 3 on developing your questioning and listening skills, and preparing for formal interviews.

Open-ended questions – questions which cannot be answered with a simple yes or no, and which generally produce longer answers.

You will need to have a good range of questions prepared as some of what you expect to ask may have been covered in the interview. It is not unusual for interviewers to start by giving you a short briefing, perhaps covering the organisation and the position concerned.

Interviewees' questions tend to fall into a range of categories, including:

- the organisation and its business;
- what the job involves;
- opportunities for your future development within the organisation, including professional qualifications, training, development and career path;
- where you are likely to be located and what scope there is for mobility in the future;
- terms and conditions of employment if these are unclear or if the salary is negotiable.

It might not be a good idea to start by asking questions about your own needs. The overriding concern of your interviewers is much more likely to be what you might do for the organisation rather than the reverse, so this list might usefully be seen as an order of priority for your interview questions.

 Activity: Developing questions for your interview or assessment centre

- Before an interview or assessment centre, prepare a list of questions that you might want to ask and put these into a priority order.

- After an interview or assessment centre, take a few minutes to review how it went. How useful or relevant were your questions and what could be improved another time?

Behavioural or competency-based interviews – interviews structured around job competencies, exploring past behaviours as a guide to anticipated future performance.

Job competencies – behaviours describing what an individual might be expected to do as part of a job.

Behavioural or **competency-based interviews**, are based upon **job competencies** and built on the assumption that past behaviours might be a good predictor of future performance. Such interviews will be highly structured and you will be marked against pre-determined criteria. Good preparation for this type of interview will necessarily involve identifying the competencies that you expect would be part of the job, and therefore would be addressed in the interview, and then preparing a good range of STARs so that you can talk with confidence in response to any question you asked. See Chapter 10 on developing content for the application process that will attract a potential employer, and particularly the material on using the STAR technique to get your message across.

Telephone and online interviews require special consideration. In the case of **telephone interviews,** these can give you the advantage of having your notes in front of you and the possibility of jotting things down during the course of the interview. The downside is that as you will not be able to read the body language of your interviewer and as will they not be able to read yours, it becomes even more important to express yourself clearly on the phone.

Online interviews are a developing area and frequently utilise webcam technology, meaning that you can see each other. In this case, how you dress and how you act will become as important as in a face-to-face interview. Online interviews have the advantage of saving on travel time and costs, but it might mean that you don't actually get to see the workplace where you might work. In some cases, telephone and online interviews are used at the preliminary stage and if you are successful, you will then be invited to a second interview or assessment centre.

If you are invited for a **second interview**, it means you're getting close to being offered a job, but it's not in the bag. For example, if an employer received one hundred applications, conducted preliminary interviews and got it down to ten for second interview, there might still only be one job on offer. So it is really well worth your reviewing what happened in the preliminary interview, asking yourself what went well, what areas were there for improvement, what extra preparation do you need to do and what you would do differently next time. If you prepared some STARs for the preliminary interview, it would be good to identify some new ones for the second interview rather than repeating everything that you said before. See Chapter 10, on developing content for the application process that will attract a potential employer, and particularly the material on using the STAR technique to get your message across.

Performing effectively at assessment centres

What are assessment centres and why do they need special attention?

An **assessment centre** can be defined as a selection procedure using multiple methods. They tend to be used by larger corporations for recruitment to graduate/management training schemes and student placements. They are also sometimes used to monitor progress and for promotion decisions. The time and cost involved tends to deter the use of assessment centres for other positions.

> **Assessment centre –** candidate assessment using multiple methods for recruitment and promotion decisions.

> **Development centre –** employee assessment using multiple methods for personal and career development.

Development centres are similar to assessment centres, but tend to be used by organisations for personal and career development rather than recruitment or promotion.

An assessment centre might typically last a full day and perhaps longer. During this time the employer will use a variety of methods to test a range of competencies which have been identified as being appropriate for the job concerned (see also Chapter 9 and the section on matching your skill set to the internship, placement or job you apply for).

Whereas a traditional interview effectively tests only a limited range of competencies such as knowledge and interpersonal skills, an assessment centre can test a variety of competencies and so the organisation can develop a more thorough appraisal of the individual applicant. There is, therefore, much less chance that anyone can 'talk their way into a job' without having the competencies needed for success in the role.

To succeed at assessment centres requires some special considerations, but the skills which you are likely to be called upon to demonstrate are for the most part the ones we have been looking at in this book and which you will have been developing both through your course and your life experiences.

Each activity you complete at an assessment centre will be scored, most probably against a range of competencies, so it may be a mistake to try and think, 'what are they looking for in this one' and then try and perform in a different way for that task. The scores will probably be weighted and then aggregated at the end of the assessment centre to produce a points total for each participant, from which the actual selection decisions will be made.

Many people find the experience of attending an assessment centre surprisingly enjoyable, especially the team and social aspects. Perhaps the most important thing to remember is that you are attending something serious, requiring your full attention and considerable energy if you are to come out well.

A consultant told us...

A consultant who has specialised in setting up assessment centres for major businesses comes to talk to our students every year. He told us that when he was attending assessment centres in his final year as an undergraduate, he had been given no preparation and found the experience very difficult.

What activities might an assessment centre comprise?

The range of assessment centre activities which you might be called upon to participate in are many and various, but they are likely to include:

- **Psychological tests** – these will tend to be either **cognitive,** which relates to testing mental states, or perhaps **psychomotor,** which test mind–body coordination.
- **Practical aptitude test/work simulation** – this will involve either doing practical tasks similar to the work concerned or real tasks which are part of the work role being tested for.
- **Role plays and re-enactments** – role plays will ask you to play a role in a fictional interpersonal situation, such as dealing with a problem customer. Re-enactments are similar but based upon real situations. In either case you may find yourself facing a professional actor, who will really test you.
- **Individual problem-solving activities** – these will test your ability to work alone. Frequently this involves an **'in-box' or 'in-tray' exercise** in which you are asked to read a number of documents within a limited time period and to sort them into priority order for action or perhaps to suggest what action would be appropriate.
- **Group/team problem-solving activities** – these will test not only your ability to solve problems but also your skill competencies in working with others in a team, and perhaps also your leadership skills.
- **Interviews** – just because you are at an assessment centre, it doesn't mean that you won't have an interview and in fact it is highly likely that you will. The interview element should therefore be taken seriously, as it might be the opportunity for you to sell yourself on an individual level.
- **Social activity** – be aware that you may be being assessed at any time – or indeed all the time – that you are at the assessment centre and, therefore, how you conduct yourself in breaks and at meal times may also be important. For example, if you take your food from the buffet and sit quietly in a corner, avoiding all social contact with other people, this might well be observed.

Cognitive – having to do with cognition or thinking.

Psychomotor – having to do with mind-body coordination.

Practical aptitude test – assessment of tasks forming all or part of a particular work role.

Work simulation – assessment of tasks similar to those found in a particular work role.

Role-play – activity involving participants in acting out prescribed roles, often within the context of a given scenario.

Re-enactment – activity involving participants re-enacting a real life situation.

Inbox/in-tray exercise – activity requiring participants to read and prioritise documents and sometimes to recommend actions.

Activity: Preparing for an assessment centre

- Take some time to think positively about a forthcoming assessment centre.
- Consider the types of activity that might be involved.
- What special considerations will you make in preparing for an assessment centre?

Handling appointment or rejection

Dealing with selection decisions

Whether you attend an interview or assessment centre, you will clearly be getting some good or bad news as a result. If you are offered a position and you decide to accept it, then it is just a matter of tying up the details of when and where you start. Alternatively, if you get a rejection it can be a very negative emotional experience – and all the more so if you truly wanted the job concerned. However, rejection can also be a positive learning experience and an opportunity to upgrade your skills for the next occasion.

Selection decisions tend to produce some very strong emotional reactions, so the emotional side needs to be dealt with and the result put in perspective. The tendency is either to feel that you failed or that the employer may have got it wrong, but neither is a useful or productive way to think about the situation. When you get a rejection, there are a number of points which may be useful to consider:

- Unlike an examination in which an infinite number of people can pass, the number of jobs on offer tend to be finite. For example, if 100 people apply for a job, 10 get short-listed for interview and you come second, this is not failure. You may in fact have been more or less equal with someone else who got the position but the employer may have made a marginal decision, such as the other person being able to start earlier.
- Remember that recruitment and selection is essentially a matching process and you might genuinely not be the right person for the particular job concerned. You may need to apply for different jobs or to different organisations where you will more likely to be seen as the right person for the job.
- Your details may be kept on file for future reference and you may be called back for another position. Many employers do this as it saves re-advertising, re-interviewing and most of the other selection costs.
- If an employer doesn't hire you, try not to see it as a problem, because there are many others you can apply to and you will have a good chance of getting a suitable position with one of these. You only need one job and the right one might be the next one that comes up.

It is important to express how you feel, however, so you may want to talk to a trusted friend. They will doubtless have an opinion to offer, such as 'they must be mad not to take you' or 'you are too good for them anyway'. However supportive your friend is, in the end you have to come to your own view and writing the experience down, as in the next activity, can really help you to off-load and **reconceptualise** the decision.

> **Reconceptualisation –** reprocessing thoughts and feelings about something in order to come to a new and updated view of it.

 Activity: Off-loading and reconceptualising the decision

- Start by writing down exactly how you feel, no matter how bad it is or how negative you are feeling. It is good to express it all.
- Try to write something positive about what you have learnt or gained from the experience.

How you get informed

There are a number of ways in which employers inform candidates. All have problems associated with the process and none are ideal. The options include:

- Asking everybody to stay until the end of the day, so that candidates can be offered the job in turn until somebody accepts. This does get things settled straight away but does, of necessity, mean that everybody has to stay until it is resolved and that the chosen candidate has to make a decision without much opportunity to consult friends and family, etc.
- Asking candidates to sit by the phone on the evening of the interviews or to be available to speak on their mobile, again so that the position can be offered to candidates in turn.
- In writing, by post or email – this inevitably creates delay, as the position has to be offered to each person in turn as some may not reply quickly and may need to be chased up.

However, if you are applying for an internship, placement, or graduate/management training scheme rather than a specific position, the process may be somewhat easier. You may get an indication on the day, but most likely you will hear by post. If you are attending an assessment centre, it will be very unlikely that you will hear anything on the day as assessors will tend to have a 'washing up' meeting after all the candidates have left, at which they will reflect on the performance of all individuals attending.

By the end of an interview or assessment centre, the employer should have told you how you will be informed of the outcome, but if not you will need to clarify this. When you are applying for a number of positions there can be real problems in juggling all the interviews and assessment centres. It may be that you get offered a job before you attend the interview or assessment centre for the job you really want. This is a real dilemma and you may have to consider accepting the first job while still participating in the selection process for the second.

Learning from the experience

If you are unsuccessful at interview or assessment centre, it is now quite normal to ask for some feedback from the organisation concerned. In many larger and more sophisticated organisations they will have information on file from which they can give you some feedback. Sometimes what you learn is that there was nothing wrong with you or the way you presented yourself, but rather that you were not seen as the best person for the particular job concerned.

If no feedback is available from the organisation, it will still be important for you to consider how it went: what went well and what could you improve upon another time? If you are applying for several internships, placements or jobs at the same time, the important thing will be to learn from each situation. If you can do this and you can improve your performance with each interview or assessment centre, securing a position will become all the more likely.

 Activity: Asking for feedback and upgrading your employability skills

- Ask the organisation concerned for feedback on your performance.
- Make a list of your strengths in the process and a list of what you could have done better.
- Consider what you might do differently another time.

Not getting the internship, placement or job can seem like a real disaster at the time but often, in hindsight, we can see that it made possible your getting something different, perhaps something better or something to which you were more suited. As stated earlier, many decisions are marginal ones, so the most important thing to do is not to take the decision personally but rather use the experience to learn, grow and move on.

Follow-up activities

Time for action – Checklist

Have you:

- considered what you need to do to upgrade your skills for interviews and assessment centres?
- thought about what you need to prepare for interview, including research and personal presentation?
- given attention to planning for success, including positive thinking and visualisation?
- recognised the importance of developing your interview skills, including preparation of STARs and your own questions to ask?
- understood what is required to perform effectively at an assessment centre?
- thought about appointment or rejection and how to handle it, including asking for feedback from employers who give you a rejection?
- thought about what you learnt and how you might use it in the future?

Further reading

Byham, C. and Cox, J. (1998) *Zapp! The Lightning of Empowerment: How to Improve Productivity, Quality and Employee Satisfaction*. New York: Random House.

Cameron, S. (2009) *The Business Student's Handbook*, 5th edn. Harlow: Pearson.

Guirdham, M. (2002) *Interpersonal Skills at Work*, 3rd edn. Harlow: Pearson.

Herbert, I. and Rothwell, A. (2005) *Managing Your Placement: A Skills Based Approach*. Basingstoke: Palgrave.

Lumley, M and Wilkinson, J. (2014) *Developing Employability for Business*. Oxford: Oxford University Press.

Pease, A. (2006) *The Definitive Book of Body Language*. New York: Bantam.

Woodruffe, C. (2007) *Development and Assessment Centres*, 4th edn. London: CIPD.

Websites to look up

- For information on careers and courses, etc:
  www.nus.org.uk/en/advice/careers
- For help with interview skills:
  www.kent.ac.uk/careers/interviews/commonquestions.htm

www.jobsite.co.uk/bemyinterviewer/index.html?utm_source=Google&utm_
medium=PSE&utm_%20term=interview+skills&utm_campaign=BMI
www.e4s.co.uk/graduate-jobs/free-interview-tips.htm
www.graduate-jobs.com/gj/gco/Booklet/graduate-job-interview-technique.jsp
- For help with assessment centres:
www.graduate-jobs.com/gj/gco/Booklet/graduate-job-assessment-centre.jsp
www.kent.ac.uk/careers/selection.htm
www.targetjobs.co.uk/careers-advice/assessment-centres

Time for review and reflection

This is your space to log your reflections on this chapter, to think about what you have learnt, how you will use it and what else you need to find out.

What were the key learning points of this chapter?
What are your strengths in the areas covered by this chapter?
What areas did you identify for development?
What have you learnt about yourself?
How will you use this knowledge?
What else do you need to learn or find out about in relation to this chapter?

12

How to Continue Developing Yourself for Your Future Success

Overview – what's in this chapter?

- Why do you need to continue developing yourself and upgrading your skills?
- Developing yourself in higher levels of education
- Developing yourself within your professional career
- Dealing with work role transitions, unexpected changes of circumstances and drawing on your own transferable skills
- Exploring self-employment and entrepreneurship as an alternative to formal employment
- Developing your commitment to lifelong learning, personal growth and development
- Follow-up activities, further reading and websites to look up
- Time for review and reflection

Why do you need to continue developing yourself and upgrading your skills?

Try completing the short self-scoring test overleaf, to assess your own level of confidence in relation to your continued personal and professional development.

Activity: Why do you need to read this chapter?

You need to self score each question on a scale from 0 to 10, where 0 is low and 10 is high.

1. How likely do you think it is that you will continue to develop yourself after higher education?	
2. How much do you know about the concept of continuing professional development?	
3. How confident are you about continuing your education by taking professional qualifications?	
4. How confident are you about continuing your education by taking higher level academic degrees, such as a masters or a doctorate?	
5. How confident are you about dealing with planned changes of work role?	
6. How confident are you about dealing with sudden and unexpected changes of work role or redundancy?	
7. How confident would you be about starting your own business?	
8. How confident would you be about self-employment?	
9. To what extent have you considered developing yourself outside of work and employment?	
10. How confident are you in planning your own future personal growth and development?	
Total score	

Interpretation

What did you score?

- Less than 50%   You definitely will find a lot of help in this chapter.
- 50%–75%   There is still plenty to learn in this chapter.
- 75%–100%   You are very confident – read on to confirm your understanding.

There will be a life after higher education and this will provide you with new possibilities for growth and development, together with opportunities to learn new skills to add to your skills set.

In this chapter we look at the opportunities afforded for your continued development both by a return to higher education and also in your professional career. In your future life there will be many transitions to negotiate in a rapidly changing world and you might even find yourself made redundant at some stage. The good news is that you now have a set of transferable skills which you can use to help you move on successfully, so that change situations can become further opportunities to grow and develop.

We also explore **self-employment** and **entrepreneurship** which are both valuable and preferable alternatives to employment for some people, for all or some of their working lives. Lastly we look at the concept of **lifelong learning**, which potentially goes far beyond both higher education and even the problem of earning a living. Finally there are some follow-up activities, some suggested further reading, websites to look up, and some space for review and reflection.

> **Self-employment –** working for yourself as opposed to formal employment by an organisation.

> **Entrepreneurship –** starting and developing your own business organisation.

> **Lifelong learning –** the concept of learning through life.

Developing yourself in higher levels of education

When you are immersed in your course it is all too easy to see the end of your course as the end of your time in education. When revising for final examinations or struggling to complete a dissertation by the deadline, you may think 'never again'. However, if you have learnt good skills as outlined in this book, you will no doubt find your next degree a lot easier than your last.

In taking a higher degree you will have to learn some new skills, but these can be seen as building upon what you did before. For example, if you wrote an undergraduate dissertation, a postgraduate thesis should not prove to be too difficult, though perhaps longer and more **academically rigorous**.

It is often good to take a break after one degree before the next, although some people like to keep going and sometimes fear stopping. Taking a break can allow you to establish yourself in your profession

> **Academic rigour –** strict adherence to normal rules and procedures for conducting academic research.

or career, but there is always the danger of not getting back into studying.

Part-time study is the route commonly adopted by students taking higher degrees and professional qualifications whilst in employment and you may find that your employer will give you some study leave and that some may pay your fees or at least make a contribution. This support is more likely to be given the more closely the degree you take is linked to your work.

Taking a vocationally orientated degree can improve your chances of both internal promotion and changing job altogether.

An ex-student told us...

One ex-student told us that he had taken a first degree in literature, he had then drifted through a series of jobs in travel and the tourism industry before finally getting into health service management. After a few years he was able to take a part-time Master's degree in this field with us, which helped him to secure a senior management position.

In taking higher degrees, such as a Master's or doctorate, you will normally be expected to learn more independently and there will tend to be less contact time than at undergraduate level. At Master's level you should look to see how much is comprised of taught components and how much is independent supervised study. In a taught masters there is normally an element of supervised dissertation work.

Research degree – higher degree completed by thesis.

If you are taking a **research degree** such as Master or Doctor of Philosophy, there will be an even greater emphasis on your working autonomously. Students sometimes talk about the 'lonely road' and you will need a high level of commitment to the project and considerable self-motivation. The project will normally be expected to break new intellectual ground, be a significant re-working of existing evidence, or perhaps both.

Supervision will be a key factor in completing a research degree. Finding supervisors who are going to be interested in your work and able to support you is so vitally important that it may influence your choice of institution more than other factors such as location and facilities, which you will be using much less than on taught programmes. Sometimes research students select a university which is quite far away from their home and work in order to get the right supervisor. Actual supervisions will be fairly infrequent, but you may need to use their facilities from time to time, so location does need some consideration.

Professional doctorate – allows professional practitioners to complete a doctorate by submission of a series of papers based on work-related problems rather than by thesis.

Professional doctorates have developed in recent years, enabling practitioners in certain professions to base doctoral work on more practical work-based problems. They frequently involve attending workshops with other practitioners in the same field and writing up a series of papers rather than a single thesis.

 Activity: Thinking about going back into higher education?

If you are considering a return to higher education it is well worth taking some time to click around websites to gather information on your options before talking to institutions directly. Here are some critical questions to ask yourself:

- Why do I want a higher degree?
- Do I have the time, commitment and motivation to complete it?
- What problems or barriers would I have to overcome to complete the course?
- At what level would I expect to re-enter education?
- What qualification would I be seeking?
- Where would I want to study and is there a specific institution or department or supervisor I would want to work with?
- How much is it going to cost and who is going to fund this?

Developing yourself within your professional career

In many work organisations, particularly the larger ones, there will be an established programme of **continuing professional development**, often known as **CPD**. This may well be closely integrated with appraisal and employee development programmes. In these cases **professional development planning** may be seen as the norm for all staff. Alternatively it might be restricted to certain types or grades of staff or there may be a requirement to opt in.

> **Continuing professional development (CPD) –** continuing your professional development after initial qualification.

A good question to ask an employer at initial interview or assessment centre, and perhaps upon promotion, is what provision will be made for your continuing professional development (see Chapter 11 on developing your interview skills).

> **Professional development planning –** process of actively planning and reviewing your professional development.

If you have a choice of jobs, a major factor in your choice might well be the extent to which your continuing professional development is likely to be supported and the potential there is for your development within the organisation. While the starting salary and rewards package might seem the most obvious attraction, particularly after some years of financial struggle as an undergraduate student, having scope for development might outweigh this in the long term.

In most professions CPD is organised by the professional bodies, but where there is no organised programme of CPD, or indeed no effective programme, you will have to take responsibility for planning your own continuing development. In this case some of the skills learnt in this book should stand you in good stead – in particular those discussed in Chapter 2 on planning your continuing personal development.

Dealing with work role transitions, unexpected changes of circumstances and drawing on your own transferable skills

In life we must expect that things will not always go smoothly. The days of a 'job for life' have now passed, so we must all be prepared for change. This will almost inevitably mean a series of **work role transitions**, but each transition can be seen as an opportunity to grow, develop and learn new skills. When we make these work role transitions we take with us many **transferable skills** and behaviours. Skills and behaviours learnt in one role will form a sound foundation for the next and can even form the basis of a new career. Each transition can, therefore, be seen as an opportunity for growth and development.

Work role transition – moving from one job to another.

If you join a large employer there may be scope to move around within the organisation, and this can provide a valuable opportunity to learn and grow. Alternatively you may want to look outside the organisation in order to see what else is on offer. It is good to practise some lateral thinking every so often and to take stock of where you are and where you hope to get to. See also Chapter 2 on planning your continuing personal development.

Transferable skills – skills learnt in one context applied in another.

Inertia – being stuck in a job or otherwise making oneself immobile.

There are often new opportunities and new directions we could take if only we took a little time to recognise them. **Inertia**, in terms of employment, is the tendency to stay stuck in the same role for no particularly good reason other than that it avoids changing. **Redundancy** is not uncommon, and while this can prove to be traumatic at the time, it can be seen as providing an opportunity to take stock and look at how you can take what you have learnt into a new role. Sometimes the new role will be less well rewarded, at least in the short term, but it may also open up new opportunities for growth and development.

Redundancy – dismissal because your job has partially or fully ceased to exist and you are no longer required.

There could be a danger towards the end of your career of becoming a **time server**, who is just 'treading water' until retirement. It would be sad if the last phase of your employment was the least fulfilling and therefore it is good if you can make a contribution until the last. One obvious area is in passing on your skills and developing those who come after you. Another may be to seek a **secondment** to another organisation, normally in the public or voluntary sector, where your skills can be utilised over a set time period.

> **Time server –** expression referring to an employee who has lost motivation and is waiting for retirement.

> **Secondment –** being temporarily transferred to another job and/or employer.

Eventually, retirement will become another transition for most of us. In many cases this can be planned and prepared for well in advance. Many retired employees use their skills set to good effect, either in the voluntary sector or in part-time employment.

Exploring self-employment and entrepreneurship as an alternative to formal employment

For much of the last part of this book we have focused upon gaining employment and developing a career. The assumption has been that you will be working for others. However, the skills that you develop in higher education and also perhaps in employment can be a basis from which you may move into self-employment and perhaps entrepreneurship – working alone or starting a business with others.

Moving out of formal employment can bring great rewards, not only in financial terms but also in respect of personal autonomy. To put it more simply, you become your own boss. However, it is important to realise that for every successful small business there are many failures. While this should not stop you, it is important to have a well worked-out proposal.

If you need to raise **capital** from banks, other financial institutions or venture capitalists, they will expect a well-researched **business plan** covering all aspects of the business including marketing plans and financial projections. Some of the skills learnt in education and beyond should help you with this, but the banks themselves often provide useful literature and support, as do local small business and enterprise units.

If you have gained marketable skills in employment you may decide to become a **freelance professional**, perhaps doing much of what you did before but for a number of organisations rather than just one.

> **Freelance –** self-employed person who is not committed to any one organisation.

Consultancy and training are popular routes and allow people to draw upon old contacts as a starting point, indeed some people even find themselves doing work for their former employer. This can be attractive to both parties as the ex-employee provides both continuity and flexibility. However, the freelance professional has no guarantee of work and must quickly establish a reputation and an independent client base.

Portfolio worker – person who may work for several organisations, may have several occupations and may mix self- and formal employment.

A further alternative is to become a **portfolio worker**, possibly mixing a variety of occupations, perhaps working for a number of employers and often working on a self-employed basis. It can be an interesting and varied life and the mix of work which you do can change over time. The downside can be when you are either in demand on all fronts and it becomes difficult to satisfy all the demands, or when everything goes quiet at the same time.

Some ex-students told us...

Three graduates who had initially worked in the public sector and who are all now self-employed told us their stories. One is a gardener and homeopath, another is running her own employment agency, while the third is both a professional gliding instructor and a central heating engineer.

Developing your commitment to lifelong learning, personal growth and development

Lifelong learning – the concept of learning through life.

The end of your studies can be a difficult time, after the intensity of student life, and for most there will be the transition into paid employment. For the majority of graduates, full-time employment will be the next big step in their life and, of course, they will want to establish themselves in their new job. **Lifelong learning** might seem at this point to be a rather abstract notion. However, we want to suggest to you that your long-term success and happiness will very likely depend upon it and that developing a commitment to learning as a lifelong activity should be a priority.

There are three main areas which you might want to consider:

- **Academic** – this would involve taking further courses (see section on developing yourself in higher levels of education above).
- **Professional/vocational** – which might include professional qualification and work-related training and development activities, normally sponsored by your employer (also discussed above).

- **Extra-mural/recreational activities** – which can include doing anything that you like, including participating in hobbies, sports, the arts, travel, etc. However, it is often the way in life that whatever you learn seems to come in useful somewhere along the way. Your current hobby might even become your next job!
- **Digital presence** – many universities allow you to maintain or export your e-portfolio when you graduate.

> **Digital identity/online presence** – your own profile on the internet utilising e-portfolios and/or professional networking websites.

A local employer told us...

The Chief Executive of a very successful medium-sized local company told us that he gladly paid for any of his staff to do whatever training they wanted, not only because it made the staff happier but also because, in the end, it always seemed to prove useful to the company in some way.

We believe that all learning has the potential to provide new opportunities and new insights. It is all too easy to get so locked into a professional career that it makes the task of making work role transitions unnecessarily difficult (see also the above section on work role transitions). Looking outside of where you are – by developing new interests, knowledge or skills – helps you to locate where you are in the world and where you are going.

Having clear aims which you can both specify and articulate would seem to be a major determinant of good health and longevity. Having an idea of where you are going and why, not only seems to give people a goal in life but also a reason for being. How often do we hear stories of people achieving despite setbacks such as illness, disability or other misfortunes?

Throughout this book we have asked you to reflect upon aspects of yourself and your skills set. Learning about ourselves is potentially a lifelong activity and in Chapter 2, when we looked at personal development planning, we made the point that the process is not just for higher education or just for employment, it is for life.

 Activity: Why stop now?

Here are two questions to consider:

- Why keep on growing?
- Why stop growing now?

Lifelong learning is an element of what might be called personal growth and development. It takes place not only in education and employment but also in the sphere of private life beyond and there is no limit to what you might do – from climbing a mountain, through learning to play the piano, to embarking on a spiritual quest to know yourself more fully. Whatever you do will develop you in some respect and you will grow as a person.

Throughout this book we have asked you to first reflect upon your skills and then actively to develop them. Now that we are almost at the end of this book, it remains only for us to wish you good fortune in your journey through life. We know all too well that life's path can be rocky at times but also that developing good skills can help you at every stage in achieving your goals.

Follow-up activities

Time for action – Checklist

Have you:

- considered why you will need to continue developing yourself and upgrading your skills after your current course of studies?
- thought about developing yourself further in higher levels of education?
- examined how you could develop yourself within a professional career?
- thought about how you might deal with work role transitions, unexpected changes of circumstances and how you could draw on your own transferable skills?
- considered self-employment and entrepreneurship as an alternative to employment?
- thought about developing your commitment to lifelong learning together with personal growth and development?

Further reading

Buckingham, M. and Clifton, D. O. (2005) *Now, Discover Your Strengths*. London: Simon & Schuster.

Cameron, S. (2011) *The MBA Handbook: Academic and Professional Skills for Mastering Management*, 7th edn. Harlow: Pearson.

Churchill, H. and Sanders, T. (2007) *Getting Your PhD: A Practical Insider's Guide*. London: Sage Publications.

Cottrell, S. (2010) *Skills for Success: The Personal Development Planning Handbook*. 2nd edn. Basingstoke: Palgrave Macmillan.

Jeffers, S. (2012) *Feel the Fear and Do it Anyway*. Revised edition. London: Random House

Lumley, M and Wilkinson, J. (2014) *Developing Employability for Business*. Oxford: Oxford University Press.

Marshall, S. and Green, N. (2010) *Your PhD Companion*, 3rd edn. Oxford: How to Books Ltd.

Moon, J. (2006) *Learning Journals: A Handbook for Reflective Practice and Professional Development*, 2nd edn. London: Kogan Page.

O'Connor, J. (2002) *The NLP Workbook: A Practical Guide to Achieving Results you Want*. London: Element.

Websites to look up

- For information on careers and courses:
  www.gov.uk/career-development-loans/overview
  www.nus.org.uk/en/advice/careers
  www.pcsexecutive.com/?gclid=CJKWz4C_pZICFQQF1Qod4la_RA

Time for review and reflection

This is your space to log your reflections on this chapter, to think about what you have learnt, how you will use it and what else you need to find out.

What were the key learning points of this chapter?
What are your strengths in the areas covered by this chapter?
What areas did you identify for development?

What have you learnt about yourself?

How will you use this knowledge?

What else do you need to learn or find out about in relation to this chapter?

References and Bibliography

Ambady, N. (1993) 'Half a minute: Predicting teacher evaluations from thin slices of non-verbal behaviour and physical attractiveness,' *Journal of Personality and Social Psychology*, 64.

Ambady, N. and Rosenthal, R. (1992) 'Thin slices of expressive behaviour as predictors of interpersonal consequences: A meta-analysis', *Psychological Bulletin*, 111: 256–74.

Baddeley, A. D. (1990) *Human Memory: Theory and Practice*. Hove: Lawrence Erlbaum Associates.

Bandler, R. and Grinder, J. (1976 and 1979), cited in O'Connor, J. and Seymour, F. (2002) *Introducing NPL: Psychological Skills for Understanding and Influencing People*. London: Element.

Belbin, M. (1993) *Team Roles at Work*. Oxford: Butterworth Heinemann.

Belbin, M. (2000) *Beyond the Team*. Oxford: Butterworth Heinemann.

Belbin, M. (2010) *Team Roles at Work*, 2nd edn. Oxford: Butterworth Heinemann.

Belbin Team Role Theory [online]. Available from: www.belbin.com/rte.asp?id8 [Accessed 18 March 2008].

Bell, J. (2010) *Doing Your Research, A Guide for First-Time Researchers in Education, Health and Social Science*, 5th edn. Maidenhead: McGraw Hill.

Berne, E. (1968) *The Games People Play*. London: Penguin.

Berne, E. (1975) *What Do You Say After You Say Hello?* London: Corgi.

Bird, J. and Pinch, C. (2002) *Autogenic Therapy*. Dublin: Newleaf.

Bloisi, W., Cook, C. W. and Hunsaker, P. L. (2007) *Management and Organisational Behaviour*, 2nd European edn. Maidenhead: McGraw-Hill Education.

Blumberg, B., Cooper, D. and Schindler, P. (2005) *Business Research Methods*. Maidenhead: McGraw-Hill.

Boud, D. (1986) *Implementing Student Self-Assessment*. New South Wales: Higher Education Research and Development Society of Australia.

Boyatzis, R. (2001) *How and Why Individuals Are Able to Develop Emotional Intelligence*, cited in Cherniss, C. and Goleman, D. (eds) (2001) *The Emotionally Intelligence Workplace*. San Francisco: Jossey-Bass.

Brain image [online]. Available from: www..science.ca/images/Brain_Witelson.jpg. [Accessed 27 March 2008].

Bryman, A. and Bell, E. (2011) *Business Research Methods*, 3rd edn. Oxford: Oxford University Press.

Bryman, A. and Buchanan D. A. (2009) *The Sage Handbook of Organisational Research Methods*. London: Sage.

Buckingham, M. and Clifton, D. O. (2005) *Now, Discover Your Strengths*. London: Simon & Schuster.

Burns, T. and Sinfield, S. (2012) *Essential Study Skills: The Complete Guide to Success at University*, 3rd edn. London: Sage.

Buzan, T. and Buzan, B. (2010) *The Mind Map Book*. London: BBC Books.

Buzan, T. (1974) *Use Your Head*. London: BBC Books.

Buzan, T. (2006) *Use Your Head*, 3rd edn. London: BBC Books.

Byham, C. and Cox, J. (1998) *Zapp! The Lightning of Empowerment: How to Improve Productivity, Quality and Employee Satisfaction*. New York: Random House.

David, M. and Sutton, C. D. (2011) *Social Research: An Introduction*, 2nd edn. London: Sage.

Cameron, S. (2009) *The Business Student's Handbook*, 5th edn. Harlow: Pearson.

Cameron, S. (2011) *The MBA Handbook: Academic and Professional Skills for Mastering Management*, 7th edn. Harlow: Pearson.

CAPLITS Centre for Professional Literacies [online]. Available from: www.ioe.ac.uk/caplits/writingcentre/criticalreview.1tostart.htm [Accessed 18 March 2008].

Carr, A. (1995) *The Only Way to Stop Smoking Permanently*. London: Penguin Health Care and Fitness.

Carr, A. (2013) *The Easy Way to Stop Smoking: Be a Happy Non-smoker for the Rest of Your Life*, 5th edn. London: Penguin Books.

Cherniss, C. and Goleman, D. (eds) (2001) *The Emotionally Intelligent Workplace*. San Francisco: Jossey-Bass.

Chopra, D. (2001) *Perfect Health*. London: Bantam.

Churchill, H. and Sanders, T. (2007) *Getting Your PhD: A Practical Insider's Guide*. London: Sage Publications.

Cialdini, R. B. (2001) 'Harnessing the science of persuasion', *Harvard Business Review*, Oct.

Cockburn, S. (2011) 'Interviews – structuring your answers' [online]. Available from:https://www.youtube.com/watch?v=0LpEKcFdcs4 [You Tube video] [Posted on 30 November 2011, accessed 3 August 2014].

Cornelius, N. (2001) *Human Resource Management: A Managerial Perspective*. London: Thomson Learning.

Cottrell, S. (1999) *The Study Skills Handbook*. Basingstoke: Palgrave Macmillan.

Cottrell, S. (2006) *The Exam Skills Handbook*. Basingstoke: Palgrave Macmillan.

Cottrell, S. (2010) *Skills for Success: The Personal Development Planning Handbook*, 2nd edn. Basingstoke: Palgrave Macmillan.

Cottrell, S. (2011) *Critical Thinking Skills: Developing Effective Analysis and Argument*, 2nd edn. Basingstoke: Palgrave Macmillan.

Cottrell, S. (2013) *The Study Skills Handbook*, 4th edn. Basingstoke: Palgrave Macmillan.

Davidson, R. J., quoted in Goleman, D. (2003) *Destructive Emotions and How We Can Overcome Them*. London: Bloomsbury.

Davis, G. (1999) *Giving Feedback*. University of Brighton, School of Pharmacy [Video material].

Entwistle, N. J. and Marton, F. (1984) 'Changing conceptions of Learning and research', cited in Marton, F., Hounsell, D., Entwistle, N. J. (1984) *The Experience of Learning*. Edinburgh: Scottish Academic Press.

Feldman, R. (2000) *Power Learning, Strategies for Success in College and Life*. Maidenhead: McGraw-Hill Higher Education.

Fiore, N. (2007) *Now Habit: A Strategic Program for Overcoming Procrastination and Enjoying Guilt-free Play*, New York, Penguin Group (USA) Inc.

Fowlie, J. A and Wood, M. (2009) 'The emotional impact of leaders behaviours', *Journal of European Industrial Training*, 33 (6): 559–72.

Gill, J. and Johnson, P. (2010) *Research Methods for Managers*, 4th edn. London: Sage.

Goleman, D. (1998) *Working with Emotional Intelligence*. London: Bloomsbury Paperbacks.

Goleman, D. (2001) 'An EI-based theory of performance' in Cherniss, C. and Goleman, D. (eds) *The Emotionally Intelligence Workplace*. San Francisco, CA: Jossey-Bass.

Goleman, D. (2003) *Destructive Emotions and How We Can Overcome Them*. London: Bloomsbury.

Goleman, D. (2013) *Focus: The Hidden Driver of Excellence*. New York: Harper Collins.

Guirdham, M. (2002) *Interpersonal Skills at Work*, 3rd edn. Harlow: Pearson.

Hawkins, P. and Winter, J. (1995) *Skills for Graduates in the 21st Century*. Cambridge: Assoc. of Graduate Recruiters.

Herbert, I. and Rothwell, A. (2005) *Managing Your Placement: A Skills Based Approach*. Basingstoke: Palgrave.

Higgins, M. (2014) 'Using the Star technique to shine at job interviews: a how-to guide', [online] Available from: http://careers.theguardian.com/careers-blog/star-technique-competency-based-interview [Accessed 3 August 2014].

Honey, P. (1994) *Learning Logs – A Way to Enhance Learning from Experience*. Maidenhead: Peter Honey Publications.

Honey, P. and Mumford, A. (1982) *The Manual of Learning Styles*. Maidenhead: Peter Honey Publications.

Hubel, D. H., Wiesel, T. N. and LeVay, S. (1977) *Plasticity of Ocular Dominance Columns in Monkey Striate Cortex*. London: Royal Society of London.

Hunsaker, P. L. (2005) *Management – A Skills Approach*, 2nd edn. Upper Saddle River, NJ: Pearson.

Jeffers, S. (1991) *Feel the Fear and Do it Anyway*. London: Arrow.

Jeffers, S. (2012) *Feel the Fear and Do it Anyway*, revised edn. London: Random House.

Kermani, K. (1996) *Autogenic Training*. London: Souvenir Press.

Kolb, D. A. (1984) *Experiential Learning: Experience as the Source of Learning and Development*. Upper Saddle River, NJ: Prentice-Hall.

Kolb, D. A. and Fry, R. (1975) *Toward an Applied Theory of Experiential Learning*. New York: John Wiley & Sons.

Kuhn, T. S. (1970) *The Structure of Scientific Revolutions*. Chicago, IL: University of Chicago Press.

Kumar, R. (2014) *Research Methodology: A Step-by-Step Guide for Beginners*, 4th edn. London: Sage

Lee-Davies, L. (2007) *Developing Work and Study Skills*. London: Thomson.

Lumley, M and Wilkinson, J. (2014) *Developing Employability for Business*. Oxford: Oxford University Press.

McShane, B. (2011) *The Few That Do: How Winners Set and Reach Their Goals*, Rossa Publishing.

Marshall, S. and Green, N. (2010) *Your PhD Companion*, 3rd edn. Oxford: How to Books Ltd.

Marx, K. and Engels, F. (1967) *The Communist Manifesto*. Harmondsworth: Pelican Books.

Mayer, J. and Salovey, P. G. (1990) 'Emotional intelligence', *Imagination, Cognition and Personality*, 9: 185–211.

Mehrabian, A. (1971) *Silent Messages*. Belmont, CA: Wadsworth.

Moon, J. (1999) *Reflection in Learning and Professional Development*. London: Kogan Page.

Moon, J. (2006) *Learning Journals: A Handbook of Reflective Practice and Professional Development*, 2nd edn. Abingdon: Routledge.

Mounsey, C. and Seeley, J. (2002) *Essays and Dissertations*. Oxford: Oxford University Press.

Mullins, L. J. (2013) *Management and Organisational Behaviour*, 10th edn. Harlow: Pearson Education Limited.

O'Connor, J. (2002) *The NLP Workbook: A Practical Guide to Achieving the Results you Want*. London: Element.

O'Connor, J. and Seymour, F. (2002) *Introducing NPL: Psychological Skills for Understanding and Influencing People*, 3rd edn. London: Element.

Oliver, P. (2013) *Writing your Thesis*, 3rd edn. London: Sage.

Pease, A. (1984) *Body Language*. London: Sheldon Press.

Pease, A. (2006) *The Definitive Book of Body Language*. New York: Bantam.

Pedler, M. and Boydell, J. (1999) *Managing Yourself*. London: Lemos and Crane.

Perls, F. S. (1951) *Gestalt Therapy; Excitement and Growth in the Human Personality*. New York: Julian Press.

Pert, C. (1999) *Molecules of Emotion*. London: Pocket Books.

Pert, C. (2007) *Everything You Need To Know To Feel Good*. London: Hay House.

Popper, K. R. (1989) *Conjectures and Refutations: the Growth of Scientific Knowledge*, 5th revised edn. London: Routledge.

Race, P. (1995) *Who Learns Wins*. London: Penguin.

Race, P. (2007) *How to Get a Good Degree: Making the Most of your Time at University*. Buckingham: Open University Press.

Ridley, D. (2012) *The Literature Review: A Step-by-Step Guide for Students*, 2nd edn. London: Sage.

Russell, T. (1994) *Effective Feedback Skills*. London: Kogan Page.

Russell, T. (1998) *Effective Feedback Skills*. 2nd edn. London: Kogan Page.

Saunders, M., Thornhill, A. and Lewis, P (2012) *Research Methods for Business Students*, 6th edn. Harlow: Pearson.

Seeley, J. (2002) *Report Writing*. Oxford: Oxford University Press.

Smith, H. W. (1998) *The 10 Natural Laws of Time and Life Management*. London: Nicholas Brealey Publishing.

Smith, M. J. (1975) *When I Say No I feel Guilty*. New York: Bantam.

Spencer, L. and Spencer, S. (1993) *Competence at Work: Models for Superior Performance*. New York: John Wiley & Sons.

Stewart, I. and Joines, V. (2012) *TA Today*, 2nd edn. Nottingham: Lifespace.

Tannenbaum, R. and Schmidt, W. H. (1973) 'How to choose a leadership pattern', *Harvard Business Review*, 51 (3): 162–80.

Thomas, G. (2013) *How to do your Research Project: A Guide for Students in Education and Applied Social Sciences*, 2nd edn. London: Sage.

Thompson, M. (2013) *Winning Strategies for Sport and Life*. London: Gabrielle Lea Publishing.

Today Programme (2012) [on line] BBC Radio 4, 14.11.2012, <http://news.bbc.co.uk/today/hi/today/newsid_9769000/9769443.stm> [Accessed 19.11.12].

Topping, K. J., Smith, E. F., Swanson, I. and Elliot, A. (2000) 'Formative peer assessment between postgraduate students', *Assessment and Evaluation in Higher Education*, 24 (2).

Tuckman, B. W. and Jensen, M. C. (1977) 'Stages of small group development', *Group and Organisational Studies*, 2 (3): 419–27.

Walliman, N. (2014) *The Undergraduate Dissertation: The Essential Guide for Success*, 2nd edn. London: Sage.

Wellington, J. (2010) *Making Supervision Work for You: A Student's Guide*. London: Sage.

Whisker, J. (2009) *The Undergraduate Research Handbook*. Basingstoke: Palgrave Macmillan.

Wilson, J. (2010) *Essentials of Business Research: A Guide to Doing Your Research Project*. London: Sage.

Woodruffe, C. (2007) *Development and Assessment Centres*, 4th edn. London: CIPD

Index